PERGAMON INTERNATIONAL LIBRARY
of Science, Technology, Engineering and Social Stu
The 1000-volume original paperback library in aid of edu(
industrial training and the enjoyment of leisure
Publisher: Robert Maxwell, M.C.

Human Growth and the Development of Personality

Third Edition

THE PERGAMON TEXTBOOK
INSPECTION COPY SERVICE

An inspection copy of any book published in the Pergamon International Library will gladly be sent to academic staff without obligation for their consideration for course adoption or recommendation. Copies may be retained for a period of 60 days from receipt and returned if not suitable. When a particular title is adopted or recommended for adoption for class use and the recommendation results in a sale of 12 or more copies, the inspection copy may be retained with our compliments. The Publishers will be pleased to receive suggestions for revised editions and new titles to be published in this important International Library.

SOCIAL WORK SERIES

Editor: Jean P. Nursten

A Pergamon Journal of Related Interest

BEHAVIOUR RESEARCH AND THERAPY
An International Multi-Disciplinary Journal

Editor-in-Chief
Prof. S. Rachman, Institute of Psychiatry

This journal focuses on the application of experimental psychology, and especially learning theories, to the modification of maladaptive behaviour, and to the improvement of learning efficacy. The main conception unifying many different theories and approaches has been the belief that behavioural disorders are essentially learned responses and that learning theory has much to teach us regarding the acquisition and the extinction of such responses. Articles describing experimental and theoretical work are published.

Human Growth and the Development of Personality

by

JACK KAHN, M.D., F.R.C.Psych., D.P.M.
formerly Community Psychiatrist,
London Borough of Newham.
Consultant Child Psychiatrist, Whittington Hospital.

and

SUSAN ELINOR WRIGHT, M.A.
Senior Lecturer in Education,
Department of Teaching Studies,
Polytechnic of North London, U.K.

Foreword by
G. M. CARSTAIRS, M.D., F.R.C.P.Ed., D.P.M.

Third Edition

PERGAMON PRESS

Oxford · New York · Toronto · Sydney · Paris · Frankfurt

UK	Pergamon Press Ltd., Headington Hill Hall, Oxford OX3 0BW, England
USA	Pergamon Press Inc., Maxwell House, Fairview Park, Elmsford, New York 10523, USA
CANADA	Pergamon of Canada, Suite 104, 150 Consumers Road, Willowdale, Ontario M2J 1P9, Canada
AUSTRALIA	Pergamon Press (Aust.) Pty. Ltd., P.O. Box 544, Potts Point, NSW 2011, Australia
FRANCE	Pergamon Press SARL, 24 rue des Ecoles, 75240 Paris, Cedex 05, France
FEDERAL REPUBLIC OF GERMANY	Pergamon Press GmbH, 6242 Kronberg/Taunus, Hammerweg 6, Federal Republic of Germany

First edition 1965

Second edition 1971

Third edition 1980

British Library Cataloguing in Publication Data

Kahn, Jack
Human growth and the development of personality.
3rd ed. (Pergamon international library: social work series)
1. Developmental psychology.
I. Title.   II. Wright, Susan Elinor
155   BF713   79-42660

ISBN 0-08-023383-X (Hardcover)
ISBN 0-08-023382-1 (Flexicover)

Printed in Great Britain by
A. Wheaton & Co., Ltd., Exeter, U.K.

And one man in his time plays many parts . . .
AS YOU LIKE IT

Contents

15.   THE SECONDARY-SCHOOL CHILD   **143**

16.   ADOLESCENCE   **152**

Foreword to the First Edition

EVERYONE who is engaged in one of the "helping professions", whether they are teachers, social workers, clinicians or clergymen or simply members of a voluntary social service agency, must encounter the recurrent problem of having to decide whether a client's experiences are truly abnormal or whether they fall within the range of common (or uncommon) occurrences. This holds true at every age and stage of human growth. Pregnant women often have to be reassured about the normality of their pregnancy, and an important function of postnatal clinics is to teach young mothers what to expect of their growing child. Nurses and doctors are quite familiar with this role, although not all of them appreciate that the time spent in this simple form of health education is just as important as their more usual therapeutic activities.

All this implies that we, the "helpers", *know* the range and sequence of normal human development, but rather often this is not the case. In our modern small family units it is possible for a young doctor or nurse to become quite out of touch with the domestic realities of living with babies, with teenagers or with ageing relatives. As a result, the constant promptings of experience which formerly were supplied by the large extended family have now to be replaced by deliberate study: but hitherto there have been few books to which one could turn. Dr. Kahn's work will prove invaluable for this purpose. He presents the reader with a well-informed account of human growth in which the maturation of the body plays an important part, but one which is overshadowed by the development of intellectual and social accomplishments and by the patterns of expectation and response in human relationships which underlie each individual's personality.

This book does not deal, except incidentally, with sickness or psychopathology, but it provides an invaluable basis for the understanding of all the vagaries of normal human development. It will help all those who are confronted by perplexed or anxious parents, patients or clients, to recognise their problems more clearly and so to offer them informed guidance: it can therefore be recommended not only to practitioners and students of the helping professions but also to every intelligent citizen who would like to have a better understanding of human nature in general and of his own personality in particular.

G. M. CARSTAIRS

Introduction to the Third Edition

THE FIRST two editions of this book were published in an era of expanding services in Health, Education and Social Services. It seemed natural that recognition of special need should be followed by the provision of appropriate services. Knowledge of human development was sought with a purpose in mind: to give a rational coherence of provision in relation to need.

This edition has been prepared in an age of cuts in spending. Many services have to fight for their very survival. It often seems that the axe is being wielded indiscriminately. It is all the more important that those who appeal for allocation of resources should have in mind a perspective of human development against which each kind of provision can be seen.

We have taken the view that value systems are more important than specific criteria; and we have taken note of the reality of value judgements in the subjects that we have dealt with.

Secondly, we have found ourselves making so many references to the multi-ethnic nature of contemporary society, that we have felt moved to add an afterword on this theme.

Thirdly, we have greatly enlarged the educational component, in order to recognize the proportion of the waking hours of the child's life which is spent in school. Furthermore, in the time which has elapsed since the first edition of this book was published, the selective system of secondary education has been gradually superseded over most of the country by the comprehensive system.

Fourthly, we have made the effort (which has been considerable in the absence of an impersonal pronoun) to delete the sexist assumption that "he" includes "she" in reference to professional workers, or to the growing child.

Fifthly, we have added an extra chapter in which we try to make explicit those theoretical perspectives which pervade the book.

Lastly, and on a personal note, we have been conscious of our position as father and daughter, working together on a book on development, in that we have become aware of how the impact of collaboration has affected our own personal development. In this, there is an implied message to readers: that we consider that growth is still possible at the respective ages of forty and seventy plus.

JACK KAHN
SUSAN ELINOR WRIGHT

Introduction to the Second Edition

THE TOPIC of human growth and the development of personality is now a recognized part of the syllabus in the training courses for social workers. It also features, although not so uniformly, in the curriculum for medical students, psychology students and the students at colleges of education. The purpose of study has to be seen in relation to the tasks undertaken by the different professions. Teachers work with children who are at some particular stage of development, and have to be aware of what went on before; and they need to have a picture of the stages still in front of the child who is at present a pupil. The helping and healing professions need knowledge of development as an aspect of diagnosis.

There are some disorders which are recognized as specific departures from the normal, and in this case the treatment is directed to the pathological process. The aim is cure. There are other disorders that are best seen as a dysfunction, and here the treatment is directed towards helping, or compensating for, the capacity which is affected. In this dimension of diagnosis, treatment may be a multi-professional affair, with the main responsibility falling upon the particular profession with specialized knowledge of some particular human function. Another dimension again is that of a deviation from a notional norm, where what is normal or abnormal is relative to the culture. The legal and social aspects are as important as the clinical ones; and, in this dimension, there is a responsibility of the helping professions to take part in the public discussions on the amount of deviation that should be tolerated. There is still a further dimension of the study of disorder which is to be thought of in terms of the provision or deprivation of the material and non-material necessities for development. At this level, the treatment would be to provide what has hitherto been omitted.

In all these dimensions, the disorder can be thought of either in terms of the individual or as the interaction of members of a group such as the family.

The choice between these different dimensions of diagnosis will depend upon the value which is subjectively attached by members of different professions to the study from one or other of the possible viewpoints.

The author's aim in this book is to call the reader's attention to a number of available viewpoints and possibly to enlarge the repertoire of methods of approach.

It is hoped that this would not lead to indecision. In fact, a diagnosis in any one of the dimensions is a decision for action. The knowledge of several dimensions is the justification for constructive cooperation between members of different professions who may be officers of the same department or of different departments, and it can allow for the organization of a treatment plan for an individual or a family on a multi-disciplinary basis. Teamwork, of necessity, involves the joint understanding of the range of knowledge, skills and responsibilities, belonging to members of different professions who all have their own kind of training and experience. It permits them to join together in ground which is common to all and yet to maintain their separate responsibilities in the areas which are exclusive to any particular one. This theme has not been dealt with explicitly in this book, but it has determined the approach to a large number of the topics which have been discussed.

In this second edition a number of additions and alterations have been made. In the chapter on adolescence the author is grateful for having been granted permission to reproduce tables on the maturational sequence, in boys and in girls, which were published by the Excerpta Medica Foundation for the International Congress on Adolescence in 1966.[1]

The chapter on infantile sexuality has also been enlarged and it has been thought worth while to extend the description of the Oedipal Situation. In order to avoid vague allusions to the original legend, the story is given in full, and comparisons are made with the Bible story of the intended sacrifice by Abraham of his son Isaac.

For permission to quote Freud's letter to Fliess in which he made his first reference to Oedipus, the author offers grateful thanks to the Hogarth Press Ltd., London,[2] and Basic Books Inc., New York.[3] The full-length account of the Oedipus story is taken from *A Classical Dictionary* by J. Lempriere, D.D., 1864.

J. H. KAHN

[1] D. J. Duche, W. A. Schonfeld and S. Tomkiewicz, Physical Aspects of Adolescence Development, in *Psychiatric Approaches to Adolescence* (edited by G. Caplan and S. Lebovici) International Congress Series 108, pp. 19 and 21, 1966.

[2] Hogarth Press Ltd., Sigmund Freud Copyrights Ltd., The Institute of Psycho-Analysis and The Hogarth Press Ltd.: Volume I of the Standard Edition.

[3] S. Freud, *The Origins of Psycho-analysis: Letters to Wilhelm Fliess, Drafts and Notes: 1887–1902,* edited by M. Bonaparte, A. Freud, E. Kris, translated by E. Mosbacher and J. Strachey, Imago Press, 1954.

Introduction to the First Edition

THIS book is based upon several series of lectures for training courses for child-care officers, social workers, probation officers and nurses, and upon courses of in-service training for health visitors, assistant medical officers of health and mental welfare officers.

The lectures followed a pattern. The first part of each session was devoted to the presentation of a theme forming part of an agreed syllabus but with a certain amount of flexibility. The remaining part of the session was devoted to questions and discussions. The freedom given to the lecturer for digressions from the main themes became reflected in the subsequent discussion, which contributed fresh material to the topic, and which created new ideas which were carried into later parts of the course.

Every course of lectures was, therefore, different. There is some difficulty in capturing the spontaneous spoken word in a printed version which remains fixed. My intention, however, is that the book should be used by the reader as a starting point for associations of ideas. These associations in the reader's mind will be his own, and will become linked with previous reading and with his experiences in his personal and occupational life.

In this way a book can become a living interaction between author and reader. It has a beginning, but we do not know the end. It has also, as its accompaniment, the ideas that *might* have been written down if there had been enough time and enough thought. Everything that one ever says is said as an alternative to something else that one *might* have said, and is listened to against the background of some other thought in the listener's mind. A new arrangement of a familiar melody may contain phrases which are very different from the source, but which owe their impact to the accompanying original sound images. The variations are created with the original theme in mind, and, at times, the theme itself is deliberately recalled in all its well-known detail. Harmonies and discords are found in the mental associations as well as in the actual performance.

Writers, like composers, sometimes wittingly or unwittingly adopt this technique. I write this in the hope of disarming criticism when either the divergence from traditional themes, or the too literal use of familiar ideas, becomes obvious and jarring to the reader.

My own conscious theme is the constancy and the repetition of basic processes in human relationships. Parent and child, teacher and pupil, professional worker and patient, all have interactions which have something in common. The transactions are two-way. Whenever someone gives, something is received by him; and sometimes the traditional roles are unexpectedly reversed. The parent suddenly finds himself dependent on the child, the teacher learns from the pupil, and the therapist receives from the patient something that is healing.

Some acknowledgements of source are made within the text. Countless other sources remain unrecognized or unremembered. Even when I quote the origin of ideas, however, I must take personal responsibility for the particular selection, and for the inevitable distortion which does injustice to the creations of others. The sources are referred to in order that the reader may make his own independent study of them.

This is not intended to be a book which tells people how to do things. The aim is to help readers to become sensitive to the dissatisfactions of themselves and others in a constructive way, and to learn to examine problems from new points of view.

J. H. KAHN

Acknowledgements from the First Edition

THE AUTHOR is glad to express his indebtedness to Tavistock Publications for permission to quote from Dr. Winnicott's *Paediatrics and Psychiatry* and "Prevention of Mothering Breakdown" by John A. Rose in *Prevention of Mental Disorders in Children* (ed. G. Caplan); Her Majesty's Stationery Office for a section from M. D. Sheridan's *The Developmental Progress of Infants and Young Children*; Faber & Faber for quotations from *The Confidential Clerk* by T. S. Eliot; and the National Association for Mental Health for permission to quote material from the author's paper to the Inter-Clinic Conference 1963, "A Wider Concept of Deprivation". Acknowledgement is also due to the writers to whom reference is made in the text.

The author owes gratitude to numerous colleagues, past and present, and amongst these is glad to mention Miss Marion Whyte, Senior P.S.W. and Lecturer in the Leeds University Department of Psychiatry, who shared in the teaching of the first of the courses which provided the basis for this book, and Dr. A. T. Ravenette, Educational Psychologist, alongside whom the author is working in West Ham. He is also especially grateful to the students who took part in various courses and who may recognize in this book ideas and phraseology which were their own contribution to discussions.

The diagram on p. 139 was designed and drawn by Dr. A. T. Ravenette.

Further Acknowledgements

MANY quotations and references have been added to the second edition and to this edition. Acknowledgement is made within the text or in footnotes.

Neither the references themselves nor the acknowledgements can ever be adequate or complete, as the subject, like the object of study, is in a continuous process of growth and change.

1

Human Needs

ONE OF the reasons for the study of human development is to find a scientific basis for provision for human needs. There are some needs such as those for food and warmth, which exist at all stages of development. Others are specific to particular stages of maturation, and are related to the acquisition of the skills and performances appropriate to each successive stage.

Assumptions on Growth

There are general assumptions about the nature of growth. It is taken for granted that some performances are innate and do not have to be taught. Others are conveyed to children by parents who represent the culture. Walking, for example, appears to depend entirely on reaching a biological stage in which the necessary skill becomes physically possible, but do we know how much an adult example is necessary to bring the potential ability into actuality? Talking, and the ability to control bladder and bowels, also are clearly related to maturation, but the transmission of the culture, by adults, in a very personal way, plays a much more important part. As regards talking especially, it seems that learning is necessary, but not necessarily teaching! Almost universally, young children are talked to, usually in a close and intimate way, and eventually the child responds in like manner.

Professional workers require a general pattern of longitudinal development (whether this takes place through maturation, teaching, or learning) in order both to understand normal growth and to find standards by which it can be said that a child attains some particular performance earlier or later than the "normal".

The idea of normality and abnormality (which merges with notions of statistical norms) emerges through comparisons of patterns of growth. The diagnosis of disorder or disease requires factors other than the rate of growth. We have to pass from the developmental framework, in which the accepted aim is to achieve optimum fulfilment of inborn potential, and enter remedial systems which provide diagnosis and treatment for abnormalities.

Home and School

In the pre-school years, children receive their care for the most part within their own families, though in highly developed countries the families have become accustomed to having access to professional services which include medical attention.

1

There are clinics, play groups, day centres and nursery schools; and there is also the domiciliary work of health visitors. These services cater in various ways both for the developmental and the healing aspects, and they supplement what is provided by the parents in the home.

For the school child, the educational services provide another factor for the developmental process. The effect of compulsory school attendance has provided a setting where the health and welfare of the child can be observed, with the possibility that any deficiencies can be made good.

Home life and school life are complementary. At first the aim was to provide, for the whole child population, what affluent parents would have provided for their children on their own initiative. Regular medical and dental inspection came to the child through services attached to schooling, although it has to be said that there is a recent tendency to return responsibility for medical and dental care to the home. The provision of school meals and milk, intended originally to ensure adequate nutrition and therefore heavily subsidized, has become thought of as a social service rather than a way of ensuring that the child was sufficiently well fed to be able to survive the school day. That, too, in a supposedly better-fed nation, is becoming less heartily presented as a characteristic of school life.

Children from severely deprived homes depend substantially on facilities provided by and through the education services, and even then remain at a disadvantage. For some of them, the school services provide the very means of survival. Yet families at every socioeconomic level now turn without hesitation to these same services for a particular need at a particular moment in the physical, intellectual, or emotional life of their children. Recent developments of medical and social services now provide comparable support for adult and child either as individuals or as whole families in the community at large.

Targets of Professional Activity

Attempts are made to identify the aspects of personality to which each professional activity is directed. Where there is disease, treatment is aimed at the pathology; where the maturational process is being hindered, activities are directed towards providing any missing factors for normal development. Unfortunately, the results of scientific studies do not lead to any simplification of the issues. As knowledge increases, the problems become more complex. Professions can no longer respectively restrict themselves exclusively either to the healing of abnormalities or to developing what is considered to be normal.

Each profession dealing with individual human beings has to take into account the stage at which an individual has arrived in developmental progress and, also, recognize any difference in some essential quality or experience as compared with that in a cross section of the population.

Moreover, the unit of study is no longer the single individual. Social workers (along with members of other professions) have been drawn into the work of healing people whose interpersonal relationships are unsatisfactory. Thus a third approach, which is directed towards the interaction, has to be added to activities aimed respectively towards pathology or to growth and development.

Professions divide themselves by their training and the skills which their members acquire, and also according to the target at which their work is aimed. But every profession tends to extend its work into areas which involve personality as a whole.

Doctors traditionally make their diagnoses in terms of abnormalities which can occur in people of any age. Pneumonia is pneumonia whether in a child or in an adult. The criteria are the physical changes which collectively are referred to as the pathology. The doctor needs to be in possession of standards by which departure from normality can be recognized. The doctor is also concerned in the developmental aspect in performances which fail to match what is expected or demanded, and needs a mental chart of the stages of development. Even though the doctors have largely shed the role of teacher implied by that title, they are still looked to for their contribution to ideas of what constitutes normality.

Teachers may be thought of mainly as providing for development of some aspects of personality. The concept of diagnosis in terms of abnormalities is seldom in the forefront of their minds, but they have to be drawn into the making of decisions to find special help for a particular need.

Social workers, whose image is of people involved in interaction with the human and material environment, have to share in ideas of remedial help and the developmental process.

The Individual and the Culture

So far, the study has been of individuals: the structure of the body and its diseases; the developmental process; and, even when studying the living and non-living environment, the viewpoint is through the eyes of the individual being studied. There is a further level of study devoted to the culture in which individuals develop and live their lives. There are aspects of normality and abnormality that are related to the culture: the level of provision below which people *feel* deprived is a feature of their particular society or culture. Many of us will remember advertisements for funds for the people of Bangladesh which read, "Your crash diet is a lot more than my normal diet".

Within our own culture, the luxuries of a previous generation are the essential needs of people of today.

There are, for example, aids to housework available to our contemporaries but which our grandparents never knew: everything from such commonly found articles as electric irons, vacuum cleaners and refrigerators—through the less frequent, such as mixers, blenders and pop-up toasters—to the more expensive washing machines, dish-washers and freezers. Many of us would feel that some of these are necessities (especially for those who both work in a full-time job and manage a home) and some are luxuries. It would, however, be very difficult to establish precisely where the line between necessity and luxury should be drawn, or even what criteria should be used for drawing it.

Interestingly enough, the one single electrical "good" which is most widely distributed in this country is the television set. It would seem that if one can afford nothing else, one needs entertainment—or perhaps consolation! The radio and the television set offer human companionship to those who may otherwise be isolated in any one of a great variety of ways.

When we talk of human needs, we shall be talking of them both physically and culturally. (The mental aspects, intellectual and emotional, will be taken up later.) But here we come to another problem. There has always been more than one culture within our society, and more than one way of describing any of them. The Registrar General has five "classes" drawn up according to "father's occupation" (except where there is no father, when the mother has, or all too often does *not* have, an occupation). Popularly, we talk about "upper", "middle" and "lower" classes. Class differences are sometimes invoked in derogatory terms in order to avoid the examination of some individual problem. A way has to be found to recognize, but not to label without thought, the variety of cultures which exist at one and the same time.

Recognizing Differences

Over the last twenty years or so, what we have been used to calling "immigrant" cultures have established themselves firmly as part of the native scene. We need to be able to study normal development within these cultures "without prejudice" (as the lawyers say) in more senses than one. We need, among other things, *not* to make the assumption that "normally" the reader of a book such as this will be "white" skinned and "middle class"!

There can be a sense in which "discrimination" is a positive recognition of differing qualities, experiences, and needs; but there is a bad sense in which the labelling of differences leads to a denial of the essential common humanity.

We must, as it were, be anthropologists in our own country, and discover for ourselves the indigenous and other hidden cultures of our own inhabitants. We must find out, in all our different cultures, what is accepted as normal and also what the hidden assumptions are. The potentialities are endless and unknown.

It is important for cultural differences to be recognized, not only by the doctor but by the teacher and the social worker—whatever their own cultural background and whether or not they are themselves indigenous.

Thus, in addition to the duality of diagnosis, there is an added dimension from the cultural background. We must now have three aspects: physical abnormalities as against "standard" patterns; maturational abnormalities in development; and social abnormalities as seen within their own cultural background.

When a particular problem comes to notice, emphasis is likely to be put on a single one of these aspects. Whenever one aspect is chosen as being the appropriate one to enclose work for a particular problem, the other two should also be kept in mind, even if only to say that it is *not* necessary to envisage them for this particular purpose.

Methods of Study

The physical approach to the study of the human body and to the treatment of illnesses has had remarkable success. Procedures, based on structural studies, in this century and the latter half of the previous century, have added to the expectation of life of our present generation, have reduced the incidence of many diseases, almost completely wiped out others, and, to a lesser extent, have increased the effectiveness of treatment of disorders of mental life—i.e. of behaviour, and of thoughts and feelings. Some such disturbances are explainable in terms of physical change, yet many seem to elude explanation in terms of physical processes. Many people still hope that eventually all human activity, including mental processes, will be explainable (and controllable) on a physical level; yet there seem to be many aspects of human life for which physical explanations do not seem appropriate. For these disturbances, another kind of intervention would seem to be necessary for treatment, and another language to describe the process.

If we wish to study the mental life of human beings as a rational process, we must make assumptions similar to those for the study of physical aspects—namely, that this too is understandable—that our thoughts, feelings and behaviour, and even our mental illnesses, make sense. Thus, we have a *psychology* of the normal which corresponds to the physiological, and a *psycho*pathology, which is the study of abnormal mental processes. In this field we become aware, too, of the importance of other aspects of life, some of which have been mentioned earlier. We become aware that a description of events is a preliminary to therapeutic intervention when disorders are apparent to the individual who suffers or to those with whom the individual lives. The description becomes the equivalent of diagnosis, and the terms in which a situation is described will often determine the type of intervention which takes place.

Organized and Unorganized Help

So far, it has been an assumption that the problems are to be studied scientifically, and that help is to be given professionally. Yet human problems have always received varying degrees of help from fellow human beings, in unorganized as well as organized channels. Professionally trained workers differ from untrained workers in that they apply their help within a disciplined framework, and are able to define the tasks which they undertake. Untrained workers may be personally gifted and do good work with the goodness of their personality. They are unable to transmit their techniques to other people unless they have studied the process of what they do. This is why many good organizations die with the death of a very talented and devoted founder. It is the professional self, not the personal self, which immortalizes the work of an organization.

If the diagnosis is in *environmental* terms, the intervention may be legal or administrative, and in some cases there may be a need to formulate the needs in these terms, to guide the individual to the social services, and to enable him or the family as a whole to utilize the appropriate provisions.

When the diagnosis is in *clinical* terms, the intervention required is a medical one. Preventive services may be applied to large groups of individuals; curative processes towards single individuals.

When the diagnosis is in *interpersonal* terms intervention is in the relationships.

It is this field in which unorganized intervention is still likely to occur, as every member of the public claims to be an "expert" in human relationships.

No community can ever deny its members the benefit of giving and receiving support and understanding on a voluntary basis, but the professional work which is to be organized by the social service departments of local authorities has far-reaching responsibilities, including activities which require the enforcement of statutory obligations.

A unique function of voluntary organizations is to explore new areas of need which are given insufficient recognition by governmental and local authority services, and to provide facilities which have not yet received official authorization. They may fill the gaps between existing services, and apply pressures for the directing of resources to neglected sections of the community. It is often the fate of voluntary organizations to have their successful movements taken over and incorporated into official services; and the enthusiastic pioneer is suceeded by those who learn to formulate the ideas in a way which can be communicated to new entrants who can develop and maintain professionalized skill.

There always remains an area of human endeavour that goes beyond theory and training and which has to be preserved by the renewal of inspiration, often by private individuals, in each generation.

Professionalism and training become specially important wherever the services are intended to be applied to the community as a whole, and where the workers have to be answerable for their standards, and where the consumer does not have an easy opportunity to refuse what is offered.

Professional Help at Different Levels: Points of Growth

Some professions have long traditions and the image is well established. Doctors, teachers and nurses receive a professional education, pass qualifying examinations, and acquire great experience in their profession. They work in their own field with the authority of their professional background. Nevertheless they are consulted by people on matters outside the range of their training and professional experience. In such matters, then, if they are to respond at all to the call for help, the response is with the untrained part of their personality, and the value of their response depends upon qualities which have no relation to their professional skill. When one deals with problems of human interaction, new knowledge must compete with the general level of untutored understanding in the general population, and there is need also for recognition of the fact that the same untutored processes will accompany the attitudes of the trained professional worker in this field, even in spite of training. All professional workers must learn to recognize the times when they respond to people's needs with their professional skill and understanding, and they must beware of confusing these with the occasions when the response is no different from what it might have been if they had never received training. At any moment they must be prepared to ask by what authority they act. They must also be prepared to recognize that they may develop a habit of seeing all problems as having an answer in one particular dimension.

Once again, we have to recall that our observations are always limited to what can be seen from one viewpoint. Our enlightenment is partial, and, even though it seems to be appropriate to a particular problem, the usefulness of any level of intervention depends upon the degree to which it can become acceptable to those to whom it is to be applied.

We must remember the other possible lines of enquiry which were referred to at the beginning, and the various levels of intervention referred to immediately above, when from time to time we may find ourselves talking about *the* "cause" or *the* "treatment needs" of some particular illness or aspect of behaviour, and when some other viewpoint might be equally relevant. We must realize that at times we are all inclined to claim the whole truth in a particular explanation of living events, yet our observations have relevance only within their own framework. Different groups of professional workers examine the problems and pursue truth in their own way, yet absolute truths and standards appear to be something that we are destined to pursue and never attain.

Where there is only one *right* way we feel secure. Doubts and uncertainties are a luxury that sometimes we feel we can do without. We need a few certainties for our daily bread and our ordinary work. We choose professions through which we direct ourselves to the helping of some particular individuals with specific problems. Professions have their boundaries and their limitations. Their rules, and their skills are based upon training which uses as much knowledge as is available.

It is when we become dissatisfied with our knowledge and our certainties that we may be ready to take the next step in personal and professional growth. It is at this point of growth that different professions have something in common. At this growing point we meet members of other professions who are having the same struggles, and who may be seeking the company of others in their ventures into unknown territory.

Levels of Description: Diagnosis

It is possible to summarize these general considerations from the point of view of the practical consequences of the study and description. Thus, human activities and problems can be said to be able to be experienced and expressed:

(1) In diagnostic terms—referring to physical abnormalities expressed as pathology in comparison with the normal structure and functioning (the anatomy and the physiology).

(2) In developmental terms—referring to stages of maturation in a particular individual and relating the capacity at one time to the stages of growth of that individual, while making comparisons with other individuals of the same age.

(3) In environmental and cultural terms—referring to material resources such as finance and housing, to occupation, recreational and educational opportunities, and cultural aspects which relate to the community as a whole and to particular cultures which exist side by side with, and which interact with, one another.

It is necessary to recognize that every disturbance or problem of individuals or families can be explained to some extent in terms of any or all of the above three categories.

Incompleteness of Provision for Essential Needs

When problems are experienced, usually a choice is made as to the area in which help is required before any approach is made to one of the helping professional services. The choice does not depend upon any absolute standards; and the response that is made will also depend upon uncertain factors such as the state of knowledge, the resources available, and upon the degree of acceptability of any particular approach both to the recipient, and the agency which supplies the help. An individual feels distress and may justifiably relate it to bad housing, unsuitable employment, or shortage of money. In some slightly different circumstances, a similar problem might be seen as the consequence of impaired physical health, and help would be sought from the doctor. In yet other circumstances, the distress would be experienced in terms of interaction within the home. A disturbed marital relationship can be given the blame for physical or mental illness or for inability to deal personally with external circumstances. Even when a disturbed relationship is incriminated as the cause of some particular person's distress, the intervention may range from legal processes, joint counselling, or complex systems of individual or conjoint family therapy. The professional worker who is first consulted may respond in the terms in which the problem is presented or may restate the problem in another framework.

Help Based on Perception of Essential Needs

No professional worker has the right to deny the reality of the problem which is first presented, but should carry the skill and authority to *add* to the original perception and thus be able to direct help into areas which previously had been unexplored. The essence of the professional response is to accept the solution which is offered in the disguise of a statement of the problem, and to be able to convert that solution (which in any case has not worked) into a fresh problem.

2

Definitions of Personality

Categories of Definition

A scientific study of personality starts with a definition of terms. There is no shortage of definitions of personality which can be used as a starting point. G. W. Allport in his book *Personality—a Psychological Interpretation*[1] devotes the entire second chapter to definitions, and there are fifty of them. Introducing these definitions he casually refers to personality as "the total manifold psycho-physical individuality", and this phrase takes in the essentials of several definitions with a more formal structure.

Etymology gives us the history of how the meanings of a word have changed and developed, thus indicating notions which are still lurking in the background. The word "personality" has been considered to be derived from *persona*, which denoted the theatrical mask used in Greek drama to indicate the character which the actor was portraying. Another possible derivation, of Latin origin, is the phrase *per sonare*, which applied to the device in the mask through which the actor projected his voice. In one case, the emphasis is on the assumed role; in the other, there is reference to what is revealed of himself by the person behind the mask. There are other meanings of the word "person", derived from the same source; emphasis on his importance ("quite a person"); representative, e.g. parson of the Church; and a special use of the word "person" is applied to part of the male body, i.e. the penis. In a legal context it may be said that, "A man exposed his person". The genitalia of a female may also be given a name which alludes to the whole personality when the words used are "her shape".

Psychological definitions are grouped in many classes, some referring to mental organization or to patterns of behaviour, and others to mental structure as described by adherents of various psychological schools. There are also omnibus definitions such as the one by Morton Prince who defined personality as "the sum-total of all the biological innate dispositions, impulses, tendencies, appetites and instincts of the individual, and the acquired dispositions and tendencies—acquired by experience".

Each definition has a value for a particular purpose in a particular setting. This idea is expressed in a formal way in William James's description of "What Pragmatism Means":[2]

---

[1] Henry Holt, New York, 1937. Revised, 1963.
[2] W. James, *Pragmatism: A New Name for Some Old Ways of Thinking*, Longman, Green & Co., 1907.

"The pragmatic method is primarily a method of settling metaphysical disputes that otherwise might be interminable. Is the world one or many?—fated or free?—material or spiritual?—here are notions either of which may or may not hold good of the world; and disputes over such notions are unending. The pragmatic method in such cases is to try to interpret each notion by tracing its respective practical consequences. What difference would it practically make to any one if this notion rather than that notion were true? If no practical difference whatever can be traced, then the alternatives mean practically the same thing, and all dispute is idle. Whenever a dispute is serious, we ought to be able to show some practical difference that must follow from one side or the other's being right."

The pragmatic approach is not the haphazard selection of ideas in quick succession for "trial and error", as some of the "error" can be avoided by doing the "trying" in imagination. This requires an awareness of different methods that could be tried. The exercise, then, is to ask "if we use this approach, rather than another one, in which direction will it take us?" Touchstone in *As You Like It* had the same idea which he expressed in the words "... much virtue in If".

Testing Theories: a Pragmatic View

John Dewey, the educationalist whose philosophical ideas have recently been revalued, uses the notion specifically with regard to scientific or empirical knowledge.[3] If theories are genuinely different from each other, they must have different practical consequences, either in some action to be taken, or in an alteration in the way in which we now see or describe a problem. (A difference to *be* a difference must *make* a difference!)

A theory may be taken as being true just so long as it is "fruitful", i.e. if it works well in predicting what will happen, and gives rises to higher levels of generalization. The history of science is the history of notions becoming discarded, particularly if no longer providing fruitful generalizations. But we must not forget that many theories stand the test for hundreds or thousands of years at a time, and the basic assumption of science is, (and has to be) that the physical universe is understandable and therefore predictable and describable.

Scientific observations need theories and definitions in order that the observers may communicate with one another in some common language. The ordinary individual has theories of personality even if the theories are not formulated in precise words. People assume that it is possible to understand another individual's feelings in certain circumstances, and they are prepared to explain, or even predict, someone else's behaviour with some degree of confidence. This implies that behaviour, thoughts and feelings follow some kind of pattern that is regular enough to justify the making of predictions. When explanations or predictions are not expressed precisely, they cannot be checked, and perhaps it is by forgetting wrong predictions, and remembering correct ones, that the ordinary individuals retain

[3] See *John Dewey Reconsidered* (Edited by R. S. Peters) Routledge and Kegan Paul, 1977—especially the paper by A. Quinton.

their faith in a capacity to put the self in another individual's place. Scientific theories are at a disadvantage against ordinary beliefs in having to be expressed in terms that can be challenged.

We are now ready to turn from the generalities of scientific theories and descriptions, and, from the wide range of available definitions of personality, to our own formulations, chosen for the purpose of work in remedial and developmental services.

Personality as an Assemblage of Qualities

This definition is selected and slightly adapted, from the large number given in the *Oxford English Dictionary:*
  "an assemblage of qualities which makes each individual unique".

This definition has the advantage of being sufficiently vague to include a large number of factors, and makes it possible to discuss separate qualities and to refer to them in turn as we trace an individual's development at each stage of life. Here there are two opposing ideas: the uniqueness which is the outstanding characteristic of individual man, and the regularities and uniformities which are the outcome of scientific attempts to impose order on nature, and, in particular, on mankind as a whole.

We can describe the separate qualities in a variety of categories. Purely for convenience, we shall use as headings *Physical, Intellectual* and *Emotional* qualities. It will be recognized that these headings cannot be discussed entirely separately; each one of them is linked with the other two. The separation is for the convenience of description and for the communication of ideas, and we need to recall that the description of separate qualities cannot include the idea of the wholeness of personality. A conceptual analysis of personality can take place in the mind, but one cannot take a human being to pieces.

Extensions of Personality

Another definition of personality refers to the popular use of the word when it is taken to describe the effect of an individual on other people. Amongst the definitions which Allport quotes on this theme, one is:
  "The sum total of the effect made by an individual upon society".

This type of meaning is applicable when it is necessary to emphasise the *social* aspect of personality. Here we take into account the image that an individual has of the self as a result of the internalization of his or her own experience of the impression that is made on others.

The social aspect is important when we wish our descriptions to go beyond the range of what is included within the skin of an individual. It is easy to recognize in terms of the second definition that an individual's personality can be different in different company. It is also possible to recognize that there are extensions of personality which go beyond the physical constitution, appearance and colouring, and include clothes, a man's pipe, a woman's perfume, the spectacles an individual wears, wallet or handbag, and such possessions as the motor-car, the house, furniture, and books on the shelves in the home. These are items by which people are recognized or which give them their own image of themselves.

When considering the effect of an individual on others, there is a popular usage of the word personality, in a quantitative sense, as when people say of an individual that he has "lots of personality" or even that he "has personality". It is rather reminiscent of the use of the word blood-pressure, only to *have* blood-pressure is a bad thing and to *have* personality is a good thing!

Personality as a Dynamic Interaction

A third view of personality is focused more directly on the relationships of individuals with one another, and with the emotional life in individuals and in groups. This class of definition includes various psycho-analytical and psychological theories of personality dealing with the mental organization of individuals and of groups. For some purposes, processes of interpersonal relationships between individuals in a family or larger groups are more important than observations in terms of the mental life of a single individual. We may find it possible to describe the family processes dealing with the family as a single unit and not as separate individuals.

There are precise technical constructions of the inner mental life (or the *psyche*) inferred from the practice of psychotherapy. The various schools of dynamic psychotherapy share the assumption of forces in constantly changing interplay between internal pressures and the external demands of the living and non-living worlds. Personality in this sense is:

"A dynamic interaction between an individual and his environment".

A further elaboration of this dynamic aspect of personality is the idea that the family, or any other group of individuals, has a unity of its own. Just as the dynamic formulations of the structure of personality are derived from the practice of individual psychotherapy, group dynamics and family dynamics have origins respectively in group psychotherapy and family treatment. In both cases, other disciplines are called upon to fill out the theory. Sociology is invoked for the study of groups and of families; and, more recently, general systems theory has been brought into service in order to deal with the complex simultaneous changes in the somewhat undefined membership of the groups or families who receive treatment under these labels.

For the purpose of description—the most useful definition is the one which refers to personality as an assemblage of qualities.

Description of the Physical, Intellectual and Emotional Aspects

The preliminary descriptions will deal with the three classes of quality mentioned earlier, i.e. physical, intellectual and emotional. The *physical* aspects of personality include body-structure—height and weight, physical appearance, colouring of eyes and hair. Some of these features (such as colouring) are determined at conception and are inherited in a manner that follows the regularities which we describe as genetic laws. Other factors are inherited in the form of potentialities or limitations. An individual's capacity for growth may be an inherited quality, but the reaching of the limits of that capacity depends upon the good fortune of receiving a diet which will satisfy optimum requirements.

Sheldon[4] made a large number of measurements of body-structure and described physical types in correlation with types of emotional reaction and predisposition to particular types of mental disturbance. These results favour the idea that body shape has fixed characteristics which are related to inherited constitutional factors linking structure with temperament. Mental processes also are linked with physiological factors such as the *metabolic* processes, i.e. the chemical interchange which follows the absorption of food, and which results in the production of energy. Different people think in different ways, and their bodies work in different ways. The difference is in the body chemistry.

Inherited factors are obviously important, but the effect of nurture has also to be taken into account when we are estimating the contribution of nature. Higher standards of food and of care have led to an increase in the average height and weight of children of comparable age during the last fifty years. On a nationwide range, the population as a whole is reaching a standard which once applied exclusively to the richest sections of the community. In times of economic distress the general height and weight decreases. Individual deficiencies may be partly determined by individual experience of deprivation of care. The same result may occur when, as a result of some types of illness, there is a failure to absorb an adequate diet even when one is available.

Furthermore, some characteristics which had been thought to be racial, and therefore inherited, may be altered when individuals of a race are moved to a different environment. For instance, the short stature of the Japanese became altered when individuals from Japan were brought up in European or American culture. This has happened in Japan itself following the gradual adoption of diets introduced from other cultures. Conflict exists, and is constantly being renewed, as to how much genetic factors determine differences in physique and in average performance in different ethnic groups. The difference in performance is a stark reality. The disadvantaged position of Negroes in the United States of America, and West Indians in this country, is beyond doubt. To impute these differences to fixed genetic qualities is highly suspect, and so-called scientific studies can never take into account all the factors.

Thus in studying the physical aspects of personality we have to recognize a wide range of differences within what is accepted as normal in any setting, and the existence of differences that are considered to go beyond the normal.

By the *intellectual* aspect of personality we mean the capacity for conscious thought and the ability to direct thoughts for a particular purpose. We think of *intelligence* as a capacity in which inheritance is believed to play the major part, and in contrast we think of *educational attainment* as referring to the amount of knowledge that an individual might have at any one moment. The importance of the role of environmental influences, going far beyond the formal educational pro-

[4] *The Varieties of Temperament*, Harper, New York, 1942.

cess, has recently been stressed alongside that of inheritance in relation to the development of intelligence.[5]

Intellectual Growth

Development implies change in a direction which is approved. It is thus more than growth. The selective aims that underlie any efforts at promoting development will affect the nature of the provision which is thought necessary to achieve those aims. Thus the idea of normal provision is relative to prevailing ideas. Granted sufficient material provision, there is an apparent inevitability about physical growth. This idea cannot be transferred to all the potentialities of performance and of emotional and intellectual development. Nobody considers it desirable to develop every single potential to its ultimate extent.

The growth of intelligence goes along with the growth of the body, although not precisely at the same rate. There is an approximate constancy of the level of intelligence as compared with that of other individuals, and therefore it is possible to arrive at a measure which indicates the relationship of an individual's intelligence with other individuals of the same age. This is not measured by an absolute figure, as height is, but by a relative figure, known as a "Quotient", which is used to compare an individual's intelligence with that of a notional average individual of the same age. The mental age is derived from the standardization of responses to a battery of tests applied to a very large child population. The child whose pattern of response is similar to that of the average of 8-year-old children is credited with a mental age of 8 whatever the chronological age.

The intelligence quotient was originally derived by taking the mental age divided by the chronological age, and multiplying by 100 (MA $\div$ CA $\times$ 100 = IQ). The calculation is based on the use of the figure 100 to represent the average. It will be obvious that a child with a chronological age of 10 and a mental age of 12 will have an IQ of 120. A child of the same chronological age with a mental age of 8 will have an IQ of 80. Modern tests by-pass the elucidation of a mental age.

The use of the concept of *mental age* is one way of describing the intellectual capacity of children whose intelligence is far above or far below the average, and has been used for communications with other professions. The use of the *quotient* was intended to provide a figure to represent the intelligence of the same individual at different ages. These hopes have not been entirely realized as the quotient does not necessarily stay constant.

For statistical purposes, description in terms of the *standard deviation* is more adequate, but this is a sophisticated approach, and its use requires familiarity with statistical methods; the standard deviation is indicated in Fig. 1. (See p. 139.)

Estimations of intelligence came into being mainly in the educational field and became linked with the capacity to benefit from educational experience. It was, therefore, natural to regard the cessation of intellectual growth as coinciding approximately with the school-leaving age, or alternatively to defer it to the age of achieving maximum physical height.[6]

[5] A. H. Halsey, Genetics, Social Structure and Intelligence, *Brit. J. Sociol.* **9**, 15–20 (1958); B. Bernstein, Social Structure, Language and Learning, *Educational Res.* **3**, 173–6 (1961).

[6] It should be stressed that the very notion of intelligence is now treated with suspicion by many psychologists, and they would dissociate themselves from the section which follows.

Some forms of test, particularly those concerned with the speed of mental operations, inferred the notion of a peak of growth in late adolescence, with a decline in adult life accelerating in old age. This, if confirmed, would have implications for career structure and for job allocation in tasks which demand the highest intellectual capacity. This idea should not go unchallenged. Intellectual capacity may well contain unused reserves, which can be developed in people of every range of intelligence and at every age, e.g. (if the conjunction is not invidious) in the severely mentally handicapped and in the very old.

The intelligence tests which are used for measurement of intelligence differ according to the purpose for which they are required. There is no test which can measure the full range of mental life, and no test can measure any quality which does not find expression in some kind of external observable performance. Psychologists used to try to devise tests for what was postulated as the inborn capacity or potentiality. The best, however, that is possible, is to aim at avoiding the use of tests which are unduly influenced by the particular educational or cultural background of individuals, unless indeed they are examining the educational or cultural background. No test can completely exclude such influences, and different tests are effective, more or less, for the purpose for which they are used. Tests used in the educational setting are intended to differentiate the types of educational needs of different children. Other tests are used clinically as part of the investigation of mental life in relation to the treatment of some mental disorder.

Educational tests usually are *group tests* which demand responses to a set of questions on paper, and the results are examined afterwards. *Individual tests* allow the psychologist to take into account the attitude of the child as well as the content of the response. This is necessarily a subjective process. All tests must be affected in some degree by the previous experience of the individual, but there are many tests which give results which are considered to be satisfactory enough for the making of comparisons between individuals who have been brought up in similar cultures and conditions. Some tests are useful in the clinical field as part of the information on which a diagnosis is made. Every test has both value and limitations for a given practical purpose.

Intelligence tests give a snapshot view. Piaget provided a radically different approach to cognitive activity by concentrating on regular definable sequences of successive stages of development.[7] Thus his study does not provide a quantitative measure of intelligence but indicates the points at which a child has arrived in his or her process of growth. He reconciles the idea of continuity with recognizable separate stages.

Descriptions of intelligence can never be fully comprehensive. Mention must be made of the stimulating idea of Liam Hudson,[8] that there are differences between people who use "divergent" and "convergent" approaches to problems. Hudson discusses originality and creativity and these notions have also been touched upon by Edward De Bono in his account of lateral thinking.

It will be seen that the essential nature of intelligence eludes precise definition. In

[7] J. Piaget, *The Child's Construction of Reality*, Routledge and Kegan Paul, 1955.
[8] L. Hudson, *Contrary Imaginations*, Penguin, 1967.

general terms, intelligence is the capacity to extract relevant information, in order to draw conclusions, when dealing with a problem, with some purpose in view.

The material for the growth of intelligence consists of the experiences of a child at home, at school, and in the environmental background. Children will differ in their intelligence level at any age just as they differ in height, and just as there are those who are tall and those who are short in height, there are some children with high intelligence and some children with low intelligence. Beyond the range of normal, there are those who are giants and those who are dwarfs. There are likewise those with intelligence so high, and perhaps so uneven in its distribution, that they are outside the normal.

Joan Freeman[9] has studied the performance and behaviour of children labelled as "gifted" and compared them with those of equal ability whose "giftedness" goes unrecognized. She showed that high intelligence in itself is not a handicapping condition, in spite of the stereotyped equation: giftedness = problems. There may, however, be unwelcome side effects on a child's development which are associated with external circumstances and the attitudes of some parents to having a gifted child. Similarly there are people whose intelligence is so low that they are unable to fit in with normal living without special educational, occupational, and (in some cases) residential care.

Intelligence may suffer along with physical qualities in the hazards in foetal life and the process of delivery. "Brain damage" has been associated with foetal infections, low birth weight, and lack of adequate obstetric care. Cigarette smoking during pregnancy has also been recognized as an important factor, and so has the taking of alcohol and drugs. Some of the abnormal processes of development of intelligence may occur in individuals of normal inheritance as a result of post-natal experiences. Deprivation of experience inhibits growth of intelligence in the same way as an insufficient diet prevents physical growth. Children who are brought up in institutions, or who are otherwise denied close and continuous contact with adults who are interested in them, show such slow development that they may be mistaken for those with congenital deficiencies in intelligence. If the deprivation is continuous, they actually *become* defective notwithstanding their original normal potential.

There can be also deprivation of a cultural kind—even the vocabulary which is available in a home or a district affects the growth of intelligence. Words are the means by which we communicate and through which we express our mental activity. Words are also the material out of which we are able to build up our thought processes and through which we perceive the world. A limited vocabulary will limit the capacity for the development of some aspects of mental life. A common language does not always exist between pupil and teacher even in indigenous communities. Without a shared understanding of the meaning of words, it is not possible to communicate abstract ideas. Education suffers when communication is hampered by separation of cultures and a failure to understand dialect, idiom, or literal translations from the child's or the teacher's first language.

The *emotional* life of an individual encompasses the basic feelings and moods

[9] J. Freeman *Gifted Children: Their Identification and Development in a Social Context*, MTP Press, 1979.

which are the product of internal mental processes, and the interactions with other people. It is concerned with the elemental feelings of love and hate, and the derivatives of those experiences, tenderness and aggression. It seems probable that the intensity with which these feelings are expressed may be an inherent quality, and that different individuals have a different capacity for emotion. There are also emotional differences between people which are the result of events in the formative years associated with temperament.

Thus the emotional aspects of personality may be a resultant of natural endowment and the experiences after birth. We could imagine an emotional quotient similar to the intelligence quotient if only we had data which were measurable. The food needed to develop the emotional capacity of a growing child is relationships of the right quality within the family leading to emotional growth which is "normal". We can also accept that there are variations which would still come within the range of normal. Normality would not depend upon absolute standards but upon what is considered healthy in a particular community at a particular time. We cannot escape the making of value judgements which are implicit in our norms, but these, also, differ in different communities.

We could also recognize that in any community some people have emotional development which is deficient, because of some inborn lack, or because of starvation of the requisite kind of relationship.

We have to consider the requirements for what we would regard as normal or optimal development. At this stage we could just refer to the idea that the emotional life includes opposing feelings at all stages, and that there are aspects which are unconscious as well as others which are conscious. There is simultaneous love and hate, one component being hidden from awareness at some particular moment. The love of a parent for a child can be accompanied by resentment at some of the burdens that the care of the child entails; or the rejection of a child, however openly expressed, may be accompanied by the opposing feelings of love and the wish to keep and to nourish the child whose presence seems so much undesired. This conflict of feelings or *ambivalence* underlies all relationships. Maturity can be considered to be the awareness of both components, the acceptance of the universality of conflict, and the readiness to take personal responsibility for the control of these feelings.

The Image and the Source

Whatever method we use in observing an individual, the result of our study is incomplete. Nevertheless, human beings have a knack of filling out a complete picture from fragmentary observations. We build up some idea of a wholeness which may be accurate, or not, even when we use a medium which leaves out everything but that which can be observed during a single moment of perception. We can see a photograph of an individual which has captured a fleeting glimpse, and yet we feel that we know how the individual will behave. We receive a little more information when we see a film at the cinema, but if it is a silent film we have observations just of actions and gestures. A sound film adds the voice, and with this further material we can recognize an individual who was seen previously in another film, and feel that we know more about him. We recognize the disembodied voice of a person on the radio, and a "personality" in a television programme may appear to us as if he were a familiar visitor to our home. The actor whom we see in the flesh, but at a distance, appears to us even larger than life because we fill out in our imagination the parts of his personality which are not observable. We often feel disappointed when we meet in person someone whom we have known only through a medium which has its limitations.

If we read a book and later see a play or film based upon it, frequently it happens that we are disappointed because our own imaginings are more satisfying to us than those of the artistic interpreter who was responsible for the production. This also happens to us with people we know when, because we have built up a fantasy of them from the limited ways in which they have appeared to us, we are disappointed by later experience of them which makes them more human and fallible. Sometimes this appears to us to be the result of their deterioration, and we may say "they have let us down".

Parents do something like this with their children, comparing them at various stages with an image which has no relation to the real child. Teachers do something similar with their pupils, doctors with their patients, case-workers with their clients, and, in ordinary social relationships, people judge their friends by an image which they themselves have created. The first impression borrows something from previous experience of other people, and this provides a number of categories into which each new acquaintance is grouped. We add in our minds something more than we can see in those with whom we are in contact. We may feel it as a personal injury whenever we are forced to alter the first mental picture. What is discussed here is given a technical shape in descriptions of "rejection" and of "transference".

Bearing in mind the fact that our observations always contain some distortion, it is part of professional work and of scientific observations to minimise the distortion. It is with the knowledge of these limitations that we trace the development of an individual through certain maturational stages of life, and discuss the innate qualities and the subsequent provisions which are necessary for development in each of the stages to which we shall refer.

Character and Temperament

There are a number of consistent features of personality that survive in each individual throughout the vicissitudes of the processes of development.

Character is the term used to describe the effective organization of an individual's capacities. The word sometimes carries a moral implication, referring to the way in which an individual is in control of activities.

Temperament refers to the prevailing moods of an individual and is dependent upon inborn factors which determine the balance of endocrine secretions. It is associated with the type of response and the degree of susceptibility to emotional stimulation. The concept is related to the postulation by Hippocrates of the four humours (blood, phlegm, yellow bile and black bile) which, in different proportions, were thought to be responsible for the constancy or changing nature of the moods of different individuals. This idea has been given fresh life within the framework of the physiological concept of *homoestasis*. The cells and fibres which constitute the central and peripheral nervous systems include two main subdivisions which are antatomically distinct and which are physiologically in opposition. These maintain the balance and influence the stability or equilibrium of the activities of vital organs and of the body as a whole. This balance, when slightly disturbed, may be restored without conscious sensation.

Psychological evidence of the existence of different basic temperaments is being provided by work such as that of Schaffer referred to in Chapter 5.

3

Theories of Personality

So FAR we have used *definitions* and *descriptions* of personality in two senses: as they are used in ordinary discourse, and also, more formally, to indicate the areas in which theoretical studies can take place. *Theories* open up new ground and we are devoting this chapter to descriptions of some theories relating to personality.

Theories can be explanatory in that they provide new metaphors for illuminating and interpreting our experience, or they can be predictive in that they allow the creation of hypotheses which can be put to the test of experimental observations.

Descriptive Theories

In this century, among the influential descriptive theories of human behaviour and experience, there have been those formulated under the labels of Behaviourism, Cognitive Development, and Psychoanalysis. Alongside these systematized theoretical models there still remain ideas about the upbringing of children and about the organization of behaviour of people of all ages, depending upon tradition, folklore, and maxims, handed down through the generations (and often no worse for that). Added to this accumulation of dicta, there are theoretical systems in which social learning is said to take place by the acceptance of the norms or values generally held within a particular society and by the adoption of approved roles in appropriate circumstances of one's life. For our purpose, we shall confine ourselves to a discussion of those theories which not only give a general picture of development but also provide a basis for professional intervention where normal functioning fails.

The name "Social Learning", as a sociological rather than a psychological theory, utilizes concepts of "norms" and "roles" which society adopts. Norms are majority values, not universal ones, and children receive them from their home, their school, their religious institutions (where such still hold sway) and, above all, from their peers. There is the implication of a well defined homogenous society, such as does indeed exist in some localities. Most of us, however, live in "pluralistic" societies in which many codes exist side by side.

Social learning does in fact take place and the theory of it recognizes the previously unnoted activities in the playground, and in family and neighbourhood life, that contribute to personal development. In spite of attempts to organize our knowledge of these processes, much of the relevant information has to be found in the original studies of individual workers such as those of Iona and Peter Opie.

Behaviourism and Learning Theory

First put forward by Hull[1] and Watson,[2] and pre-eminently promoted by Skinner,[3] the theory of Behaviourism is based upon a stimulus–response explanation. On this Hull organized his comprehensive "Learning Theory" to explain the acquisition of all human characteristics. Given the "input", the "output" can be predicted. In common with other developmental theories, inferences can be drawn as to how any particular individual reached his or her present state. The theory is most notable for its claim to work forwards towards predictable (and predicted) future characteristics. Skinner pungently insists that such people as psychiatrists and philosophers have tried to explain human behaviour without making detailed observations of actual human actions. He takes for granted the notion of "an action", and of how one picks out (and labels) an action from surrounding behaviour. Desired notions can be reinforced, and undesired ones extinguished. Working mainly with pigeons, Skinnner has found that rewards (such as food) work much better than punishments (such as giving electric shocks) in reinforcing desired actions and extinguishing undesired ones. No response at all, works best for extinguishing undesired actions, and *erratic* reinforcement makes any kind of behaviour persist for a long time.

The behaviourist model seems to us to be inadequate as a total explanation of human behaviour, if only because it has no need for the notions of consciousness or intention. For example, if one describes the movements of a leg, what is it that distinguishes swinging to and fro from kicking? As any child knows, one of these descriptions is an exoneration from the consequences.

The advantage of theory is that experiences are formulated for general use, and the insights can become a recognized, interpretive model. Learning theory has become a basis of some of the procedures used in psychiatry, social work and education.

Within psychiatry, the theory has been applied under the label of "behaviour therapy" or (as we prefer) "behaviour shaping" to the treatment of phobias, obsessional states, and some of the so-called anomalies of sexual behaviour. In social-work practice, behaviour-shaping techniques can be introduced to clients who are willing to accept a contract to carry out procedures, under the instructions of the worker, aimed at inducing an approved pattern of changed behaviour. In education, formal programmes of learning can be set up, and teaching machines can be employed, for the imparting of that kind of knowledge in which the truth of the information is never in doubt.

When the aim is that of changing behaviour to a more satisfactory but predetermined form, or whenever it is necessary to develop a specified skill, there is no need to consider any underlying mental state, nor to take into account the personality as a whole. The proof of the effectiveness is in the performance which can be achieved.

[1] C. L. Hull, *A Behaviour System*, Yale University Press, 1952.
[2] J. B. Watson and R. Rayner, "Conditioned emotional reactions", *J. Exp. Psychol.* **3** (1920).
[3] B. F. Skinner, *The Behaviour of Organisms*, Appleton-Century-Crofts, 1938; B. F. Skinner, *Science and Human Behaviour*, Macmillan Co., 1953.

The brevity of this section should not be taken as any absolute judgement of the importance of learning theory in the understanding of human development or as a basis for possible interventions. The reader who chooses to give it a greater emphasis in the explanations of human behaviour and its modifications is advised to go direct to the original sources or to writers who are more immersed in them than we are.

Some references have been given in the previous pages. Therapeutic implications will be found in:

V. Meyer and E. S. Chesser, *Behaviour Therapy in Clinical Psychiatry*, Fenguin, 1970.
D. Marholin II (Editor), *Child Behaviour Therapy*, Gardner Press, N.Y., 1978.
I. M. Marks, *Fears and Phobias*, Academic Press, 1969.
Also, learing theory has influenced family therapy in the work of:
J. Haley, *The Uncommon Therapies*, Norton, N.Y., 1973.
S. Minuchin, *Families and Family Therapy*, Harvard University Press, 1974.

Cognitive Growth Theory

Cognitive theories focus on the development of intellectual capacity and on the ability to use and understand symbolic representations of thought.

PIAGET'S DEVELOPMENTAL PSYCHOLOGY

The most influential theorist of cognitive development is Jean Piaget. He has collected thousands of observations of children's responses to various tasks or problems. In tracing the developmental progress, he maintains that younger children cannot fully understand abstract notions (such as that of conservation of volume: the amount of liquid does not change if poured from a container to one of another shape). More constructively, and more strikingly, he takes the wrong answers that children give and shows that they form a consistent pattern. The wrongness of the answer ceases to have a derogatory implication because, at each stage, children have identifiable and predictable ways of thinking which are valid within that stage of growth.

The essential idea is that the stages through which children pass before reaching maturity are invariable. In their central characteristics, they are as distinct as the larva/chrysalis/imago sequence of an insect, but with the very important difference that the transition is gradual and that in some particulars the stages overlap.

Summaries of Piaget's work do not do justice to his rich accounts of the life of childhood. His observations include the child's own commentary on a performance: the "why" as well as the "how" and the "what".

Piaget distinguishes three main *stages* in the development of children's thinking.

In the *sensori-motor* stage (age 0–2 years) the apparently simple motor responses to external stimuli become embodied in a matrix of experiences. Thus, apprehension of the stimuli lays the foundation for comprehension of the external world, and of one's personal responses to it.

The second main stage is the *pre-operational* stage (ages 2–12 years), where there is progress from intuitive processes of thought towards the mastery of logical and abstract thinking. At first, the child is mainly concerned with his or her own impressions of experience of the outside world, and only gradually begins to realize that there are points of view other than one's own. This early intuitive phase includes magical interpretations of external appearances.

Later, within this same stage, comes the phase of *concrete operations*, where the actual handling of physical objects is essential for the building up of a framework of concepts, although the developing concepts are not yet brought together into any complete or coherent theoretical system. Gradually, physical skills, accurate and relevant observations, and the use of language in which to describe one's experiences grow interdependently (along with neurological development). It is during this phase that the child begins to acquire principles of conservation, that is, that such properties as volume, mass and quantity remain constant when material is rearranged but not actually added to or subtracted from.

In this phase, the child learns also through play (amongst other activities) that rules are a cooperative creation, rather than something imposed by adults acting in the name of some intangible authority.

The third and final stage is that of *formal operations* (age 12 to adulthood). At this stage the young person begins to be able to cope with totally abstract chains of reasoning. The separate fragments—of knowledge, of attitudes and of interpretations—are brought together into an ethos and into a theoretical system which may contain many contradictions, but which has some coherence. The potential is there (and for a few is realized) to sort out and reconcile the contradictions.

Piaget's system is pervaded by the notion of *adaptation* which is so diversely interpreted that all we can do is to give our own interpretation of it. It is a dual process of *assimilation* and *accommodation*. Both of these must occur for adaptation to be complete, but whether they happen concurrently or consecutively is not clear. Assimilation refers to the altering of an already conceived frame of ideas to admit new experiences from the outside world; and accommodation to the modifying of perceptions in order to invent patterns of thought and to impose them upon external reality. Thus, all perception is a creative distortion of experience.[4] From this creative aspect of perception we can infer that the results of advanced scientific experiments are not discoveries but inventions.

We do not wish to imply that theory making is confined to the highest level of thought. George Kelly has pointed out that human beings are scientific experimenters from infancy onwards.[5]

The final stage in Piaget's formulation, however, refers to the capacity for sophisticated theorization.

The idea of sequential stages of intellectual growth is important in the educational setting and in every diagnostic process which takes account of human development.

Piaget's actual stages have come in for some reassessment, as also have the contexts in which his observations have been made. Margaret Donaldson maintains that many children show certain kinds of abilities (especially in the area of mathematics) much earlier than Piaget has supposed.[6] She adds the idea that when a

---

[4] In this interpretation of Piaget, we have linked his ideas with those of classical Gestalt psychology.
[5] G. Kelly, *The Psychology of Personal Constructs*, Norton N.Y., 1955.
[6] M. Donaldson, *Children's Minds*, Fontana, 1978.

task has personal significance, a child seems to be able to leap through some of the boundaries of Piaget's stages. Her work emphasizes what has always been implicit in Piaget's own writings: that the stages must not be kept rigidly separate, nor the ages associated with them be taken as universal.

The central idea, that children of the same age could be at different stages of intellectual development has become part of "common sense".

We shall be discussing Piaget's ideas again, in later chapters, with a more specific reference to education.

Psychodynamic Schools

There are a growing number of psychodynamic schools in which there are two purposes: one is to provide a general theoretical explanation of human behaviour and the development of personality; the other is to put the theories to practical use in methods of treatment for specific mental disorders. In many cases the aim has been extended to relieving distress or to finding solutions for problems of living. Thus, psychodynamic schools go beyond those psychiatric ideas which distinguish clearly between the pathological and the normal, and, in fact, draw from the pathological to find explanations for purpose and meaning in everyday actions.

All of them owe their origin to *Freud's* psychoanalytical formulations, even if indirectly. Some schools are in the direct line of Freud's teaching; some are called "Neo-Freudian"; some are "Anti-Freudian"; some would be glad to call themselves "Non-Freudian"! None of them could have existed without Freud.

The term *psychodynamic* has been given a general application to all psychological schools which acknowledge the existence of a changing balance of mental forces in the processes of the mind.

Freud described "mind" in the language of physics, physiology, economics and history. In just the same way, the modern neurophysiologist will use the computer, which is a product of the human brain (or should we say "mind"?) in order to explain the functions of the human brain (or mind). Freud's models are not concrete entities with an independent physical existence, but they are analogies taken from the features of some human achievement. *The value of a model, or an analogy, is in its appropriateness in providing understanding of a function, for a purpose, and within a context.* Some of Freud's models are discussed below.

THE DYNAMIC MODEL

The term *dynamic* implies, in Freudian writings, the idea of *instincts* which are innate, unlearned and universal. When aspects of *animal* behaviour are described as instinctual, they are specific to species, unlearned and serve some biological purpose. (Much of the theory of instincts has had to be altered as a result of the discoveries of ethologists, beginning with the work of Konrad Lorenz.) Freud's theory of instincts was related to sexual drives, aggression, social behaviour and (later) death.

Linked with the instinct theory was the concept of *ambivalence* which involves the simultaneous existence of two opposing, contradictory and irreconcilable attitudes, even though only one of them might find overt expression. The model therefore had to include this idea of conflict, with descriptions of defences against the anxiety which results from the pressures of the repressed component of the conflict, viz. projection, displacement, regression, fixation.

THE TOPOGRAPHICAL MODEL

Here, the mental apparatus is divided, as if spatially, into three systems: Conscious, Pre-conscious and Unconscious. Freud himself never used the term "subconscious".

Within this model, *repression* is the means by which the ideas attached to instincts are denied access to consciousness. The emotions themselves cannot be unconscious—only the ideas to which they are attached. For repression to take place, the "unpleasure" of the conflict must be stronger than the pleasure of the satisfaction obtained from instinctual behaviour.

THE STRUCTURAL MODEL

The *Ego, Id* and *Superego* were described as structures in the mind, and gradually replaced, or supplemented, the topographical divisions. There is now a welcome tendency to think of these terms as referring to mental processes rather than to concrete entities with a specific location.[7]

Ego (which means "I") refers to the conscious self in action. *Id* (which is impersonal, i.e. "it") is not only the repository of contents repressed from consciousness, but is also the reservoir of all the creative and destructive potential which has not yet achieved consciousness. *Superego* (described more fully in Chapter 8) contains all the prohibitions and obligations absorbed originally from parental injunctions, but it also includes the individual's own constructions of fantasied retaliation for the presumption of wishing to derive instinctual satisfaction. The Superego is an internal structure which embodies and elaborates all the concrete and abstract sources of disapproval.

THE HISTORICAL MODEL

The *historical* model allows us to refer to Freudian ideas in relation to stages of development. Briefly, these are: first the *narcissistic* state, before the infant has acquired an external frame of reference; next come the *oral, anal* and *genital* stages, culminating in the *Oedipal Situation*, which expresses, in dramatic form, the complex personal relationships of child and parents. Following the so-called *latency* period, *puberty* heralds the onset of *adult sexuality*.

The value of this model is that one can read backwards from anomalies of emotional life, and trace them to earlier events in specific stages in psychosexual development.

[7] There are, nevertheless, some neurophysiological findings which locate specific mental functions in specific areas of the brain. It would be possible to bring some Freudian formulations into this framework.

TRANSFERENCE RELATIONSHIPS

Some ideas which arose out of the study of the interaction between psychoanalyst and patient have gained a more general application. *Transference*, and *counter-transference* were terms first used to refer to distortions of the relationship of patient and therapist. The patient thinks and behaves irrationally towards the therapist, carrying (transferring) attitudes from previous situations. The term "positive transference", covers the idealization of the therapist. The term "negative transference", applies to perception of hostile, destructive powers in the therapist.

Both aspects of the transference are in the image of previously distorted perceptions of parents as a primary source, and they also derive from secondary transference figures, such as teachers, doctors and other people in authority.

Modern treatment accepts and utilizes the transference as a living example of the enduring patterns of the patient's interpersonal relationships.

Not all the interactions can be attributed to transference; there is a reality aspect of the relationship and, moreover, there is the counter-transference which is the irrational component of the therapist's approaches and responses to the patient.

The exploration of counter-transference is as essential in treatment as is the interpretation of attitudes and relationships of the patient. Greenson[8] has dealt creatively with the whole issue of transference and counter-transference.

CHOICE OF MODEL

It appears to us that insufficient value has been given to Freud's inconsistencies! He allowed himself the freedom to change his concepts from time to time, and to introduce ideas that were at variance with his own existing formulations. He was not inhibited from subsequently re-using ideas that he had hitherto discarded. In the corpus of his library of major works, there is no unitary theory that can represent the whole. Yet attempts have been made to freeze the ideas into a single doctrine (or a dogma). It would be better to think of them as a foundation on which the manifold theory and practice of psychoanalysis continues to be built.

In our attempt to survey psychoanalytical theories, we are aware that some of our statements are incomplete and they will be unacceptable to many writers within psychoanalysis. They do not fully represent our own thoughts on the subject matter! At no point should we claim that our own, or anyone else's, ideas are definitive, comprehensive or unchallengeable.

Freud's developmental ideas are referred to briefly here, and outlined more fully in the chapter that follows. Indeed, we go so far as to use them as the prevailing account of the early years of childhood. This does not mean that all other accounts are excluded; Piagetian and Freudian ideas can fit happily together, whereas, in our view, a strict Behaviourist approach would conflict with both.

The essential contradiction in Freud's writings is that of the idea of *determinism*, which he introduces over and over again to explain the sequence of mental events, as against his practice of treating individual patients as being *free* agents.

[8] R. R. Greenson, *The Technique and Practice of Psychoanalysis*, Vol. 1, The Hogarth Press, 1967.

It is true that many patients are figuratively imprisoned by their past history, and behave *as if* compelled to repeat the behaviour which led to failure and distress. Freud's form of treatment was not a way of providing an excuse for a continuation of such behaviour, nor was it a way of "curing" it. Rather was it a means of increasing, through understanding, the patient's ability to take responsibility for finding alternative ways of responding to external events. In this sense, it differed from traditional medicine, where the patient is ill, and the doctor does the curing. Psychoanalysis, instead, became a cooperative venture in which the responsibility rested finally on the "patient", notwithstanding the popular misconception that it is a process in which the therapist takes over and reshapes the patient's behaviour and personality.

Many of the post-Freudian developments have been evolved specifically to overcome the residual deterministic components in the main structure of psychoanalysis.[9]

Freud himself struggled continually to escape from his dynamic formulations, and to return (not very successfully) to a physical and physiological framework.[10] He had an excuse for this which we have not: he had lived half his life in the pre-Freudian era.

There is now a whole range of psychodynamic schools of thought, some described as humanistic or existential, and some are frankly political. Some attempt to avoid even the mention of mental disorders, and aim to take the treatment of mental distress completely out of the traditional medical framework. Some would oppose any current system of therapy, as representing the constraints of organized society. Thus, some stoutly oppose the notion of diagnosis. Others take a further logical step and resist the idea that any one person can be a therapist to another. Many of their ideas are of inestimable value in challenging comfortably held assumptions about the nature of personality, and of human behaviour and interactions. If we, personally, cannot go along with many of them, we must concede that what may appear to us to be an overstatement is necessary in order to make some important points. Even to list such examples inevitably distorts the message of each by inappropriate juxtaposition. The reader may be familiar with the writings of some (no doubt with some misconceptions) of the following: R. D. Laing, F. Perls, T. Szasz, I. Illich, A. Janor and C. Rogers.[11]

Other Psychoanalytical Theories
(1) Anna Freud and Melanie Klein

We return now to the main stream of psychoanalytical teachings. Both *Anna Freud* and *Melanie Klein* have, in different ways, regarded themselves as being in the direct line of Freud. Both carried out their main work with children and yet

---

[9] See D. J. Smail, *Psychoanalysis: A personal approach*, J. M. Dent, 1978, for an exposition of the mechanistic components in much psychoanalytical writing.

[10] For a summary of Freud's persistent themes, and a description of many of his models, see Kahn and Nursten, *Unwillingly to School*, Pergamon Press, 1964.

[11] See J. Kovel, *A Complete Guide to Therapy*, Pelican, 1978 and D. J. Smail, Op. cit., for critical surveys of the field. See also Bibliography (p. 215) for original sources.

have made contributions to the understanding of adult mental life. They are different in their approach to transference, and to the utilization of ideas of unconscious processes.

ANNA FREUD

Anna Freud has enlarged the topographical model, and has chosen to study the ego processes (which are sometimes referred to as being superficial compared with the unconscious Id and Superego processes). She deals with them at unexpectedly profound levels. In her work with children, she adds the dimension of her own experience, as a school teacher, to the understanding of normal development.

What she did was to show that disequilibrium in the course of development is not *necessarily* pathological, and may do no more than prepare the ground for individual differences in personality.[12] Her treatment methods have included a direct use of procedures borrowed from education, and her concepts of normal development have enriched the procedures for the therapy of mental disorder.

MELANIE KLEIN

Melanie Klein's therapeutic approach was to go direct to the unconscious processes, even in the youngest child. She assumed that interpretation should be directed towards the deep origins of disorders, and she constructed a model which she applied to the earliest stages of infancy. She took up ideas which Freud and Karl Abraham expressed in the context of the origins of depressive states, and she elaborated them into the *object-relationship theory of personality structure*. Personality is looked upon as if it were built up by the incorporation of "good" and "bad" objects—the objects being mental representations of people, or parts of people (e.g. the breast or the penis). The infant perceives good experiences and bad experiences of the mother (in the first place) as coming from separate persons. The integration of the mother into one person who can be both good and bad is the first step during early infancy towards the integration of "the self" as a person with both good and bad qualities. In the early unintegrated state, there is confusion about good and badness in the perceptions which the infant has of both parents. The infant cannot tell what is inside or what is in the external world. Gradually, personality grows, through the process of *introjection*, which is the "swallowing" or incorporation of objects (or representations of objects), and *projection*, which is a way of experiencing one's own internal feelings as if emanating from someone or something in the external world.

Nowhere better than in Melanie Klein's work has the intensity of infantile feelings been demonstrated, and linked with adult envy, greed and the need for reparation.[13] Moreover, her object-relations theory illustrates how the paranoid and depressive disorders of adults have their parallel in the paranoid and depressive feelings in normal development during early infancy.

[12] See A. Freud, *Normality and Pathology*, Hogarth Press, 1966.

[13] See M. Klein, Our Adult World and its Roots in Infancy, Ch. 1 in *Our Adult World and Other Essays*, Heinemann, 1963; and Love, Guilt and Reparation, in Klein and Riviere, *Love, Hate and Reparation*, The Hogarth Press and the Institute of Psychoanalysis, 1937.

Fairbairn used the idea of object-relations in a deliberate attempt to restate Freudian theories.[14] Concentrating on instinct theory, he recalled Freud's concept of instincts as seeking *satisfaction.* Fairbairn's contribution was to state that instincts sought *objects.* This has usefully emphasised the two-person nature of many kinds of sexual satisfaction, and points to the long lasting mutual attachments so often involved in sexual fulfilment. Fairbairn goes on to construct complex patterns of object relationships which are each characteristic of some particular pathological syndrome.

Other Psychoanalytical Theories
(2) Reich, Rank, Stekel, Adler, Jung, Erikson

One person only can be *first* in the development of a new interpretative framework. Freud was not only the founder of psychoanalysis, he also produced a massive and influential corpus of work. Others, who made original contributions to psychodynamic theories had to stress their divergence from Freudian ideas in order to exist in their own right. Either they had to acknowledge an orthodoxy of psychoanalytical thinking (incidentally, Freud himself could say "Personally, I am not a Freudian") or they had to hew out for themselves the shapes of ideas that were unknown to Freud and his close followers. Some of them, famous in their time, like *Reich, Rank* and *Stekel*, survive through attempts to revalue the relevance of their work to the contemporary scene. *Adler*, who studied the disadvantaged, has suffered from the disadvantage of having had many of his ideas absorbed into psychodynamic thought, often without acknowledgement.[15]

JUNG

Jung remains as one of the giants of early psychodynamic developments, and there is an ever increasing interest in some of his basic ideas.

Jung's analytical psychology has grown in importance in the understanding of what is universal in human experience (the archetypes), of the mystic and the spiritual, and of the urges towards integration of the personality which can receive fulfilment especially in the latter part of life.[16] Jung brought into Western culture the wisdom of Eastern religion and philosophy, and offered a necessary balance to the *logical* analysis that has always been the basic principle of the reasoned statements of Western thought. (There has also always been a mystic approach in Western culture, but it has not been dominant over the centuries.) Eastern thought provides ways of experiencing that are different from those of the Western tradition, and it contains metaphors for experiences and states of consciousness that cannot otherwise be expressed.

[14] W. R. D. Fairbairn, *Psychoanalytic Studies of Personality*, Tavistock Publications, 1952.
[15] H. F. Ellenberger, *The Discovery of the Unconscious: The History and Evolution of Dynamic Psychiatry*, Penguin, 1970.
[16] C. G. Jung, *Collected Works*, 2nd ed., 12 vols., Routledge and Kegan Paul, 1966.

ERIKSON

Among more recent contributors to the development of psychodynamic theories, Erikson stands out through his introduction of a cultural dimension into the study of individual personality. His most valuable contribution is the idea of a "life-task" in every stage of development, each one characterized by polarized forces stemming from the community. Each phase involves a *psychosocial crisis* between two basic attitudes (e.g. Trust v. Mistrust, Integrity v. Despair). These are discussed in terms of immediate personal relationships, in relation to the wider community, and the (Freudian) psychosexual stages of development. Erikson has eight phases, which stretch through childhood into adolescence and adult life; and leave a "task" still to be performed in middle age. The successful performance of the "life-tasks" needs the ability to acknowledge the polarities of opposing forces as realities; and not to attempt a false reconciliation. The eight phases are set out in a table which is called a worksheet, as Erikson regards his ideas as developing and subject to change.[17] He deals mainly with the ego development of the individual in a setting which includes the hazards of parental, communal and cultural forces.

Theory and Practice

The theories so far considered provide both a picture of the development of personality, and a statement about the mental processes which exist in an individual at some critical point in life. The theories are put to use, both in improving the circumstances in which children are brought up, and also in the therapy of psychiatric disorders at any stage of life.

Some theories concentrate on the analysis of the forces existing at the point of encounter of observer and observed. *Kelly* has shown that each individual is a "scientist", exploring or construing the relationships existing at that moment. His theory of *personal constructs* can be utilized both for the understanding of behaviour and also for the discovery of alternative forms of behaviour to add to one's repertoires.[18] Thus, personal construct theory has found a place in new developments in psychiatry, in psychology and in education.

The Notion of Development

Before we go on to discuss the various stages of development, we should pause for a moment to examine the notion of *development* itself. It is usually taken for granted in works on "Child Development" that we know what this title means. There is an implication, seldom brought out, that it is different from either change or growth. It is growth in a desired or normal direction. Like growth, it needs "nutrition", and often the problem is to decide what *is* normal development, and what is or might be necessary provision for that development. Do children need, for

---

[17] E. H. Erikson, Identity and the Life Cycle: Selected Papers, *Psychological Issues* (Monograph), I:1, International Universities Press, N.Y., 1959. See also H. W. Maier, *Three Theories of Child Development*, Ch. 2, Harper and Row, 1965.

[18] G. A. Kelly, *The Psychology of Personal Constructs*, Norton N.Y., 1955.

instance, close contact with the mother to provide for normal language development? If so, then children who do not get it are not just different: they have suffered a *lack* of provision, a deficiency. Sociologists have warned us of the dangers of labelling as a deficiency any departure from middle-class norms, but we must also be aware of the equal danger of not noticing actual deficiencies of provision, which could, if suitable help is offered, be remedied. A doctor who diagnoses malnutrition is also making a value judgment about what should be the normal diet of child or adult. The judgement will to some extent be relative to what is available. It is important and necessary to make value judgements about what should be normal provision in all areas of growth and development, otherwise there would be no basis ever for a decision that some individuals or sections of the community are in need of help, nor any way of assessing the kind of help that is required.

4

Developmental Stages

Individuality of the Baby at Birth

Descriptions of a baby as a separate individual usually refer to helplessness and dependence. In descriptions of relationships with the mother, it is stressed that the baby needs the mother (or substitute for her) for very survival. All this is true, but it is equally important to be aware of the fact that even at birth the baby has a vigour and an assertiveness which gives a life of his or her own. In the image that a mother has of a baby, even in the stages before she becomes pregnant, there may be a picture of a plump, happy but helpless child lying contentedly on a soft pillow. The strength of her unborn baby may be surprising and at times alarming.

A mother's image of the baby is not a snapshot but a moving picture, yet it may omit some of the essential sequences. One mother might envisage the infant exclusively as a grown-up, pursuing a career with independence and with an ability to take some of the burdens that older parents can no longer carry. To another, the main picture of the child might alternate between a passively dependent chubby baby and a later edition who would have the ability to separate, but who would still prefer to keep in contact with her. One could hypothesise also on the tensions of the child who might have need for someone who can give comfort at the frequent moments of discomfort or distress, alternating with a need for self-assertiveness and for a freedom from the imposition of conditions which limit activity.

Dependence and Independence

During pregnancy the mother becomes aware of something that is within her but which has a separate life. The baby is cushioned within the mother from many of the discomforts of extra-uterine life. It receives the benefits of the chemical interchange in the mother's blood stream, and there are some variations in body processes which depend upon the changes in the mother's metabolism. The child has a separate circulation of blood with a barrier between it and the mother's circulation, but some of the constituents, which are in solution in the plasma of the blood stream, pass through this barrier and provide the child with nourishment and with oxygen.

There is a separateness as well as a union. In the later stages of pregnancy the child has physical movements which the mother cannot control. The kicks which she experiences are as independent of her as they would be if she were kicked from outside.

32

The process of birth still leaves the child dependent upon the mother, but it emphasizes the processes of a separation which becomes more complete with each further stage of the child's development.

At birth the child has some physical accomplishments in his or her own right. Within seconds air is taken in, with what seems to us to be a struggle, and then breathed in and out. The child can cough and sneeze in a way which helps to clear the air passages when mucus threatens to obstruct them. He or she can wriggle, and thus prove that the muscles give the power of movement, and can grip with considerable strength a finger put into the palm of the hand. The child can cry, and thus call attention to the needs for relief of physical discomfort or the distress of loneliness. Most important of all, is the ability to suck.

These accomplishments are necessary for survival. There are other qualities which, at this stage, are merely potentialities to be developed later. Some of these would seem to be patterns of behaviour which are already laid down, and which merely await physical maturation for their full expression. Other potentialities depend for their fulfilment upon the physical, intellectual and emotional experiences which are the material for their growth.

At all stages we have the mysterious phenomenon of a single process serving simultaneous and opposing functions, e.g. the intra-uterine movements which give notice of separate existence and, at the same time, provide a communication between unborn child and mother.

Nature and Nurture

We have those capacities and accomplishments which are due to nature and those which are due to nurture. Sometimes it is difficult to distinguish between the influence of one or the other, and some qualities may have a contribution both from inheritance and from post natal experience.

The *physical* characteristics in the various stages of development are described in terms of body-structure and capacity for movement. *Intellectual* life is represented in the learning in general about the outside world and the more formal learning which is called education. The stages of *emotional* development are more difficult to define, and our descriptions depend more upon inference than on direct observations in measurable terms. Each physical and intellectual stage has its counterpart in emotional development, but the different aspects may develop at different rates in any one individual.

Developmental Norms

Many workers in different professional fields have made observations on developmental stages regarding the behaviour patterns and responses of the child, week by week, and month by month. A. E. Gesell has written extensively, alone and with collaborators, giving the results of an enormous number of recorded observations of many aspects of infant development. He describes "norms", which are averages, against which any individual child can be measured in what is called

"Developmental Diagnosis",[1] and it is maintained by Gesell and his co-workers that "it is possible to diagnose in the first year of life nearly all cases of amentia, cerebral injury, many sensory and motor defects, and severe personality deviations". They state that "human organism is a complicated action-system, and an adequate developmental diagnosis requires an examination of four fields of behaviour representing different aspects of growth. These four major fields are:

(1) Motor behaviour.   (3) Language behaviour.
(2) Adaptive behaviour.   (4) Personal-social behaviour."

The detailed description of the infant's growing capacity, supplemented in some publications by illustrations, gives a good background of knowledge for the precise diagnosis of the present capacity of the child, and this has been shown to have some predictive value of future progress. R. S. Illingworth, who supplements some of Gesell's findings with his own extensive paediatric experiences,[2] summarises the literature, and describes stages of normal development and its variations including the mental development associated with various physical defects. Illingworth discusses reasons for the demand for "norms" in child development:

"To satisfy the intellectual curiosity of parents about their children especially after a previous stillbirth or a family history of mental or physical handicap."
"In cases of adoption and to estimate the possibility of some inherent handicap."
"Following injury or infection in a newborn baby, to be able to follow the development made in later stages."
"In cases where there are problems of behaviour or food difficulties to be able to take into account mental and physical defects."

Parents sometimes come under criticism for using the timing of the developmental landmarks of the child for the purpose of competition with other parents. A point is scored when one's child sits up, talks and has achieved toilet training in advance of the neighbour's child. It is the game of keeping up with the Jones's baby. Rather than criticism there should be understanding of the anxiety about the progress of their babies when parents are cut off from the traditional sources of knowledge and reassurance that used to come from the older generation in large families. This lack of background information applies especially to parents of handicapped or defective children. They do not know what to expect when the child's development is delayed, and even the professional workers, whose help they seek, often seem to be without mental guidelines within which they can discuss a particular child.

In the case of adoption we have the controversial point as to whether adoptive parents have the right to the exclusion of deficiencies in the children they adopt.

The Need to be a Parent

Yet there is every reason, as Illingworth says, to consider it to be a double tragedy for a husband and wife, who have been unable after several years of

---

[1] A. Gesell and C. Amatruda, *Developmental Diagnosis*, Paul B. Hoeber Inc., 1960.
[2] R. S. Illingworth, *The Development of the Infant and Young Child, Normal and Abnormal*, 6th ed., E. S. Livingstone, 1975.

marriage to satisfy the normal desire to have a child, to adopt a child who subsequently appears to be mentally defective. Some adoptive parents deliberately choose a handicapped child, and there are others who are prepared to take their chance along with natural parents, but it seems to be justifiable to attempt to protect the ordinary range of adoptive parents from the burden of handicap that could be detectable at the time when placement is arranged.

Those adoptive parents who consciously put the needs of some parentless child before the rewards that come from a child whose progress lies within conventional expectations, may look for a child who is apparently disadvantaged by belonging to a racial or cultural minority and possibly carrying also some genetic hazard. If the acceptance of this burden also satisfies some personal need in the adoptive parents, it is none the worse for that. This is the material out of which all kinds of altruism are created. For many prospective adoptive parents at the present day, there may be no choice. The availability of abortion reduces the number of unwanted live births. Illegitimacy no longer seems to be quite the burden or handicap it once was. Fewer babies are available for adoption than ever before. The normal healthy baby, even if illegitimate, is likely to be retained somewhere within the extended family. Those who want to adopt a child may find themselves expected to take one that carries some physical or social handicap. Some prospective adopters get the impression that they are being called upon to pay a price for assuming the rights and obligations of parenthood.

Childless couples are in a double trap. Adoption brings its potential hazards for parents and child; continued childlessness has to be accounted for in constant questioning from relatives and friends, and in every professional encounter. The successful adoptions seem to pass unnoticed. Barbara Tizzard has added an entirely new dimension to the perspectives on adoption.[3] She demonstrates that adoptive parents need not aim at providing a continuation of an idealized life of the child with the original parents. Life in the adoptive home has its own values. Even after the age of three, good "parenting" can repair much of the damage of earlier experiences. Some of the worst results come from injudicious attempts to restore the child to the natural parents in instances where this is an entirely unrealistic aim.

Desire to Differentiate: Organic and Emotional Causes of Disorders

Where injury of infection or problems of behaviour call for investigation, professional advisors and parents alike are often anxious to be able to distinguish those disturbances which are due to inherent causes and organic factors, from those which are due to emotional ones. Any theory of causation leads to inferences which are either satisfying or disturbing to the parents. If the condition is inherent it is nobody's "fault", but is likely to be thought of as uncorrectable. Of acquired disturbances, the organic ones are thought of as less blameworthy than the emotional ones. If relationships within the family are thought to be responsible for emotional disturbances, the parents feel guilty and seek confirmation of their fear that their

[3] B. Tizard, *Adoption: A Second Chance*, Open Books, 1977.

behaviour towards the child is responsible, and may even attract blame in order to refute it.

These comments are made because of the doubts as to the advisability of the use of "norms" as standards *by parents in order to judge their child, in such a way that they feel that they or the child are good, when he or she is level with or in advance of, the norm, and bad if lagging behind.*

Emotional attitudes with regard to the use of developmental tests are somewhat similar to those with regard to the use of intelligence tests. Individuals who do not get a particular desired result from tests feel that it is the test itself which threatens the future of their child. The validity of the tests is challenged, and the purpose often misunderstood. For this reason one requires to know their limitations and special values. As with intelligence tests, it can be held that no assessment should be made for the information of a parent unless there is the opportunity for discussion of the results with the parent by a worker who is familiar with the child as well as with the standards.

With this proviso it can be said that professional workers who deal with children will find it invaluable to have knowledge of developmental norms, and Illingworth gives ample evidence for the statement that the developmental tests "can detect mental retardation and neurological conditions with a considerable degree of certainty". He adds "There is little evidence that mental superiority can be detected in infancy."

Charting the Stages

Dr. Mary Sheridan, who carried responsibility within the Ministry of Health in relation to the special provisions for handicapped children, has produced a very clear chart of observations on "The Developmental Progress of Infants and Young Children".[4] The categories that are given under the headings Posture and Large Movements, Vision and Fine Movements, Hearing and Speech, Social Behaviour and Play, seem to be more related to the everyday activities of children than the headings used by Gesell.

The work covers the age range of 1 month to 5 years, and an extract covering the period from 1 to 6 months is reproduced by permission (pp. 38–9). It will be noted that the records of progress are arranged under the four headings in vertical columns. It is therefore possible to read expected average performance at any one age by reading across the pages, and the progress in one quality by reading vertically downwards. It is the experience of many students that it is easier to comprehend the developmental progress by following one quality at a time rather than by attempting to maintain the picture of the relative progress of each quality at any one time. Perhaps this is partly because of the knowledge that the different qualities grow at different rates (the child may grow in physique at a greater rate than in intellectual performance), and partly because of the fact that our span of attention is limited. An individual's personality is a complete whole, but the capacity to study it seems to be limited to observations on a very narrow range of activity. Having

[4] *Reports on Public Health and Medical Subjects*, No. 102, H.M.S.O., 1960.

got a picture of each quality in turn, it may then be possible for the student to turn back occasionally and to attempt to bring two or three different aspects into relation with one another. This limitation in our capacity to observe when trying to understand any subject will accompany us and hamper us in all our studies.

There are other ways of describing developmental stages. *Biological stages* are those which depend upon maturation of inborn capacities, *cultural stages* are patterns imposed upon the individual in each particular society, and the two are superimposed. Psychoanalysts describe *stages of psychosexual development* under the headings of *Oral*, *Anal* and *Genital* in accordance with the successive predominance of sensitivity of different areas of the body during the early years.

Talking is the stage when the infant,[5] who had previously been able to communicate with the mother in a private language of gesture and inarticulate sound, uses the code which allows communication with a wider world. Walking marks the division between the stage when the infant is carried about, and the stage when there is freedom to move independently. The progress serves both the physical needs of the individual and the social needs of the family. Each of these new capacities marks a stage in which there is opportunity to form relationships within a widening circle of other individuals.

Transition between Stages as a Crisis or Stepping Stone

Some stages, such as school entry, are a further mark of the progress from life in the family to life in the outside world. Further stages in each individual life, where there is a transition from one stage to another, include transfer from one school to another, puberty, school examinations, school leaving, entry into occupation, courtship, marriage, moving house, illness, deaths of relatives and close associates, and the changes in middle and old age.

Every change is to some extent a crisis. Early methods of satisfaction are outlived, but the desire for them may remain as accompaniments to later satisfactions as we pass through them. The various landmarks have been spoken of as "crisis events",[6] and there may be emotional disturbance of greater or lesser intensity at each stage. There can be regret, anxiety, or depression during the crisis of giving up an old status and an old satisfaction, and there is a point of instability between the two phases of life. This is literally true in the process of learning to walk. A child who has learned to stand, holding on to someone's hands or a piece of furniture, has to take a few steps into the unknown before reaching the safety of another hand or another piece of furniture. Inevitably the child falls, yet it is rare to show anxiety unless that anxiety is conveyed by the adult at hand. The child falls and falls again, getting up with great determination, and begins to walk again. The new accomplishment and the new freedom is sufficient reward.

Sheridan has spoken of the landmarks as "stepping stones", and this imaginatively refers to the passing to the new level of satisfaction of the next phase. The

---

[5] The word "infancy" is derived from the Latin "infantia" which means inability to speak.
[6] E. Lindemann, Recent Trends in Preventive Child Psychiatry, in *Emotional Problems of Early Childhood* (ed. G. Caplan), New York, 1955; G. Caplan, *An Approach to Community Mental Health*, Tavistock Publications, 1961.

AGE	POSTURE AND LARGE MOVEMENTS	VISION AND FINE MOVEMENTS
1 month	Lies on back with head to one side; arm on same side outstretched, or both arms flexed: legs flexed, knees apart, soles of feet turned inwards. Large jerky movements of limbs, arms more active than legs. At rest, hands closed and thumb turned in. Fingers and toes fan out during extensor movements of limbs. When cheek touched, turns to same side; ear touched, turns away. When lifted head falls loosely. Held sitting, head falls forward, with back in one complete curve. Placed downwards on face, head immediately turns to side; arms and legs flexed under body, buttocks humped up. Held standing on hard surface, presses down feet and often makes reflex "stepping" movements.	Stares expressionlessly at brightness of window or blank wall. Shuts eyes tightly when pencil light shone directly into them at 1–2 inches. Follows pencil flash-lamp briefly with eyes at one foot. Notices dangling toy or rattle shaken in line of vision at 4–6 inches and follows its slow movement with eyes from side towards mid-line on level with face through approximately quarter circle, before head falls back to side. Beginning to watch mother's nearby face when she feeds or talks to him.
3 months	Now prefers to lie on back with head in mid-line. Limbs more pliable, movements smoother and more continuous. Waves arms symmetrically. Hands now loosely open. Brings hands from side into mid-line over chest or chin. Kicks vigorously, legs alternating or occasionally together. Held sitting, holds back straight, except in lumbar region, with head held erect and steady for several seconds before bobbing forwards. Placed downwards on face lifts head and upper chest well up in mid-line, using forearms as support, and often scratching at table surface; legs straight, buttocks flat. Held standing with feet on hard surface, sags at knees.	Visually very alert, particularly preoccupied by nearby human face. Moves head deliberately to look around him. Follows adult's movements near cot. Follows rattle of dangling toy at 6–10 inches above face through half circle from side to side, and usually also vertically from chest to brow. Watches movements of own hands before face and beginning to clasp and unclasp hands together. Recognizes feeding bottle and makes eager welcoming movements at it approaches his face. Regards still objects within 6–10 inches for more than a second or two, but seldom able to fixate continuously.
6 months	Lying on back, lifts up head from pillow. Sits with support in cot or pram and turns head from side to side to look around him. Moves arms in brisk purposeful fashion and holds them up to be lifted. When hands grasped, pulls himself up. Kicks strongly, legs alternating. Can roll over. Held sitting, head is firmly erect, and back straight. Placed downwards on face lifts head and chest well up supporting himself on extended arms. Held standing with feet touching hard surface bears weight on feet and bounces up and down actively.	Visually insatiable: moves head and eyes eagerly in every direction. Eyes move in unison: squint now abnormal. Follows adult's movements across room. Immediately fixates interesting small objects within 6–12 inches (e.g. toy, bell, wooden cube, spoon, sweet) and stretches out both hands to grasp them. Uses whole hand in palmar grasp. When toys fall from hand forgets them or searches only vaguely round cot with eyes and patting hands.

HEARING AND SPEECH	SOCIAL BEHAVIOUR AND PLAY
Startled by sudden loud noises, stiffens, quivers, blinks, screws eyes up, extends limbs, fans out fingers and toes, and may cry. Movements momentarily "frozen", when small bell rung gently 3–5 inches from ear for 3–5 secs with 5 secs pauses: may move eyes towards sound. Stops whimpering to sound of near-by soothing human voice, but not when screaming or feeding. Cries lustily when hungry or uncomfortable. Utters little guttural noises when content. (*Note.*—Deaf babies also cry and vocalise in this reflex way, but if very deaf will not show startle reflex to sudden noise.)	Sucks well. Sleeps most of the time when not being fed or handled. Expression vague, but tending to become more alert, progressing to smiling at about 5–6 weeks. Hands normally closed, but if opened, grasps examiner's finger when palm is touched. Stops crying when picked up. Mother supports head when carrying, dressing and bathing.
Sudden loud noises still distress, provoking blinking, screwing up of eyes, cry and turning away. Definite quietening or smiling to sound of mother's voice before she touches him, but not when screaming. Vocalises when spoken to or pleased. Cries when uncomfortable or annoyed. Quietens to rattle of spoon in cup or to bell rung gently out of sight for 3–5 secs at 6–12 inches from ear. May turn eyes towards sound; brows may wrinkle and eyes dilate, may move head from side to side as if searching vaguely for sound. Often licks lips in response to sounds of preparation for feeding. Shows excitement at sound of approaching footsteps, running bath water, etc. (*Note*—Deaf baby, instead, may be obviously startled by M's sudden appearance beside cot.)	Fixes eyes unblinkingly on mother's face when feeding. Beginning to react to familiar situations—showing by smiles, coos and excited movement that he recognizes preparations for feeds, baths, etc. Responds with obvious pleasure to friendly handling, especially when accompanied by playful tickling and vocal sounds. Holds rattle for few moments when placed in hand, but seldom capable of regarding it at same time. Mother supports at shoulders when dressing and bathing.
Turns immediately to mother's voice across room. Vocalises tunefully, using single syllables e.g., ka, muh, goo, der. Laughs, chuckles and squeals aloud in play. Screams with annoyance. Shows evidence of response to different emotional tones of mother's voice. Responds to baby hearing tests at 1½ feet from each ear by correct visual localization, but may show slightly delayed response. [Tests employed—voice, rattle, cup and spoons, paper, bell; 2 secs. with 2 secs. pause.]	Hands competent to reach for and grasp small toys. Most often uses a two-handed, scooping-in approach, but occasionally a single hand. Takes everything to mouth. Beginning to find feet interesting and even useful in grasping. Puts hands to bottle and pats it when feeding. Shakes rattle deliberately to make it sound, often regarding it closely at same time. Still friendly with strangers but occasionally shows some shyness or even slight anxiety.

keeping in mind of these two separate ways of looking at the developmental landmarks serves the practical purpose of calling our attention to the fact that some individuals and some families need special help on these occasions.[7]

It is not always possible to pass through the landmarks and critical events in triumph, even with help. There are the disasters of incurable handicaps of genetic origin which increase in severity as life goes on. There are the incurable diseases of children in which death is a constant prospect. Particular individuals and the family surrounding them need to have their depression recognized and as much of their burden as possible, shared. Lindy Burton entered sensitively into these themes.[8] But even here there are contradictions which must be recognized. A parent who learns of the fatal illness of the child begins the mourning immediately, but the child may live longer than the grief can be sustained. The continued survival exhausts the emotional responses. The next task is to come to terms with the fact that the child who is dying is also living. At all ages an individual who is dying is perceiving, thinking and feeling and there are new perceptions, thoughts and feelings almost to the last moments. Development still continues.

Thoughts about death might well have been reserved in this book entirely to the concluding chapter, but the reference here is an acknowledgement of the fact that death can take place at any age, and that the care of the dying is an acknowledgement that life is continuing.

[7] J. K. W. Morrice, *Crises Intervention: Studies in Community Care*, Pergamon Press, 1976.
[8] L. Burton, *Care of the Child Facing Death*, Routledge and Kegan Paul, 1974.

5

The Suckling

Breast Feeding as a Reunion with Mother

It is a traditional custom to put a baby to the mother's breast immediately after birth. The process of birth may have been distressing to the mother. In some cases the mother accepts labour in its literal sense as a job of work in which she actively participates, and looks upon each pain as the product of her own activity which is bringing the desired result nearer. Sometimes intensity of pain or the anxiety of the mother calls for active intervention on the part of the medical attendant. Anxiety increases, and yet almost invariably after completion of the birth processes, which is marked by the expulsion of the placenta or afterbirth, there is a look of tranquillity and satisfaction on the mother's face which is something that goes beyond mere relief.

The baby has been subjected to considerable pressure in the process of birth, and has had the abrupt ending of the supply of oxygen and food from the mother's blood. There is an initial struggle for the first breath of air. Feeding comes later, and the feeding reunites mother and baby at a new level. Imaginatively we can picture the baby in the first distress wishing for something to relieve and comfort, and what is wished for then materializes—almost as if she were the creation of the need. Ever after, in distress, we reach out for comfort, and hope to match the kind of realization of that first reunion of baby and mother.

The feeding process begins, and this satisfies a multiplicity of needs of both the mother and the child. The mother needs to give suck as the child needs to suck, but there can be many reasons why a mother may not be able to feed her child at the breast, and why she may not even wish to. The inauguration of the flow of milk is slow. For the first three days after the birth of the baby the fluid which comes from the breast is not milk but colostrum. It is a thinner fluid and there is less of it than of the milk which will come later, but the baby has enough reserve of food for this period. The sucking of the nipple at this stage stimulates the flow of milk, and is thought also to help the process of involution of the muscles of the uterus which had become enlarged during the months of pregnancy.

Establishing the Flow of Milk: Sign
Release Phenomena

The establishment of the milk supply is now thought to depend upon a precise mechanical stimulus which occurs when the size of the baby's mouth and the size of the nipple have a certain relationship, and a measurement of these relative sizes was carried out by Mavis Gunter[1] in relation to the success or failure of breast-feeding. This is thought to be one of a series of phenomena where something is set going by a mechanical process which is important in the tie between mother and child. These processes were first discovered in the study of the behaviour of animals with their young, and the science in which there is an attempt to correlate observations on the nurturing of young animals with those on the human infant is called "Ethology".

Lorenz, in a book called *King Solomon's Ring*,[2] was one of the earlier writers on this subject. (The book was so named because of the legend that King Solomon wore a ring which enabled him to understand the language of animals.) Lorenz kept a number of different animals within his home and observed their behaviour, and then studied it by altering the circumstances. For example, the young geese follow the mother immediately after being hatched from the egg. It is a behaviour pattern which has survival value. Lorenz noticed that the pattern of following was set going by the sight of the first moving object which, in fact, was usually the gosling's mother. Lorenz found experimentally that the goslings would follow any other moving object which came into the line of vision immediately after hatching. A dog or even a moving rubber ball would be treated by the goslings as if it were the mother. When Lorenz arranged that he himself became the first moving object to be seen, the goslings followed him and continued to do so even into their adult life.

It would seem that there are certain processes which set going a kind of behaviour, and other processes which inhibit them when the behaviour is no longer appropriate. The substitute mother is lacking in some of these processes including that which later sets the offspring free.

Another example is the opening of the beaks of young nesting birds at the moment that the mother (or father) arrives with a worm. This occurs not on the sight of the mother or even of the worm carried in its beak, but as a result of the vibration caused when the parent bird alights on the side of the nest, and it can be reproduced experimentally by touching the edge of the nest.

These processes are called "*Sign release phenomena*". Different forms of behaviour depend upon a particular stage of maturation in the young and upon the appearance of some outside stimulus or sign. They are "species specific", i.e. there are different kinds of behaviour and different signs in different kinds of animal.

These phenomena occur in the behaviour of the human infant and mother, and have been described by John Bowlby.[3] The sucking at the breast is one only of these phenomena. In addition, the baby's smile, the baby's cry, the baby's clinging with the hand around the neck of the mother, are all activities which arouse something in the mother for which she is ready, but which needs a stimulus for it to be released.

There is a level of mothering which exists as a potential in every individual which is part of the general sympathy and compassion for other human beings, and there also is mothering which is intellectual and which can be studied. In addition to all

[1] Instinct and the Nursing Couple, *Lancet* 1, 575 (1955).
[2] K. Lorenz, *King Solomon's Ring*, Methuen, 1952.
[3] The Nature of the Child's Tie to his Mother, *Int. J. Psycho-Anal.* 39, 350 (1958). See also *Attachment and Loss* (Vol. 1 *Attachment*), The Hogarth Press, 1969.

this, there are the built-in processes, described above, which need some particular occurrence for development and release. Successive stages of mothering are roused by the developing activities of the baby: not just what the baby is doing, but the fact that what the baby is doing is changing from day to day. The older term "imprinting"[4] has now been largely superseded by "bonding" which refers to both parties in the tie.

The process takes place in stages. A stimulus brings part of the mothering process into being, further development reinforces the tie, and still further development on the part of the child is the stimulus to release the tie and permit the child to separate.

This kind of explanation enables us to understand the mother of the child who suffers from some handicap and who does not develop at the normal rate. The mother of such a child may not be able to develop some of the normal responses, or to release her child from herself at later stages, because the necessary stimulus never arrives. The inappropriateness of the tie at different stages may be what we refer to when we say that she rejects or overprotects the child.

This particular topic was introduced at this point in order to explain the fact that some failures to establish breast feeding have purely mechanical causes. A mother may wish to feed the baby and fail, and then she feels inadequate. There are other mothers who do not want to feed their babies, and is has become known that it is possible for the wish not to feed the baby to lead to failure in the production of milk. Thus it is often implied by the professional attendant (doctor or midwife) that a mother who fails *could* feed the baby if she only wanted to. A feeling of guilt is thus added to the feeling of inadequacy. It is said that she "rejects" her baby, but perhaps it is the professional attendant who is rejecting (towards) the mother.

Mechanical and Emotional Factors

When breast-feeding is first established, difficulties can arise from lack of knowledge of the simple mechanics of holding the baby to the breast. Most mothers have had no experience of seeing other mothers breast-feeding their babies—families are small and breast-feeding in other homes is private.

Sometimes a baby is held at the breast in such a way that the baby's nose is embedded in the breast,[5] and the baby has to let go of the breast with the mouth in order to continue to breathe. Sometimes such a baby will pummel the breast in efforts to get the mouth free while still wanting to suck, and the mother will say the baby is "fighting the breast", or, more simply, is "refusing" the breast. Such a mother feels deeply hurt, by what she feels to be the baby's deliberate behaviour. Breast-feeding is broken off and, although the mother blames the child, she just as unfoundedly feels guilty herself.

Breast-feeding has become one of the topics which arouse partisan feelings. Most studies of the baby's mental life are conducted on the assumption that the baby's feeding takes place at the breast. Most writings for the lay public state the value of

[4] R. A. Hinde, The Nature of Imprinting, in *Determinants of Infant Behaviour*, Vol. 2 (ed. B. M. Foss), Methuen, 1963.
[5] There is a similar effect if the baby's upper lip is pressed against the nostrils.

breast-feeding for the infant, and sometimes make reference to the value that the mother herself receives from the process. Reference is made to the universality of breast-feeding in primitive races. It has recently been suggested that this universality is achieved only at the expense of high infant mortality, which means that where breast feeding is not established, the infant simply dies![6]

Jelliffe and Jelliffe[7] have presented a reappraisal of the role of human milk and breast-feeding in both the developed and the developing countries of the world. "Concerns with global food supplies, with the need for the regulation of child spacing, with the prevention of infectious diseases, with the economics of infant feeding, with newer knowledge of mother–neonate interaction, and with continually emerging information on the specific nutritional needs of young infants all overlap into the question of breast-feeding, as does recent awareness of the need to try to achieve a balance between technology, biology and tradition".

Artificial Feeding: Rational and Irrational Reasons

Bottle-feeding remains prevalent, in spite of teachings to the contrary, in any country where facilities for artificial feeding exist. Perhaps bottle-feeding is like contraception. It seems to be practised wherever the techniques are available. It seems to be inevitable that where the opportunity occurs, people separate off certain biological aspects of sexual and reproductive life that are unwanted, and retain those which seem at the moment to be considered essential, valuable, or satisfying.

Professional attitudes are influenced by the personal self as well as the professional self of the doctor or nurse in charge of the family. Sometime the professed attitude is that of supporting breast-feeding, but the attitude which in practice comes in response to the mother's enquiry is the personal one which supports that part of the maternal feelings which finds breast-feeding difficult. In a study[8] of reasons given by mothers for their adopting artificial feeding, many of the reasons given by mothers for taking the baby off the breast were explanations which they hoped would be acceptable, and which would answer implied criticism.

Among the large number of unspoken reasons, there is the undoubted convenience of bottle-feeding which permits the mother some freedom from the constant tie in that it is a process which can be carried out by other people. Moreover, a mother may take the baby off the breast because of her fears that her milk is not good enough for her child, and often this erroneous view is supported by professional attendants. In small drops all milk looks thin compared with the opaque liquid seen in depth in the bottle, and perhaps human milk is in any case less opaque than cow's milk. The belief of milk "not being good enough" or not "suiting" baby is part of every woman's fear of not being quite good enough, or of being in some way inadequate. There are also the associations of breast-feeding (involving

[6] M. Mead, *A Cultural Anthropologist's Approach to Maternal Deprivation—Deprivation of Maternal Care*, p. 50., W.H.O. Public Health Papers 14, 1962.
[7] D. B. Jelliffe and E. F. Jelliffe, *Human Milk in the Modern World*, Oxford University Press, 1978.
[8] L. J. Newson and E. Newson, Breast Feeding in Decline, *Brit. Med. J.* 5321 (1962).

the nipple in a mouth) with sensuality; and women who feel that *any* deep sensations are bad will feel frightened by the association of this experience with sexuality.

Other women are afraid that breast-feeding will alter the shape of the breast, and so it does, to some extent; and, if a woman's image of herself is that of the profile in which youthful breasts are a prominent but delicate feature, she will find herself unable to accept the next stage of her development.

A more recent factor in bottle-feeding has been the medical emphasis on hygiene and sterility of everything brought to baby's mouth. Bottles can be boiled, powdered milk comes out of tins and is free from bacteria. The composition of the feed can be modified according to the prescription of the revered doctor, and the mother actually sees the level of milk in the bottle going down, and knows that it is passing into the stomach of her baby. It has the right composition, and the right quantity, the right temperature with a guarantee of freedom from infection.

All these latter reasons can justify those feelings in her which favour her wish to discontinue breast-feeding, but some of the wish for close contact with the baby remains. Even when the baby is fed with the bottle, the baby may be held close to the mother's body and feel her heartbeat, be sensitive to her confident embrace, and smell her presence. There is an abundance in mothering which spreads into the feeding of the baby whether at the breast or with the bottle. In this country the incidence of breast-feeding will vary according to social class, ethnic origin and personal value systems, but at present it is the practice of the minority.

Vigour of Baby's Sucking

The baby's part in the feeding process is studied by direct observation, and inferences are drawn from what we see in the light of our ideas regarding the development of personality. A baby feeds at the breast or at the bottle with the mouth, and the baby is an active participant in the taking in of the milk. A baby sucks vigorously. This fact is responsible for both the satisfactions and the anxieties that mothers have about breast-feeding. The fantasy that a mother might have had about her baby in the days before her marriage or during the time of her pregnancy is likely to be of a passive and helpless child, and the feeding process is pictured as the milk passing peacefully into the baby's mouth and down the throat. The baby's sucking, however, is a very vigorous process, and at this early stage it emphasizes the conflict between dependence and separateness.

The sucking process serves many purposes for the baby. The baby *feeds* with the mouth, the baby also *feels* with the mouth, experiencing a sensation which is stimulating and pleasurable within the act of feeding. Sensation is at its most intense level in a young baby with regard to objects which touch the mouth. The mouth is the point at which the baby makes contact with the outside world and, if that contact is with the nipple, it is the mouth which is the point of union of the baby with another person. It is at this point, therefore, that the baby becomes aware of the limits of the body, and of the distinction between what belongs to the self and what is outside. This sensation would seem to be the first area through which the baby is able to perceive, and, for some considerable time afterwards, any object which is put into a child's hand is taken immediately to the mouth, presumably to distinguish it by its shape as well as by its taste.

The contact of mouth with nipple—or with the teat which is the substitute of the nipple—is associated with the pleasure of feeding. It is the sensation of loving contact with another individual. It is a means of getting satisfaction which can be recollected in dreams, and one may see a baby continuing with sucking movements when falling asleep. It is a sensation which can be reproduced by self-stimulation when a baby sucks the thumb, or the stimulation can be provided by someone else who puts a dummy teat in the baby's mouth. Sucking gives the sensation of love which can be experienced with another individual, or as something deriving from the stimulation of recollecting it.

This capacity to derive sensual satisfaction with the mouth becomes partly superseded, as people grow, by other satisfactions, but it remains with us as an essential core. We celebrate important occasions with meals or with drinks; and we give ourselves comfort when we smoke or when we continue to suck our thumbs, our pipes, or our pencils, or when we chew gum which has no nutriment but merely taste. The word "companion" implies someone with whom one has shared bread.

Primitive Levels of Satisfaction and Frustration

The vigour with which feeding takes place provides another aspect of the activity which is concentrated on the mouth. The baby sucks vigorously and assertively. The mother feeding the baby at the breast, who is unprepared for this, may even feel that the baby is attacking her. There is good evidence, in the reconstruction of infant life which takes place when older children or adults regress in mental illness to infantile levels, that babies themselves have some awareness of fantasy of destructive power in the process of emptying the breast. It is also true that there are primitive levels of thought and feeling in all of us in which there is a wish to make reparation for the attack which we make on the source of our feeding and of our satisfaction.

To summarize simply, *the baby feeds with the mouth, feels with the mouth, loves with the mouth and attacks with the mouth.* There are various stages of mental life which can be described in different terms according to the particular theory of personality development which is held by the person making the observation. This stage, where the feeding process plays such an important part in the physical, perceptual and emotional life of the baby, is called *The Oral Stage* by those who adopt psychoanalytical viewpoints.

There are further stages described within this framework, and many different mental processes are attributed to each stage. It is possible, however, to find the rudiments of all the later processes in this early stage. The stage includes fundamental biological drives which serve the function of maintaining life and of giving satisfaction. The process is also linked with the contact between human beings and with the fantasies that we have about these contacts as well as the realities of them. The process is also linked with the restrictions which are imposed upon human beings from the earliest stages after birth. We begin to live in a world which is ordered and arranged by other people who are guided by custom. Feeding is provided sometimes according to the child's needs and demands, and sometimes according to ideas conveyed through the mother as to when the child should be fed and when food should be withheld. Babies may develop a rhythm which is satisfactory to them, and which fits in with the framework provided for them.

Feeding Routines

There has been a change in feeding patterns. Differences of feeding patterns in different races or different cultures have been noticed by anthropologists, and these have been equated with different types of personality in the adult members of the community. There have been changes in feeding patterns in the last few generations in this country. It has been suggested that there is a pendulum swing from rigid feeding schedules to on-demand feeding. The rigid pattern held sway particularly in the 1930s.

Possibly the changes are more complicated. The feeding pattern prevalent a couple of generations ago, according to descriptions and recollections, depended upon the proximity of the baby to the nursing mother who fed the child at the breast. The child was fed at irregular intervals on demand or at the whim of the mother. Rigid schedules perhaps began with the opportunity for regularity which was provided by artificial feeding. Regularity became associated with the goodness of mothering and with virtue in the baby. Regular hours and regular amounts were prescribed, and mothers were forbidden to feed even a crying (and presumably hungry) baby if there was still half an hour to go before the time of the next feed. Night feeding was prohibited and mothers were told, "Once you give a feed to a baby in the night, you will have to go on doing so". Good mothers were terrified to give way to what they were told were their baby's improper demands.

A reaction from this has been, in more recent years, the system of "on-demand" feeding, which was considered to be a return to the feeding processes of a previous generation. Perhaps the difference in the mother working to this system is her complete subordination to the baby's cry.

It might be possible to describe variations of this "on-demand" system which would make a fourth level, namely, a fairly regular rhythm of feeding which allows for variations of the individual baby's needs, and variations of any particular baby's needs on different days. It is surprising how, under some such regime, both baby and mother become adapted fairly quickly to a regularity which is convenient, but which is sufficiently flexible to make allowance for variations in the appetite for food and comfort.

It is thus evident that in this period of early feeding of the child we have all the variations of problems which can occur in the search for satisfaction and for approval, or of the need to love and be loved, even when it involves accepting the restrictions and the accompanying feelings of rebellion against having to conform.

On the mother's part, this period includes a miniature representation of the conflicts which she will continue to have about having a child who is dependent upon her and at the same time trying to separate; and of her own feelings about wanting simultaneously the incompatible rewards that come from another creature's dependency and independence.

Feeding has been described in detail because it is the most important activity in the development of the child, and because in it can be concentrated every possible pattern of personal adjustment and interpersonal interaction. The baby is in the meantime acquiring experiences of the outside world, and learning to distinguish through perceptions the difference between what goes on within and what goes on in the outside world of objects and people. The baby makes attachments to the mother and to other individuals, and these depend upon different stimuli—the mother's face in full view with both eyes visible stimulates the smile—the profile is not sufficient. The mother responds to the baby's smile as does everyone else. The baby's cry is a particularly important communication, and is perceived as such. It can be a signal of discomfort to which the mother or some other individual responds. It can be a call for a feed, or it can be interpreted on occasions as "temper". Many people become abnormally sensitive to the baby's cry, having been led to believe that babies spend their time feeding or sleeping, and, if awake and crying between feeds or in the night, they feel that something is wrong, either with the baby or with themselves. It should be noted that the young baby has no way of communication other than by crying. Baby battering can sometimes be interpreted as the mother's response to a cry that seems to be inordinate and beyond her capacity to satisfy.

Patterns of Infant Care

The baby's cry becomes another activity which, like the feeding, is an issue between parents and children. Parents are told to ignore the baby's cry in order that he or she should not become "spoilt". The importance of regularity of feeding and sleeping is that from the early stages it is thought that the baby should be forced into a pattern of behaviour which is acceptable. Mothers even fear that the child who cries for comfort, or who refuses a feed, will become delinquent if she gives in and becomes indulgent. Others fear equally terrible consequences if the baby's needs are not anticipated in such a way that there is never a reason to cry.

Some mothers are at the mercy of the latest professional pronouncement. Some mothers cheat a little and find an excuse for responding to the baby's needs for food or comfort. In a study of infant care in Nottingham,[9] what was reported to health visitors was different from what was reported to university staff who had no professional relationship with the mothers. They could admit giving a night feed or comforting the crying baby to a non-professional person, but tended to tell the health visitor what they thought she expected them to do.

The baby develops other needs. He or she is happier in the pram when propped up so that outside objects can be seen; and moving shadows of the leaves of a tree are more satisfying than the fixed outlines of walls, and still less satisfying is the emptiness of the visual field when the baby lies flat in the pram.

An active baby makes demands for food, warmth and many other stimuli, but there seems to be a tradition in describing babies as "good" when demands are minimal. They are described as "easy" and "content". If someone asks mother

[9] J. and E. Newson, *Infant Care in an Urban Community*, Allen & Unwin, 1963. (*Patterns of Infant Care*, Penguin, 1965.)

about a baby "Is he good?" the expected answer, quoted in this study, is "Yes, he is very good. I hardly know I have got him." This is somewhat reminiscent of the idiom of some wives in describing the absence of sexual relationships. They say, "My husband is very considerate"!

Schaffer,[10] who studied the behaviour of babies in the temporary separations which occur when they are left for short intervals in their prams, records the comment of one mother whom he interviewed. "When I take him out for a walk in the park he just will not lie in his pram like other babies. He has to be propped up so that he can see everything that is going on. The hood has to be left down in case he misses anything, and the moment the pram stops he begins to cry."

Schaffer suggests that there is an optimal amount of stimulation which differs from infant to infant, and that it is a function of mothering to supply this optimal amount. But mothers, too, differ in their sensitivity to the infant's call, and some say, "I cannot bear to hear my baby cry, and have to pick him up the moment he starts".

Schaffer[11] also reported the wide differences in the reporting of the liking and disliking of physical contacts in the form of cuddling, hugging and kissing. Mothers varied in their needs for these contacts, and babies in their response to them.

An important study of individual differences, covering work over a span of twenty years, has been recorded by Sibylle K. Escalona.[12]

She found it possible to distinguish between active and inactive infants. Active infants are those whose behaviour involves the whole body; they require little in the way of background stimulation and are able to respond at their most mature level to the routine caretaking contacts of maternal figures. The mere presence of objects and toys within reach and sight can draw responses from the active infant. Inactive babies draw their stimulus and satisfaction from activities of parts of their own bodies; they overcome distress unaided by sucking their fingers, by rocking, and they begin to scan the immediate environment for visual and auditory stimuli. This capacity to find comfort can lead to a vicious circle. The inactive infants need more stimulation than the active ones in order to reach the same level of social awareness, but they are the ones that get the least attention.

An important generalization was made from analysis of the conditions under which infants first show visual attention to their surroundings. A moderate degree of stimulation favours development; too strong an arousal leads to regression.

The mother, in particular, varies her response at this early stage to the infant's changing needs. She introduces variation and intensifies those actions which, at one moment, are pleasing and reduces her activity when the stimulus is too great. Social encounters with siblings and fathers are less accommodating; the infant may be "... bounced, tickled, tossed, or teased by the offer of toys withdrawn just before they are grasped...". It is the non-maternal contacts which provide the growing infant with the experience of having to accommodate to an unaccommodating world.

[10] B. Foss (Ed.). *Determinants of Infant Behaviour*, II, Methuen, 1963.

[11] H. R. Schaffer and Peggy E. Emerson, *The Development of Social Attachments in Infancy*, Child Development Publications, Indiana, 1964; and H. R. Schaffer, *The Growth of Sociability*, Penguin, 1971.

[12] Sibylle K. Escalona, *The Roots of Individuality*, Tavistock Publications, 1968.

It is to be noted that there is an increasing tendency for fathers and other members of the family to supply aspects of parental stimulation which at one time were attributed almost exclusively to the mother. Also, some importance must be attached to the experiences, though comparatively few in number, of upbringing in kibbutzim, communes and squats.

6

Toilet Training

DIVISIONS in the developmental stages are made under different headings by observers who have different standpoints. There is a difference in the outward behaviour between an infant who has to be carried from place to place and the toddler who can move on his or her own initiative. There is a difference between the baby who babbles in a manner intelligible only to those who communicate in the same baby language, and the young child who has acquired the speech which is understood even by strangers.

Walking is a *physical* landmark, talking an *intellectual* one even though it depends upon physical maturation and emotional relationships.

Toilet Training as a Social Demand

The acquisition of control of bladder and bowel is a step in *social* life and implies conscious conformity to rules laid down by others. Control of bladder and bowel functions also has *physical* and *emotional* aspects. Control of bladder and bowel function becomes important wherever mankind lives in large communities. The excreta can carry infection, and indiscriminate passing of urine and faeces and careless handling can be a danger to the community. Excreta become associated with dirt, disease and danger.

Control of the process of elimination marks the stage when the child begins to take responsibility for carrying something out which is not a personal need, but a duty imposed upon the individual because of the needs of the group in which he or she lives, and the needs of the larger community which contains the group.

The attitudes to the products of elimination are always complex. Separate from the body, they may be looked upon as carrying danger, but the process of elimination itself can carry with it a feeling of goodness and of healthiness and, at the moment of elimination, the products themselves can be regarded with satisfaction as a sign of healthy body activity. Health is often judged by the regularity and the quantity of urine and faeces.

Maternal Attitudes to Products of Elimination

In early infancy the baby's urine and motions are looked upon benevolently. They are so close to being a part of the baby's body that the mother handles them without fear or distaste and often with a considerable amount of affection. The first

51

motions after birth are called meconium, and they are different from the faeces which are formed later in that the substance is completely free from bacteria. Shortly after birth when the child is fed with milk at the breast or from the bottle the bowel products change in character and begin to contain some of the fat from the milk. The motions are often a pale yellow in colour and quite sweet to smell, and mothers handle the napkins with satisfaction and without fear when changing a napkin which contains the child's motion or which contains the urine.

Digestive disorders may alter the character of the "stool" (as it is sometimes called). Green, loose and scanty motions may be a sign of underfeeding the baby. A hungry unhappy baby with loose stools soon produces an unhappy mother who becomes anxious about the child's feed, and the mother may even be tempted to dilute the feed in the belief that the milk is too strong for her baby. This is where the mother needs reassurance as to the goodness of her milk if she is feeding at the breast, and of the goodness of her mothering if she is feeding the child with the bottle, and she may need practical information about some of the processes of feeding.

Gradually, as the child is given mixed feeding, the motions change in colour and character, and begin to resemble the more adult faeces. They begin to have the characteristic smell of motions, as a result of the activity of bacteria which become the normal inhabitants of the bowel.

The mother may still feel safe in handling these more mature stools but begins to feel that it is necessary to be more careful of her disposal of them and in her cleaning up of the baby, of herself and of the utensils. Gradually her attitude to these products alters, and as the baby shows signs of physical development and intellectual awareness, she is able to give some of the responsibility for the disposal of the motions and urine and is able to seat the child on the lavatory. The little boy is able to stand and direct his urine into the pan, if it is low enough, and the little girl is able to choose a time to sit on the seat for the passing of urine or for her bowel action.

Maturation of Nervous Pathways

There are steps of physical development which have to be reached before a child can be said to acquire this kind of control. It apparently depends upon maturation of nerve fibres which go to the muscles which control the "sphincters" (the name given to the muscles around the openings of the bladder and the bowel).

The nerve fibres in general are able to work efficiently when they acquire a myelin sheath, and this maturation takes place at different times in nerves to different parts of the body. The fibres to the muscles controlling elimination mature somewhere around the eighteenth month of life, and then the child is able voluntarily to initiate contractions in the abdomen which set going the process of relaxation of the sphincters and expulsion of the excreta. Previous to this the emptying of bladder and bowel is reflex and involuntary.

Reflex contraction of bladder and bowel muscle tends to take place throughout life whenever a certain degree of distension is reached. Voluntary contraction of muscles assists this natural and more primitive process, and voluntary control inhibits the process. In the early months of life the reflex emptying of bladder and bowel may appear to be unpredictable, and therefore there are wet and soiled napkins. There are, however, some patterns of regularity, and some indications that the process is about to take place can be observed. There is a tendency to empty bladder and bowel as the result of a series of reflexes when food enters the stomach. The contents of the different parts of the bowel are, in turn, passed on a stage further in a kind of shunting process. The bowel is thus likely to expel some of its contents, and simultaneous bladder contractions lead to a passing of urine.

The mother who places a child on the "potty" shortly after feeds may succeed in catching the products, and take pride in the dry and clean napkins. On other occasions she may notice the beginning of the elimination when the baby flushes and the rate of breathing alters. Quick recourse to the potty saves the napkin. Sometimes mothers who in this way train themselves, rather than the baby, take a pride in what they think is the baby's achievement, and equate it with the goodness of the baby. The danger here is that the inevitable accident becomes badness in the baby. Another danger is that there is a difficulty in the mother's adaptation for the transition to the stage when the baby has the capacity to control the passing and the withholding of urine and faeces. The pattern of the baby's behaviour has changed, and yet the mother is still seeking the same result.

Battles of Will

If regularity has become an issue, and if the mother feels that it is necessary for her rather than the baby to control the regularity of the passing of the urine and motions, the baby is likely to get satisfaction from resisting her demands as soon as he or she is capable of doing so. Battles begin over toilet training in the same way as they can occur when food is offered too rigidly in timing and quantity.

The young infant learns to retain the stools even when laxatives are given up to the point when the motions become so loose that they have the consistency of diarrhoea and can no longer be controlled. Alternatively, the infant may pass the motion at an inconvenient time and place at the very moment that the mother has given up the struggle.

Tension, Relief and Gratification

During the end of the second half of the first year or during the second year, the baby has learned to distinguish sensations in connection with the passing of urine and faeces, and there is a pleasure in the relief of the distended bowel and bladder with the emptying at what seems to be the right time. There is a pleasure in the sensation of the passing of urine and motions, and these sensations begin to rival those of the mouth as a source of gratification.

Psychoanalysts refer to the *anal* period of psychosexual development and also they pay attention to the importance of sensations and fantasies in connection with the urethra. These orifices (anus and urethra) become, for the time being, an important focus of emotional experience. There is a sense of gratification when elimination is satisfactory, or of discomfort and pain when the timing or the nature of the product has altered in some way—such as when the urine is too concentrated or infected, or when the motions are too hard or too loose.

The thoughts and fantasies about the actual products are complex because the action of elimination is thought of as good and sometimes the products themselves are thought of as good or, alternatively, actions and products are thought of as bad and dangerous.

The products are a part of the child's body and the goodness or badness is of the self. These products are an extension of the personality into the outside world. While the child was first experiencing the sensations of feeding, and learning the limits of the self, it must have been hard to distinguish where the mouth began, as there was a continuous passage of milk between the mouth and the nipple or bottle. When sensation first developed at the bowel orifice, it must have been difficult to determine where the body ended as the products passed outwards. Moreover, just as feeding is not entirely a personal activity but a relationship between the child and the mother, elimination also is a kind of relationship, because the mother communicates approval or disapproval of the child by her attitude to it. According to folklore, this approval is reciprocal, and a baby will wet in the arms of someone who can give sufficient confidence as to permit complete relaxation.

Bowel Activity as a Communication

Thus, elimination serves a biological function for a child, and it can also be part of the loving contact between the baby and the one who is caring. Fantasies about the products themselves enter into the structure of the later mental life in terms of goodness or badness, and even shape delusional feelings which are present in some degree in the normal individual and in more intense form in the mentally disturbed. Many people continue to think of urine and faeces as poisonous even when they are in their body, and they seek to find medicines or physical procedures such as washouts to cleanse themselves. More fancifully still, they can think of these products as dangerous to other people. Popular and trendy speech reveal these depths of feelings in the use of the names of products of elimination to describe people in a deliberately offensive way. In contrast to the careful wording of the previous sentences, it is interesting to note that in some ostentatiously modern literature the language is deliberately explicit and the pages are spattered with the word "shit". Alongside these attitudes there is pride in the achievement of urination and defaecation, and boys in particular take pride in quantity and direction in the passing of urine!

These are features of which every individual has some knowledge. Such ideas become exaggerated in mental illnesses when social controls are removed.

There are some who are not mentally disturbed but who derive character traits from the degree of importance given to the toilet care during this period of training. Cleanliness is next to godliness, and dirtiness is sin; and the close anatomical association of bladder and bowel with sexual organs connects the sin of dirtiness with sexual guilt (and, incidentally, links sexuality with the toilet). Some people react to this so strongly that cleanliness and orderliness become their chief virtue. They are tidy in their appearance and in their work, and often put these characteristics to good use. Sometimes individuals carry the tidiness and carefulness into every field of activity and become miserly, or the same process may take more abnormal forms when the individual is so fearful about the power to damage people by dirt or untidiness that he or she develops obsessional rituals to protect others from the consequences of hidden powers of evil.

There are milder degrees of these processes which find justification in various cults concerning food and the control of movements of the bladder and the bowel. Many people regard regularity as a sign of health and go to great lengths to ensure it for themselves and their children, and, as mentioned above, the more that attention is paid to the activity, the more it can become an activity in which battles are fought between child and parent. Thus, bladder and bowel activity can succeed oral activity in providing individual gratification, and in addition, communication both of a loving and of an aggressive nature.

Control as Stage of Development

Bladder and bowel control serves the further function of marking a stage of maturity, and temporary or permanent regression to more infantile states can be indicated by a return to the uncontrolled infantile habits. Enuresis (wetting) and encopresis (soiling) can have many explanations when they occur at different stages of an individual's life, and it is always necessary to take into account that such a symptom can have a meaning as part of the interaction between individual and family as well as having a purely personal or clinical significance.

Enuresis

This is one of a type of problem which deals with control in the individual, and in which the symptom resembles immaturity. The change from immaturity to maturity is one about which parents are seriously concerned and yet, at the same time, a child's lapses into greater degrees of immaturity are looked upon partly as humorous. Grown-ups refer to their own occasional loss of control in temporary illness, or following indiscretions, with good-humoured tolerance which sometimes conceals intense anxiety. Loss of control is a serious insult to one's image of oneself, and the ideas are important symbolically—we speak of a "leak" of official secrets.

Parents sometimes look upon enuresis in children as an indication of their own failure, or as inherent defectiveness in the child. Professional people tend to look upon it as a disease entity and look for a single causal factor. Enuresis, however, is a condition which is best looked upon as (to adapt a phrase used by Sir Aubrey Lewis in a slightly different context) "a patch of *family* biography".

We should not give the name enuresis to bedwetting at too early a stage. There are many reasons for the failure to acquire control, or for the loss of control after it has been acquired:

(1) *Low intelligence*. This is the equivalent of continued immaturity. Mental handicap does not inevitably lead to continued enuresis, but the process of acquiring control should be expected to proceed more slowly than with a child whose intelligence is within the normal range.

(2) *Unsatisfactory social conditions.* For example, in overcrowded homes where several children sleep together in one bed with inadequate bedding, if one or more of the children is enuretic, there is no incentive for any of the others to acquire control. In such homes there may be inadequacy of parental care, and a lack of consistent control of any kind. The cause of enuresis here is inadequate training and care.

(3) *Excessive training.* Undue attention to the activity of processes of evacuation causes increased sensitivity of the bladder to its contents. The bladder acquires a lower threshold of capacity and has to be emptied more frequently than normally. If a child is afraid of punishment for wetting the bed, or is told in the daytime not to ask to go too frequently to the lavatory the effect of the anxiety may increase the need to go. People are familiar with this even as adults in social situations and within the normal range of familiar activities. An example of this is of the child who develops the habit of asking to go to the "loo" immediately on arrival at a strange house on a visit with mother. After several instances of this behaviour, the mother gives strict instructions before setting out, not to ask to go immediately on arrival. The extra precaution is taken of a last visit just before leaving home, but before reaching the bus stop the child needs to go once again! This type of anxiety can set a pattern in a more serious way when the occasional inevitable lapse is taken as a serious fault.

(4) *Temporary regressions.* Children return to infantile behaviour patterns during emotional stress of any kind or during physical illness. This can occur at times of school examinations or disturbances affecting other members of the family. The birth of a younger child can cause a return to bedwetting in an older child either as a result of unconscious rivalry, or even as deliberate imitation of the baby who shows no signs of control yet receives lavish attention.

(5) *Fixation at infantile level.* Some children remain immature in a way that partly satisfies unconscious wishes of their own and of their parents. Often this is an interaction, particularly between mother and child, and occasionally both father and mother are closely linked together with the child in an overprotecting relationship. One example of this was of a 13-year-old girl who had been enuretic since the age of 3. At the time the parents had been advised to lift the child at night to pass urine, and up to the age of 13 this was still being carried out by mother and father together each night. Napkins were fixed and refixed by father and mother together as part of the attention to this girl.

More frequently the close relationship is one between child and mother alone, and in some cases the bedwetting is a call for attention from the child to its mother. It has been said that some children cry with their eyes and some cry with their bladders.

(6) *Aggressiveness.* Although as described above the symptom can be partly satisfying to the parent and child, it could also be an outlet for anger against the mother, or an expression of conflict. It is the mother who has to wash the sheets, and, in some cases, this is discussed bitterly within the family and with the child, and sometimes the child is asked to wash the sheets and to make his or her own bed. Occasionally the child who wets the bed regularly at home is perfectly dry at the home of a favourite aunt (this, incidentally, proves the fruitlessness of a con-

tinued search for the cause of enuresis in the mechanics of micturition). Sometimes enuresis proves a necessary safety valve in a disturbed family relationship, and an illustrative case is that of a child of 9 brought to a clinic for continued nocturnal enuresis. She was a shy, pretty, only child of middle-class parents in a pleasant suburb of an industrial town. Enuresis was the only symptom. Her intelligence quotient was 85, and she was being coached by her mother for the Secondary Selection Examination which was to take place in eighteen months' time! She had to get up at seven each morning and do an hour's arithmetic with her mother before going to school. All this she did obediently but without apparent benefit. She and the mother attended the clinic three times, but visits were stopped because they interfered with attendance at school. Supposing some treatment had been available which could have "cured" the enuresis, the effect might have been disastrous. The bedwetting was the one way in which this girl could allow herself to rebel.

(7) *Orgastic.* The passing of urine has its own pleasure which is related to sexual sensation. Some children openly admit that they like the sensation of warm urine at the moment that it is being passed. Moreover, a boy approaching puberty may pass urine for the resemblance of the sensation to that caused by seminal emissions, and sometimes to conceal an emission which has occurred.

There is a wide range of types of treatment in current use. Some of the methods are based on theories which are in direct opposition to the theories on which others are based. Many children have had a number of these very different methods of treatment and, therefore, before coming to any particular method, have already had a history of the trial and failure of other methods. Each method must have its successes, and one could ask what proportion of cases get better, and at what stage? One might also ask whether recovery at any particular stage is directly related to the remedy being applied.

Successful results coming from a variety of different kinds of treatment may have one thing in common, and that is the arrival by the individual concerned at a particular developmental stage when control becomes possible or acceptable. Treatment thus becomes related to maturation. It is not a process where something that went wrong has become remedied, but rather a process which helps development which has been delayed in that particular respect.[1]

---

[1] R. F. Barbour *et al.*, Enuresis as a Disorder of Development, *Brit. Med. J.* 5360 (1963).

7

Infantile Sexuality

DESCRIPTIONS of sexuality which are entered into for the purpose of marking out stages in the development of emotional life usually deal with the topic as a phase in infancy which follows oral and anal phases. The importance of sensation in different areas or zones of the body is linked with gratifications, frustrations and with fantasies. Theories of infantile sexuality were built up within a framework which assumed the existence of instincts which link psychic experience with the physico-chemical economy of the body.[1]

Sex Differences: Physical Basis

The physical nature of the sex differences requires more attention than is usually given to it, and the sex of the infant has its importance, to both parents, long before the time when the infant has even the most shadowy consciousness of sexual identity. Notwithstanding jokes about "la différence", it is too often taken for granted that human beings can be referred to with a male pronoun while making occasional acknowledgements of the existence of the female. The English language, with its lack of a neutral pronoun, makes it difficult to avoid this fault, the Sex Discrimination Act notwithstanding! True equality of the sexes is a social aim rather than a biological fact and in this section it can be pointed out that there are differences in the rate of development of physical and intellectual performance, in the time of reaching maturity, senescence and death; and these differences have a personal and social importance. The sex difference exists in the first single cell resulting from the union of the ovum with the spermatozoa. It continues to exist within the constitution of the chromosomes in every cell of the mature body. Each human cell has forty-six chromosomes, of which forty-four are in identical pairs, the remaining two determining the sex of the individual. These special chromosomes are designated "X" and "Y". Where the cell contains two "X" chromosomes the individual is female. Where there is one "X" chromosome and one "Y" chromosome the individual is male. While still within the womb, the development of the foetus proceeds in directions determined by this chromosome constitution. The

---

[1] E. Glover, *Psychoanalysis*, Staples Press, 1939.

58

embryo with an "XX" constitution gradually takes the characteristic shape which includes ovaries, a uterus and the female external genitalia connected with the vagina. An embryo with chromosomes having an "XY" constitution begins to develop testicles and a penis.[2]

The body tissue which carries both primary and secondary sexual characteristics shows very little development until the time that puberty is reached, but there is no period of life in which the sexual characteristics do not affect the totality of personality, including the process of growth.

Sexual Organs and Sexual Roles

Anomalies of physical sex characteristics exist, sometimes leading to erroneous sexual attributions. A female infant with an enlarged clitoris may be brought up as a male. A male infant with a cleft in the penis may be brought up as a female. Sometimes the error is not recognized until puberty, and, occasionally, surgical help is needed to assist in the establishment of appropriate sexual functioning.

This is not what happens when people seek a *change* of sex. Most of these are psychological rather than physical anomalies, and here the surgery, in the case of the male, can be a deliberate castration, plus the creation of an artificial vagina, in order to assume the semblance of a female. The publicity surrounding "sex changes", with or without operation, is an indication that traces of problems of sexual identity are almost universal. Moreover, the actual shape and function of the sexual organs are a focus of fantasy. The male organ can be imagined as hurtful to the female, and vice versa.

The comforting aspects of the sexual organs may be taken for granted, but do not frequently find expression except in poetry, mythology and religion.[3]

Rates of Growth

Measurements of the comparative maturity of development as between the sexes are based on examination of the bone structure, and it has been stated that "girls are on the average ahead of boys in skeletal maturity from birth to adulthood".[4] At birth, boys are four to six weeks behind girls in skeletal age, and girls maintain their lead and reach adolescence and final mature size some two years before boys. The longer and later adolescence of boys gives them a final advantage in height and weight at the adult stage.[5]

[2] Some chromosome anomalies are associated with congenital diseases. For example, some cases of Mongolism are due to what is called "trisomy", i.e. one chromosome in a pair has at some stage been subdivided, making three chromosomes instead of two in that position. Some other anomalies are linked with abnormalities of the sex chromosome structure where, for example, there is a genetic constitution of XXY, XXX, or XYY. In some of these cases there are abnormal shapes of sexual organs and doubtful sexual identity, but in some instances there appears to be a normal sexual identity, including fertility.
[3] "Thy rod and thy staff they comfort me." Psalm 23:4 AV and RV.
[4] G. A. Harrison *et al.*, *Human Biology*, Oxford University Press, 1964.
[5] J. M. Tanner, *Foetus into Man*, Open Books, 1978.

Cultural and Biological Factors

Differences have been noted in the rate of intellectual development between boys and girls and in the responses to the teaching of different subjects at school. There is a welcome tendency to attribute these differences to cultural factors, including that of the forward look, on the part of all concerned, to the adult gender function in our society. It scarcely seems likely, however, that the vital biological distinction is, in itself, not without its effect on the potentiality of the male and female to respond in a different way to similar stimuli.

The sexual differences inevitably lead to differences in the experience of the infant within the family and the social setting. Parents frequently would choose for their first child a boy rather than a girl and, less frequently, a girl rather than a boy. They may vary their preference for subsequent children. Even when there is no apparent preference, and when the child of either sex receives full acceptance, there seems to be some kind of response from the child that carries approval according to its sex. Vigorous feeding is more readily approved in a boy than in a girl. Mathematical failure at school carries less disapproval in girls than in boys; and, in boys, mal-adaptations to family standards is more likely to find expression in undesirable behaviour than it is in girls.

These brief references to the basic differences between the sexes tend to empha-sise that sexuality is something which enters into every aspect of life, and that it is something which has consequences for the interactions within the family from the very moment of birth. Having said this, we can now take up again the sequence in the stages of psychosexual development within the framework of psychoanalytical theory, which assumes that adult behaviour has its roots in infancy.

Sensual Pleasures: Intensity of Sensual Experiences at Different Stages

It takes a considerable time before children have a complete sense of identity and of the limits of their own body. Each movement that the baby is able to make is repeated until it is mastered and then, as if to increase the satisfaction, it is made more complicated. Each sensation is recaptured in the attempts to repeat the ex-perience or to enjoy it in fantasy; and the child learns how to explore the body. The baby has learned that pleasure comes to the lips from contact with other indi-viduals, with the mother's nipple or the mother's face, and from the kiss that he or she is encouraged to give to members of the family. Infants are able to enjoy the contact of food and to revive the pleasure by sucking the thumb or the dummy teat. They have also learned that denial of the desired pleasure is possible, and that some of the pleasurable sensations seem to be disturbing because they are so overwhelm-ingly intense. They have discovered that there is both gratification and anxiety in the contacts between themselves and mother or nurse at the moment of the sen-sation of the passing of urine and faeces. They may experience some satisfaction in the feel of a wet or soiled napkin against the skin, or they may learn to think of it as bad and dangerous. The sensations become partly a personal property and partly a communication between self and others.

Genital Sensitivity

The next stage in the exploration of personal and inter-personal experiences is the discovery that the genital organs are especially sensitive. Boys and girls alike learn that there can be a kind of pleasure from the touching of the genital organs. Pleasure can be produced or enhanced by movements of the body which cause rubbing of these parts. This pleasure reaches a height during the second year of life and the accidental discovery leads to a deliberately produced pattern of pleasure and excitement. The nature of the sensation has the quality of overwhelming intensity to a greater extent than in any other previous experience. The accompanying anxiety can be increased when the activity is noticed and disapproved by the parents.

Communication of Guilt

Mother and father alike may be disconcerted by the sexual nature of a young baby's play with himself or herself. It seems so inappropriate, so out of keeping with the ideas of childhood innocence. The residues of guilt which the adult has with regard to mature sexual enjoyment seem to be activated when the parent is confronted with this activity in a young infant. Disapproval is conveyed to the baby boy or girl in looks, words, or physical punishment. The primitive guilt which the baby has already begun to experience in his or her abandonment to the depths of sexuality becomes reinforced by the parents' underlying attitude, even when they are not overtly disapproving. Perhaps the sexual stimulation has already followed the pattern of oral and anal sensations in appearing both as a personal gratification and also as a process of communicating with others. The satisfaction can become associated, therefore, with fantasies in which other individuals are involved. Stimulation can be produced by the child alone; but stimulation also occurs during toilet care and cleansing when the same parts are handled by the mother (or the individual who does the nursing). The person who condemns the pleasure is also the one who takes a share in stimulating it. Gratification and frustration become associated with the love and hostility with which child and adult communicate with one another.

The sexuality differs from the oral and anal (and urethral) activities in having no immediate biological function at this stage. Fantasy reigns supreme, and the adult to whom sexuality has a more physical fulfilment, may find the infantile sexuality to be incomprehensible. The adult contributes to the sexual role of the baby girl or boy, and the response of baby to parent is affected by the parental attitudes. The girl or boy learns to recognize that girls and boys are treated differently, and each learns to recognize the personal gender role.

The sexual sensation in the genital organs has so far followed the previous pattern of sexuality. Oral, anal and genital phases follow one another in sequence at separate periods, but sensations in these three areas can be experienced simultaneously. Freud described the infant as "polymorphous perverse", implying that in a way that is similar to the perversions of abnormal adults, the normal infant can derive sensual satisfaction from many different parts of the body.

Emphasis on sexual differences has been necessary in order to establish the fact that there *are* differences. Emphasis on differentiation can be carried too far, or made too rigidly. These days, most people recognize that each individual carries some characteristics generally attributed to the opposite sex.

Here, girls are perhaps more fortunate than boys in having the approving label of "tomboy". There is no approving female designation for "feminine" qualities in a boy—unless the word "unisex" has eroded the rigidity of the stereotype. Parents can help their children to find a more secure sexual identity, if they are not compelled to exclude qualities of the other sex.

Masturbatory Activities

Deliberate self-stimulation in order to achieve sexual sensation is masturbation, and this can occur in baby boys and baby girls. A stage is reached where there is a flushing of the face and a holding of the breath similar to that in adult orgasm. Sometimes the rubbing is continued without a climax ever being reached. Occasionally the child learns that the use of the hand is disapproved but is able to get a similar sensation by rocking the body, even to the extent of shaking the cot. A more remote displacement of the activity is head banging. A child may bang the head for long periods and continue even when this produces pain. Perhaps pain serves the purpose of satisfying guilt feelings by giving an in-built punishment for the activity which is also a pleasure.

Masturbatory activity is universal in the second year of life, and it persists into later stages of childhood. Parents may quite naturally be worried by these activities. Some parents succeed in denying that it ever occurs, some try to distract the child with some other activity, but most babies or infants lose the habit spontaneously when the world becomes a more interesting place and when they no longer need to find their solace from their own body.

Children who are severely punished, or children who are left too much alone, are more likely to continue with the habit. *Very* severe punishment or withdrawal of love may, equally, have the effect of inhibiting sexual activity to such a degree that subsequent sexual maturity is never achieved. It is understandable that parents should be concerned about the persistence of masturbation as they themselves have recollections of adolescent sexual activities and fantasies which seemed to serve no *immediate* biological purpose. It is only in recent years that "normal" adults of both sexes have been prepared to admit that masturbation continues as an addition to heterosexual or homosexual experience, and sometimes as the only sexual activity. The sensations and the fantasies *do* serve a purpose as a blueprint for the more mature sexual activities of adult life.

8

The Oedipal Situation

STAGES in the emotional development of an individual, as revealed in psychoanalytical studies, are given names which depend upon the area of the body which at any one time is predominantly sensitive. The early stages in the child's expanding experience of the self and of the outside world, are labelled *oral, anal* and *genital*. Satisfaction and frustration are localized successively in the mouth, excretory organs and the genitalia.

The historical progress is referred to as "Psychosexual development". The word "sexual" is used in a general sense, and this use is justified by the continuing nature of sensuality in the separate stages. The sensations may appear overwhelming at times, and at all stages tension can be followed by gratification, with disturbing as well as pleasing overtones.

The three stages are usually described separately, but they are not clearly divided from one another, and early kinds of satisfaction survive as a central framework for each successive stage.

When the infant first becomes aware of the complex sensations around the genital organs, these become associated with the primitive recognition of his or her sexual status. The child begins to interact, in fantasy, in a different way with each parent. In general, the child develops a specific and intense attachment to the parent of the opposite sex. The parent of the same sex becomes a rival.

This stage has been described as the *Oedipal Situation*. Originally it was referred to as the *Oedipus Complex*, but the word *situation* appears preferable when the process takes the normal course, complicated though that may be. Freud used this label in order to refer to the Greek legend which was the subject of the play *Oedipus Rex* by Sophocles. In this drama, it was prophesied at the time of the birth of Oedipus that he would kill his father and marry his mother. He was, consequently, to have been put to death, but, being abandoned instead, he was brought up in the belief that his foster parents were his real parents. The means adopted to avert the prophesied fate led to its fulfilment. When Oedipus came to adult life he met, quarrelled with, and killed his father, and married his mother, in ignorance of their true identities.

Myths as Patterns of Regularly Occurring Human Situations

The use of the label "Oedipus complex" is a familiar part of psychological language and, for that matter, of present-day humour. The first mention of it appeared in a letter written by Freud to Wilhelm Fliess in 1897. Freud was a somewhat reluctant discoverer of the contents in the hidden depths of the human mind. Fliess

63

was a Berlin physician and biologist with wide interests and it was to Fliess that Freud turned as someone to whom he could unburden himself in letters which gave a day-to-day record of his work and his thoughts about it. It became a painful experience to Freud that each new patient made him the recipient of childhood memories of scenes of seduction by grown-up persons—most frequently by the parent of the opposite sex. At first, he had taken the memories as clear evidence of historical fact, but later he learned of instances where there was independent evidence that the incidents could not have taken place. He was so shaken by this discovery that his immediate thought was that he must now abandon his methods and his theories, but afterwards it occurred to him that there must be some reason for the fact that human mental processes could consistently produce these fantasies in almost identical patterns. He had begun to conduct his own analysis, making private records of his own apparently undirected thoughts, communicating the basic ideas to the distant and idealized personality of Fliess. He wrote:

> "So far I have found nothing completely new, but all the complications to which by now I am used. It is no easy matter. Being entirely honest with oneself is a good exercise. Only one idea of general value has occurred to me. I have found love of the mother and jealousy of the father in my own case too, and now believe it to be a general phenomenon of early childhood, even if it does not always occur so early as in children who have been made hysterics. (Similarly with the "romanticism of origins" in the case of paranoiacs—heroes, founders of religion.) If that is the case, the gripping power of *Oedipus Rex*, in spite of all the rational objections to the inexorable fate that the story presupposes, becomes intelligible, and one can understand why later fate dramas were such failures. Our feelings rise against any arbitrary individual fate such as shown in the *Ahnfrau*,[1] etc., but the Greek myth seizes on a compulsion which everyone recognizes because he has felt traces of it in himself. Every member of the audience was once a budding Oedipus in phantasy, and this dream-fulfilment played out in reality causes everyone to recoil in horror, with the full measure of repression which separates his infantile from his present state..."[2]

Freud had turned to the Greek myths for his literary prototype of the complex and turbulent tangle of family relationships. The original story of Oedipus is not of the delicate family romance in which a 4-year-old boy says to Mummy, "When I am big I am going to marry you"—not even when the boy adds that at that time Daddy will be a little boy or that Daddy will go away. The Oedipus story is of incest, murder and rape, and it is not lacking in details of basic human situations which are relevant to problems of personal identity, of parentage and the special case of adoption.

Present-day Implications

There are some hidden or unexplored depths of the story. One of these is the tacit assumption that, because of the prophecy, the parents of Oedipus had the

[1] *Die Ahnfrau*, the title of a play by Franz Grillparzer.
[2] S. Freud, *The Origins of Psycho Analysis: Letters to Wilhelm Fliess, Drafts and Notes: 1887–1902*, Imago, 1954.

right to put Oedipus to death in order to avert the prophecy. This part of the story usually passes almost unnoticed. Even today, in many parts of the world a child may be murdered for being the wrong sex or being one child too many. In this century, and in this country, babies were murdered in the big cities for the sake of a few pounds of an insurance policy taken out with this in mind. The laws regarding life insurance had to be altered.

The Oedipus Legend in Full

At the time when Freud was formulating his theories, scholars of all European countries were united by knowledge of classical literature. Today this knowledge can no longer be assumed and it may be possible to understand some of its implications better if a fairly full account of the story is given. The following is quoted from *A Classical Dictionary* by J. Lempriere, D.D., published in 1864:

"ŒDIPUS, a son of Laius, king of Thebes, and Jocasta. Being descended from Venus by his father's side, Œdipus was born to be exposed to all the calamities and persecutions which Juno could inflict upon the posterity of the goddess of beauty. Laius, the father of Œdipus, was informed by the oracle, as soon as he married Jocasta that he must perish by the hands of his son. Such dreadful intelligence awakened his fears, and to prevent the fulfilment of the oracle, he resolved never to approach Jocasta; but his solemn resolutions were violated in a fit of intoxication. The queen became pregnant, and Laius, still desirous of averting the evil, ordered his wife to destroy the child as soon as it came into the world. The mother had not the courage to obey, yet she gave the child as soon as born to one of her domestics, with orders to expose him on the mountains. The servant was move with pity, but to obey the command of Jocasta, he bored the feet of the child, and suspended him with a twig by the heels to a tree on mount Cithæron, where he was soon found by one of the shepherds of Polybus, king of Corinth. The shepherd carried him home, and Peribœa, the wife of Polybus, who had no children, educated him as her own child, with maternal tenderness.

"The accomplishments of the infant, who was named Œdipus on account of the swelling of his feet (*oidéw tumeo nous pes*), soon became the admiration of the age. His companions envied his strength and his address, and one of them to mortify his rising ambition, told him that he was an illegitimate child. This raised his doubts; he asked Peribœa who, out of tenderness, told him that his suspicions were ill founded. Not satisfied with this, he went to consult the oracle of Delphi, and was there told not to return home, for if he did, he must necessarily be the murderer of his father, and the husband of his mother. This answer of the oracle terrified him; he knew no home but the house of Polybus, therefore he resolved not to return to Corinth where such calamities apparently attended him. He travelled towards Phocis, and in his journey, met in a narrow road Laius, with his arm-bearer, in a chariot. Laius haughtily ordered Œdipus to make way for him. Œdipus refused, and a contest ensued, in which Laius and his arm-bearer were both killed. As Œdipus was ignorant of the quality and of the rank of the man whom he had just killed, he continued his journey, and was attracted to

Thebes by the fame of the Sphynx. This terrible monster which Juno had sent to lay waste the country (*vid.* Sphynx), resorted to the neighbourhood of Thebes, and devoured all those who attempted to explain without success the ænigmas which he proposed. The calamity was now become an object of public concern, and as the successful explanation of the ænigma would end in the death of the Sphynx, Creon, who, at the death of Laius, had ascended the throne of Thebes, promised his crown and Jocasta to him who succeeded in the attempt. The ænigma proposed was this: What animal in the morning walks upon four feet, at noon upon two, and in the evening upon three? This was left for Œdipus to explain; he came to the monster and said, that man, in the morning of life, walks upon his hands and his feet; when he has attained the years of manhood, he walks upon his two legs; and in the evening, he supports his old age with the assistance of a staff. The monster, mortified at the true explanation, dashed his head against a rock, and perished.

"Œdipus ascended the throne of Thebes, and married Jocasta, by whom he had two sons, Polynices and Eteocles, and two daughters, Ismene and Antigone.

"Some years after, the Theban territories were visited with a plague; and the oracle declared that it should not cease till the murderer of king Laius was banished from Bœotia. As the death of Laius had never been examined into, and the circumstances that attended it were never known, this answer of the oracle was of the greatest concern to the Thebans; but Œdipus, the friend of the people, resolved to overcome every difficulty by the most exact inquiries. His researches were successful, and he was soon proved to be the murderer of his father. The melancholy discovery was rendered the more alarming, when Œdipus considered, that he had not only murdered his father, but that he had committed incest with his mother. In the excess of his grief he put out his eyes, as unworthy to see the light, and banished himself from Thebes, or as some say, was banished by his own sons."

The Oedipus story contains elemental themes which are repeated amongst the great by the prudent slaughter of the young who might grow up to be rivals, and by the usurping of power by the young who could not afford to wait to inherit it. The rivalries across the generations are matched by those between siblings. Stories of brotherly love are told side by side with the story of Cain and Abel. Freud might have used Bible stories had he known them as well as he knew the Greek myths.

Abraham, Isaac, Ishmael and Sarah

The Bible story of the readiness of Abraham to sacrifice his son, Isaac, has some of the same elements as the Oedipus legend, including Divine intervention into human affairs.

In the authorised version (Genesis 22: 1 and 2) the story begins, "And it came to pass after these things that God did *tempt*[3] Abraham, and said unto him, Abraham: and he said, Behold here I am. And he said, Take now thy son, thine only son Isaac,

---

[3] Our italics.

who thou lovest, and get thee into the land of Moriah; and offer him there for a burnt offering upon one of the mountains which I will tell thee of."

The story continues with the account of the preparation for a sacrifice. When the altar was complete, Abraham "bound Isaac, his son, and laid him upon the altar, upon the wood". When he stretched out his hand and took the knife to slay his son, an angel of the Lord called on him to stop, saying, "Now I know that thou fearest God, seeing thou hast not withheld thy son, thine only son, from Me".

This story is usually quoted as an example of Abraham's willingness to sacrifice to God what was dearest to him. It could equally well be told as the turning away from human sacrifice. There is, however, yet another meaning to be found. The first words of the chapter were, "And it came to pass *after these things*".[4] One should, therefore, turn to the preceding chapter which deals with the birth of Isaac in Sarah and Abraham's old age, and the casting out of Ishmael and his mother. Sarah had believed herself to be barren and had offered her handmaiden, Hagar, to Abraham so that he could have offspring. As so often happens following adoption of a child by an infertile couple, they subsequently had a child of the marriage. At the time that Isaac was weaned and when Abraham made a great feast, Sarah "saw the son of Hagar, the Egyptian, which she had born unto Abraham, mocking". She asked Abraham to cast out the bondwoman and her son so that "the son of this bond-woman shall not be heir with my son", "and the thing was very grievous in Abraham's sight because of his son". During the night, Abraham received reassurance from God that from the seed of Ishmael He would also make a nation, "because he is thy seed". Yet Hagar and Ishmael were cast out into the desert and only survived by miraculous intervention.

In the description of the preparations for the sacrifice of Isaac, it is said that "and Abraham rose up early in the morning...", presumably before Sarah was awake.

Could the hidden meaning of the story be that Abraham was, in effect, saying to Sarah, "You made me get rid of *my* son. Now I shall get rid of yours"?

Maturation as an Historical and as a Personal Process

Myths and legends provide metaphors which help the understanding of nuclear situations that are repeated throughout history. We like to believe that the modern civilized man has acquired control over passions that found freer expression in the early history of the human race and in the infancy of present-day human beings. Thus the behaviour of parents of "battered babies" can be better understood in terms of extreme immaturity, in which the demands of the new-born infant are in competition with those of the adult, but at the level such as that of the rivalry of a slightly older infant sibling. At a more mature level, the competition between the adolescent and the adult generation could be said to represent the search by youth for answers to riddles of the universe in dimensions which still seem to be forbidden by and to the older generation.

[4] Our italics.

Emphasis by Omission

All these myths, legends and metaphors add meaning to observations of human behaviour because they select a salient element for particular emphasis. For that reason these special descriptions always leave something out. At first what is left out is that which is so obvious that it is taken for granted, but new knowledge sometimes takes us into dimensions which exclude the original level of understanding. The stories selected for psychiatric enlightenment leave out consideration of the tender love of parents for each other, and for their children, and of brotherly love as a reality.

We can turn once more to the Bible (Jeremiah 31: 19)[5] for an illustration of parental love:

Is Ephraim a darling son unto Me?
Is he a child that is dandled?
For as often as I speak of him,
I do earnestly remember him still;
Therefore My heart yearneth for him,
I will surely have compassion upon him,
    saith the Lord.

The Biblical quotations and interpretations given above provide an attempt by the authors to place the descriptions of the Oedipal situation in a wider context of human thought and levels of maturity. It is intended to emphasise that explanations can exist in different dimensions, using different assumptions, and arriving at different conclusions. The usefulness of any particular metaphor is to provide a theory which is internally consistent and coherent. Sir Denis Hill[6] pointed out that Freud attempted to treat neurotic symptoms by discovering that the neurotic symptom had meaning. He quotes Medawar,[7] who stated that scientists are constantly building explanatory structures, telling stories, which are scrupulously tested to see if they are stories about real life.

We can therefore return to the Oedipus story as the drama selected for the psychoanalytical explanation of some aspects of living.

Acting the Drama in Fantasy

The kernel of the drama is enacted in fantasy in the lives of young children when they become aware of the sexual differences between the parents. For either boy or girl, the mother is the first object of love, but subsequently the situation develops in different ways according to whether the child is a boy or girl.

A boy is fed, fondled, gratified and denied by the mother. The sensations of his own body become related to her activities as well as to his own. He prolongs the sensations by reproducing her actions in his imagination, and elaborating them. He begins to desire exclusive possession of her, and these desires seem to become fulfilled whenever his father is absent. His father's presence becomes a threat to his

---

[5] Soncino Press 1949, English Text by the Jewish Publication Society of America.
[6] Sir Denis Hill, On the Contribution of Psychoanalysis to Psychiatry: mechanism and meaning, *Brit. J. Psych.* (1970).
[7] P. B. Medawar, *The Art of the Soluble*, Methuen, 1967.

claim for sole rights. He resents the contacts that he notices or imagines between father and mother. He may try to come between them by pushing the father away, or even, in desperation, seeking the company of his father if that will separate father from mother.

With a girl, this interaction takes a different course. She too is at first dependent upon, and closely attached to, her mother. As she develops, she becomes aware of her own feminine role, and so do her parents. She turns from her mother and claims her father as her special property and future husband.

The fantasies find words in which they can be expressed towards the end of the second year and during the third year of the child's life.

Repression of Sexual Component

The mental experiences become associated with tension in the sexual organs which by now have become sensitive. By this time, the child will have noticed disapproval, and sometimes will have experienced punishment, whenever any interest or excitement is shown in connection with the sexual organs. Feelings of guilt are aroused, and these become associated with the desire for possession of the mother or father respectively.

The sexual nature of the feeling becomes repressed. The boy who wished to destroy his father gradually invents games of make-believe in which he pretends to *be* his father. Later still, he is content to model himself for future development on the reality of his father. Similarly, a girl begins to imitate her mother when she no longer wishes to usurp her.

The process is more complicated still when there is more than one child. Two children of the same sex cannot have exclusive possession of one parent. Even in infancy, the second one has to take the parent who is still unclaimed—whatever the sex. When there are many children, there are a variety of possibilities, and an older child might become a subsidiary mother or father, and enter into interactions with the younger children in a way that is reminiscent of the rejection and accepting attitudes of a parent with a child.

Parents as Participants: Abnormality

The process becomes truly abnormal when parents enter actively into the situation as a result of their own abnormal needs. Parents may be rivals of each other, and they may encourage the love and jealousy which the child may show respectively towards them. There is a play-off of love and hate, and there may be envy of any preference shown to one parent or the other.

Normally the child is partly aware of the fantastic nature of these feelings. If the feelings are fostered and nurtured by the attitudes of the parents, the child may begin to think of them as both real and frightening. A boy inflates himself in fantasy to adult size, makes a brave show, and finds himself inadequate. There is terror under his grotesque assumptions. Worse still, the parents may enlarge their own image of the child, and deal with him as if he were offering a serious threat. Parents sometimes present a ready-made fantasy to a child, and, when he accepts it in a literal way, they are as dismayed as the child is.

Sometimes when a father dies, a well-intentioned adult will say to a boy of, say, four years "You will have to look after mother now". The boy expects himself to have an adult masculine strength, and fails according to his own standards. When a living father is considered to be unsatisfactory, a mother may turn to her infant son for male comfort. The child may then model himself on the very qualities of his father that his mother rejects. The mother then says "He is out of control". He defies her and shouts back at her, and she is afraid that he will overwhelm her. The child, meanwhile, has also drawn upon himself the criticisms of neighbours and perhaps his teacher, but within himself he is terrified because he well knows that he is playing a part which is beyond his real capacity.

Parents sometimes fear the sexuality that is revealed in the words and the behaviour of their young children. Some good parents fear the assertiveness that is culturally associated with masculinity. A boy is described as "... lovely when he was a baby. He was so cuddly." At the age of 3 or 4 years, his normal curiosity and vigour is thought of as an abnormal and undesirable aggression. His masculinity is deliberately attacked, and he may even develop feminine qualities in order to propitiate one of his parents.

In similar fashion, a girl may respond to her parents' unspoken wish for a boy, and adopt a sexual role on masculine models.

Normally, however, the early emotional interaction which is based on the unequal relationship of child and adult is given up. The repression of this kind of sexual imagery begins to shape a system of internal controls which is called the *Superego*. Freud stated "The Superego is the heir to the Oedipus Complex."

Latency Period

The historical description of stages of psychosexual development, in classical psychoanalytical terms, includes a *latency period*. This begins at around the age of 5 years, following the resolution of the oedipal situation and (in Freudian concepts) the formation of the superego. It ends with the onset of puberty, which brings biological reproductive capacity and the reactivation of sexuality. Puberty is the stage where either further repression or conscious control of sexuality becomes necessary, but it is implied that during the latency period sexual fantasies are in abeyance.

The latency period is thus, approximately, the stage between the age of 5 years and a point between 11 and 15 years when sexual maturity becomes apparent. It corresponds to the early school life when the child's mental activities are becoming roused by experiences and perceptions of the world of ideas and of material objects. It is implied that the child's mental life is predominantly conscious and intellectual.

One wonders whether the postulation of a latency period was the last concession that the early analysts felt compelled to make to the myth of childhood innocence! It is true that so much of the child's waking life is spent within the school that there is less opportunity than before for the emotional turmoil of family relationships. The inner fantasies, whenever they are revealed, are nevertheless shown to be rich in elaboration of ideas about birth and death, and about the complicated physical interaction between the individuals of different sex.

If we insist upon assuming the existence of a latency period, it should perhaps be postponed to that stage of life which was referred to in an epitaph on the tomb-stone of a woman who had died at the age of 80 years. "During the last ten years of her life," it stated "she was the model of virtue."

Continuity

Melanie Klein's[8] innovations in psychoanalytical theory deliberately disturbed the Freudian time-table in the historical model of mental development. She brought the Oedipal Situation forward into the early months of infancy. She assumed the existence of intense anxieties during the processes of birth and in the adjustment to the postnatal situation. Happier emotions follow the gratification of being fed and the comfort of warmth.

The capacity to love and the sense of being persecuted have deep roots in the earliest mental processes. Melanie Klein followed up her observations of infancy with conclusions drawn from later childhood, adult life and old age.

There is an overwhelming and disturbing character about the desire for gratifi-cation, and sometimes a feeling of guilt accompanies its fulfilment. Many of the restrictions, controls and self-denials which govern people's lives are self-imposed rather than the result of external limitations and punishments.

The Superego of some individuals can become more intolerant (and irrational) than the degree of strictness of the parent would appear to justify. There are some people, indeed, who punish themselves for every success, or who manage to achieve failure at the moment that success comes within reach.

The basis of envy, greed and gratitude as enduring character traits is laid down, according to Melanie Klein, in the satisfactions and frustrations at the breast.

The discoveries of mental processes, described in analogies for which this new technical language had to be created, have enlarged our understanding of a wide range of human activities. There are by-products of psychoanalytical studies which began with Freud with the purely utilitarian purpose of treating illness of the mind. The same disciplined process of search for meaning has been applied to the examin-ation of poetry, drama, and other art forms, and also to economic transactions, politics, and to people's attitudes to their religious ideas.

Psychoanalytical terms have been referred to and briefly explained, but as a general rule these terms will be avoided. This is because many of the words have acquired widespread currency, and are used in an undisciplined way. When words are used in an undisciplined way it is for the purpose of *avoiding* understanding of the ideas to which the words are meant to refer.

[8] M. Klein, Our Adult World and its Roots in Infancy, in *Our Adult World*, Heinemann, 1963.

9

Rejection: Reappraisal

THE USE of a particular word to describe a process in human behaviour occurs whenever a new way of looking at a process has come into being. The word "Rejection", applied to an aspect of the relationship between mother and child, had shock value when first used. After the word came into common use it became so much a stock phrase that it has been used more to avoid thinking about the subject than to face the problems involved. Jargon[1] is sometimes used in a way that is like putting labels on unopened parcels in order to have an excuse for not looking inside to see what is really there.

In one sense this chapter is obsolescent in that the word "rejection" has almost ceased to be thought of as an "all or none" process. The term is still used professionally (but perhaps not so much as, say, thirty years ago) and rejection is still a fact of family life. There is, however, less tendency to use the term as an explanation for all disorders in children, and, moreover, attention has been given to extreme forms under the label of "child abuse".

Our aim here is to discuss some of the hostile components of parental feelings, before going on in the next chapter to "acceptance".

In order to make the problem more real, and to give it flesh and blood, here are extracts from two newspapers:

"The 25-year-old mother of three children, Mrs. . . ., wants to find a home for a fourth baby she is expecting in July.

"She would not part with her 7-year-old son . . . or her 3-year-old daughter . . ., but she said last night: 'I don't like babies. I think they are terrible things. They all scream their heads off.'

"Mrs. . . . and her husband insist that they could not afford another child. Their third child, a 21-month-old girl, is in the care of the . . . Council.

"Mrs. . . . said she had asked the Almoner at . . . Hospital if she could have this baby adopted. The Almoner replied that she was shocked but she would see what she could do.

'Later the hospital said they were not prepared to help me. We wrote to an evening paper to see if we could get help through its columns. We would like the child to go to a good home where there are no other children—to someone who deserves a child.'

---

[1] The word "jargon" originally meant the twittering of birds, and, like bird song, it can be used to claim territorial rights.

72

"As Mrs. . . . spoke her two children remained in the room watching television. Amid all the questions and answers, they kept their eyes on the television set. But they know about the child to be born and have been told that it will have to be 'given away' or they will not be able to have a holiday this year.

'Babies are a full-time job. Two are quite enough and this house is not made for a big family. Big families cause squabbling and the father goes off for a drink to get some peace,' said Mrs. . . . 'We are a very happy family and I do not want to have anything to spoil it'."

2nd Article.

"*Mrs. . . . wants her baby back*"

Decision to give child away regretted

"Mrs. . . ., aged 26, the housewife who with her husband decided to give away their baby before the child was born, has refused to sign the adoption papers for the girl who is now with her prospective foster parents.

"Mrs. . . . said yesterday, 'I never thought it would happen to me. But I keep on thinking about the baby and wishing I hadn't given it away. I can't sleep at night and I lie awake worrying whether she is all right. I suppose it is the mother instinct. After all, she is my own flesh and blood'."

Such cases are faily uncommon although similar stories are reported from time to time. Great indignation is aroused, and newspapers consider them worthy of report.

Revealing the Basic Attitudes in Professional Workers

This particular case is quoted because one of the newspaper accounts happened to appear on the morning of a lecture given as part of a course for social workers. It was read out to the group at the beginning of the lecture. The students had themselves read different versions in their separate newspapers and there were comments such as "She was a monster", "She was not fit to have a baby", and a discussion of this item continued to occupy the second part of the session following the lecture. The discussion became heated, and some of the participants, who had already had long experience of social work in various capacities, were unwilling to discuss the motivation of the person concerned in anything other than critical terms. Amongst explanations given was that it was a planned attempt to get money from newspapers which would be willing to pay for the story of her life. It was only the discussion of the reasons involved when a newspaper finds the topic worthy of space, and perhaps of payment, that enabled them to refer to their own feelings about such events.

Hidden Acceptance in a Rejecting Mother

Is it possible to recognize that the rejecting mother, who shocks us by her attitude, is also partly a mother who has accepting feelings which are mainly hidden

H.G.D.P.—D

from herself, and that, conversely, the ordinary accepting mother has hidden rejection feelings? In practice there appear to be qualitative differences in behaviour, but the feelings behind the actions are part of something that is universal.

Universality of Rejection

Every mother who has a baby, has a baby instead of something else. There is always some sacrifice involved. There are physical burdens of pregnancy and childbirth; the responsibility that both parents have for the care of the young child; the sacrifice of leisure and recreational interests; the financial cost which could have gone to some material possession; the possibility that having the baby might mean that the mother has to give up the satisfactions of a career with its day-to-day enjoyments and its long-term ambitions. Yet all these may be gladly given up for the fulfilment that comes from parenthood.

It is easier to describe what a parent gives up in a material sense or in other personal satisfactions when having a child, than to describe the nature of the satisfaction which occurs in the interaction between the parents and the child whose changing responses give a new experience to the parent at each stage. Parents are more likely to tell their friends about the anxieties and burdens, the loss of sleep, feeding troubles, the sitting-in night after night, the worry about illness, than to find words for the sense of fulfilment. It is culturally acceptable to emphasize the disadvantages and also to delay marriage and to delay the having of children until certain material standards have been obtained. For many people there is a conventional list of possessions which may include a certain amount of capital, a house, particular articles of furniture and household equipment and perhaps a car. When these have been acquired (and then only) do some couples permit themselves to turn to the thought of having a family. With some, the postponement is for the purpose of enjoying a particular kind of social life. With others it is so that both husband and wife may continue a career for which they have prepared themselves and which gives other rewards as well as financial ones. The deferment of having a family may help to maintain mobility which permits professional advancement.

Where contraception is reliable and in widespread use it might appear that the association of sexual intercourse with possible conception requires a conscious effort of thought. Parenthood may have to follow a deliberate decision, which becomes harder to make the longer it has been delayed.

There are degrees of importance which different people attach to other gains against those of having children. In all these cases, however, the more intangible urge to seek the satisfaction of the new experience of the child, which is born out of their union with one another, is present even when it is unacknowledged. Thus we return to the thesis that rejection is a question of degree, and the important problem is to recognize those degrees which are so severe that we are entitled to call them pathological.

Competing Needs

It is necessary to call attention to the reality of external factors which increase the stress on some young parents of today as compared with those of a previous generation. At one time, the extended family of all social classes gave practical support, and those who could afford it had paid domestic help. The modern parents may be isolated, and domestic help is either unobtainable or too expensive for all but the wealthiest, and yet, more than ever before, husband and wife may have responsibilities which take them from their homes. There is a need for facilities for feeding and napkin-changing in public transport and waiting rooms. The offer of such services would obviate the necessity for criticisms of parents which are frequently made without sufficient understanding of the circumstances in which they have to live.

Pathological Situations

Situations which carry an unusually high probability of abnormal rejection can be classified as follows:

(1) FACTORS RELATING TO THE MARITAL
SITUATION OR STATUS

(a) A pregnancy that is illegitimate. In such a case there may be an almost complete rejection, or, paradoxically, a most intensive degree of attachment with a mother who does not have to share a child with another parent.

(b) A pregnancy that is the cause of marriage. This is more likely to be a factor where the marriage would not have taken place at all but for the pregnancy. There may be much less disturbance where pregnancy merely brings forward the date of a marriage previously intended, but even here the recriminations between the parents and their respective families may add to the burdens during the pregnancy and early months of the child's life.

(c) A pregnancy, whether planned or unplanned, that causes the postponement or the end of a mother's career, leaves the child with the burden of responsibility for the unfulfilled ambitions.

(d) The existence of marital disharmony, where the pregnancy provides a tie to the marriage, either deliberately sought for this purpose, or occurring unplanned. Having the child for any other purpose than its own sake is a poor basis for parenthood, and, although it is sometimes "prescribed" as a way of healing a marriage, it is more likely to add to the total disturbance than to cure it.

(e) Mixed marriages. Differences of colour, race, religion, nationality, social class or intelligence level can occur, and such marriages may be well founded if they are entered into by the partners with some basis of identity with one another. There are, however, some such marriages which are entered into more *because of the differences* than because of anything that the partners have in common. It is as if the differences are sought as part of rejection processes which already exist, but which in the first place apply to the family of origin. A son or daughter who rejects some aspect of the personality of the parents or the family background may seek company with an individual who stands out in contrast to them. In such a case, the marriage may not be wholehearted on either side. The rejection process eventually involves the partners themselves. The having of a child brings to light the fear that the child may have an undesirable quality representing the marriage partner.

It may be worthwhile here to recall the universality of all these processes, and to remind ourselves that there is always, even in the "normal" marriage, some degree of rejection of the partner. How often do we hear in our ordinary lives, when the child misbehaves: "How like your mother!" or "How like Uncle Jim!"

(2) FACTORS CONCERNING THE CHILD

(a) A child of the wrong sex—particularly after two or three children of the same sex.

(b) A child of the wrong intelligence level, either below or above the parental level.

(c) A child with some hereditary defect. This applies to handicapped children with all kinds of defects—physical, sensory or intellectual.

(d) A child who has some crippling illness occurring after birth.

All these instances represent, to some degree, a failure of the child to become the fantasy child of the parent. This process can be even more intense if one child has died. The parents may immediately seek another child to replace the one that was lost. Any shortcomings of the living child are met with the belief that these would never have been present in the child which had died and, in fact, where one child out of a number is lost, it is often felt, and sometimes said, to the others, that "the best one went" and that any of the others could have been more easily spared.

Adoption brings in problems of its own, but the problems have a resemblance to those which have just been outlined. There may be the wish that the adopted child should be a special child of the parent's fantasy. Parents of adopted children expect trouble. They are advised to enlighten the child regarding the facts of adoption and a formula is sometimes suggested "that other parents have to take what God sends them, but we chose you out of a lot of children". Far from being reassurance to adopted children, this is an attempt to tell them that they should be as special and outstanding as the parents expected when they chose them out of so many. Enlightenment should be given, not as something separate, but as part of the explanations of the facts of birth. Children cannot know what it is to be adopted unless they also know how babies ordinarily become members of a family by being born to the mother in the family. A second point with regard to adopted children is that they should not be deprived of standards of behaviour or of the punishments that are applied to ordinary children within the family; an adoptive parent might say "I could have punished him if he had been my own." In such a family, not to punish is to deprive. A third point is that such children should no more be expected to show gratitude for being in the family than a child who is born into the family.

The processes of rejection which are so universal include the begrudging to the child of the results of the parents' personal efforts. The baby is competing with the parents for the limited resources available. It is conceivable that this begrudging is more likely to apply to a child of another father and another mother who is taken into the house and adopted as the family's own. Such children, born of other parents, become heirs to the adopted parents and sometimes the adoptive parents question their wisdom of having embarked upon a course which leaves most of the accumulation of their life's work to be enjoyed by someone not of their own blood. It is no wonder that there are special problems in adopted children when they become adolescent and express the kind of rebelliousness which most adolescents go through. The marvel is that so many adoptions work successfully and give happiness to both parents and child.

(3) FACTORS CONCERNING THE PREGNANCY AND DELIVERY

(a) Physical illness affecting the mother's health—toxaemias, threatened abortions.

(b) Complications during the confinement necessitating surgical attention at the time or later.

(4) FACTORS RELATING TO DEEP EMOTIONAL DISTURBANCES OF EITHER PARENT

(a) Fears in the mother regarding the confinement including fantasies of physical harm to her body. These are sometimes increased by the exchange of old wives' tales which touch on fundamental fears.

(b) Fear of loss of attractiveness due to alteration in the figure—particularly with regard to the abdomen and breasts.

(c) Fears associated with the repudiation of sexuality, the pregnancy providing evidence to the world that sexual contact has taken place.

(d) Fear of having an abnormal child, which in some degree is universal, is more intense where the mother is overwhelmed by feelings of inadequacy of or badness within herself.

(e) Immaturity of either parent. There can be rejection of the pregnancy and of the child when either mother or father is immature and would therefore feel a rivalry with the child for the attention of the other parent.

(f) Deep feelings of sexual inadequacy in the mother or father which may be associated with guilt concerning masturbation.

Rejection Processes

Methods of expressing rejection feelings can take many forms. Some choose not to have children (or not to marry) but social pressures still make it "normal" to marry and have children. The single and the childless have to bear the burden of these pressures or yield to them and have children they do not actively want. Those who *do* want children, and are unable to have them, bear a double burden.

After conception has taken place, rejection may be shown by the attempt to procure an abortion. The Abortion Act of 1967 (implemented in 1968 in all parts of the United Kingdom except Northern Ireland) made it possible to consider social reasons for the termination of a pregnancy. Before then, in addition to this comparatively recent legal abortion on health grounds, large numbers of illegal abortions were performed under unsafe conditions, carrying the risks of severe injury or even death.

At present the ease with which it is possible to obtain a legal abortion varies widely in different parts of the country. There are some areas where medical *men* seem actively antagonistic to the very idea. Emotions are highly charged on both sides of the issue. One can understand the feelings of many women that they themselves should have the right to choose whether or not to have a child. ("Abortion is no man's business.") One can also understand the feelings of nurses and doctors under pressure to carry out an operation not entirely without risk, on request, and not in consequence of some form of diagnosis. There is also some resentment which comes partly from the side-tracking of ethical issues on which values differ, and partly from being expected to be merely the technician.

Any woman who wants an abortion is in a predicament. There is the emotional difficulty in arriving at her own decision; and, if the decision is to seek termination, there is the practical problem of finding implementation. All this in a situation where the immediate benefits must be weighed against the long term possibilities of guilt feelings, loss of self-esteem, and the burden of having to reveal the occurrence in subsequent relationships and medical treatment!

The problem is complex for the professional worker and for the individual woman. No available choice is satisfactory. What is really required is for the pregnancy not to have existed, and to terminate it is not quite the same thing. It has to be recognized however that social and professional pressures against the contemplation of abortion make it seem to be "anti-abortion" to attempt even to discuss some emotional hazards of a decision either to keep or to part with a child (by abortion or adoption).

If the "right to choose" is a justifiable demand, it has to include the right to choose wrongly.

Once a child has been born the most extreme form of rejection is infanticide. This is or was accepted practice in some cultures, and in our own legal system it is recognized that a mother's reaction to her newborn child may be affected by factors not present in other periods in her life. The verdict of infanticide is different from one of murder and applies to cases where a woman causes the death of her newly born child at a time when she had not fully recovered from the effect of giving birth to such child.

The more usual ways of expressing attitudes of rejection are:

(1) *Open rejection.* The child is neglected, handled roughly, spoken to sternly, criticized for every action and sometimes openly blamed for change of family fortune or alteration in mother's health.

(2) *Overprotection.* Here the child is guarded from danger, from infection and from contamination by undesirable habits which other children at school or in the neighbourhood may have. Attention to body process is maintained at a high level, but the normal activities of the child are restricted as being possibly dangerous. Education, recreation and social enjoyment all become limited. The process is even more dangerous to the child than open rejection because the child finds it harder to protest against what is done for his or her own good.

(3) *Indulgence.* There is a level of indulgence which is carried out out of love, which is relatively harmless; but there is another level which is carried out as the result of apathy and which is a form of deprivation. A child who is "bought off" with some material gift as a substitute for parental attention gets no satisfaction from the gift, and is deprived of the appropriate level of the restraint which parents offer as part of the standards of their families.

Rejection Feelings: Reality and Fantasy

Rejection may be felt by the child in cases where it actually exists, and also it may be imagined in cases where there is no apparent reason. The death of a parent may be interpreted in the child's fantasy life as desertion by that parent. The child may even feel in some ways guilty and responsible for the loss of the parent. Many mothers threaten that they will run away when the child is naughty, and some attribute their illnesses to the child's misdeeds. Divorce or separation of parents (so frequent nowadays) can have similar effects, especially if quarrels between the parent preceded either of these events.

The child who is left with just one parent is deprived of the benefits and support that could have been obtained from the missing parent, and has other deprivations too. The remaining parent is not able to fulfil his or her *own* role in attempting to fulfil both. The child who loses a father also loses a mother, because the mother, in attempting to be the head of the house, is unable to give the relaxed and confidently affectionate mothering of which she might have been capable before. Sometimes a single surviving parent is too demanding of the child and seeks a level of companionship that would be appropriate in a marriage partner. The child then feels inadequate in that he or she cannot realise the parent's expectation.

A child taken to hospital may interpret this as being deserted by the parent, particularly if there has not been adequate explanation, and if he or she is not visited frequently in hospital. The effects of separation from the mother, or deprivation of maternal care, have been the subject of monumental work by John Bowlby and others.[2]

When another child is born into the family this may lead to actual or fantasy rejection of the older child. In some cases, the parents concentrate all their attention on to the new arrival, and the first child is neglected. Some feelings of neglect and rivalry exist, however, even when parents make efforts to prepare the first child

[2] J. Bowlby, *Maternal Care and the Mental Health*, W.H.O., 1958; *Child Care and the Growth of Love*, 2nd ed., Penguin, 1965; *Attachment and Loss*, Vol. I, The Hogarth Press, 1969. J. Robertson, Film, *A Two Year Old Goes to Hospital*, Tavistock Child Development Research Unit, London, 1952.

and share their concern between the older and the younger one. The older child may still wonder why it was necessary for them to have had another child, and may come to the conclusion that it was because of not being good enough. There seems to be no escape from these feelings; and the only child who has not been supplanted may still have fantasies of other children being born in the family and taking *his* or *her* place in the family. The realization of the actual experience of having a brother or sister generally is not so disturbing as the fantasy, and perhaps the greatest reassurance comes in a wider family network when the arrival of a new baby is not a rare and shattering event.

Balance of Rejection and Acceptance; Mothering Breakdown and Distress

We must return to the recognition of the fact that concentration on processes of rejection and the outlets of its expression may divert us from recognition of the process of acceptance, which, like rejection, is always present. Acceptance shows itself in the provisions for a child's development; the mothering or parenting process is a balance of rejecting and accepting attitudes. In this sense mothering or parenting can be looked at as quantitative. Rejection ceases to be an "all or none" process, and it becomes easier to understand that there are circumstances which temporarily affect the ability of the parent to make provision. John A. Rose compiled a series of contingencies[3] that seemed to be, singly or in combination, the critical stress associated with mothering breakdown and subsequent pathogenic mother–infant interaction.

(1) Multiple births.
(2) Children born within ten to twelve months of each other.
(3) Dislocating moves in pregnancy or the new-born period involving changing geographical areas and the need to find new ties.
(4) Moving away from a family group or back to the group for economic reasons at a critical period for mother and child.
(5) Unexpected loss of security by reason of job losses, to husband; to the pregnant woman.
(6) Marital infidelity discovered in the prenatal period.
(7) Illness in self, husband, or relative who must be cared for at a critical period.
(8) Loss of husband or of the infant's father close to the prenatal period.
(9) Role reversal if a previously supporting person breaks down and becomes dependent.
(10) Conception and course of pregnancy related to the loss of a person with whom there was a deeply significant tie.
(11) Previous abortions, sterility periods, traumatic past deliveries, loss of previous children.
(12) Pregnancy health complications when occurring at a given time.

---

[3] *Prevention of Mental Disorders in Children* (ed. G. Caplan) Tavistock Publications, 1961.

(13) Experience with close friends or relatives who have had defective or injured children.
(14) The juxtaposition of conception with a series of devaluing experiences.

All the contingencies listed above will be seen to increase the burden on the mother—or, alternatively, to deplete her of some of the resources from which she gives to her child. Thus rejection, and acceptance (which we shall discuss next), may be seen to be partial aspects of the transactions between parent and child, and these transactions are reciprocal.

In the case of battering parents the rejecting component of the relationship may appear to be so unadulterated that immediate separation of the child from the parents may be required as a life saver. After the child has been removed, and not before, the accepting component in the parents should be searched for, recognized and developed.

There are some cases where the accepting component is sufficiently evident to justify work (and supervision) with the intact family group.

Up to the present, the attention to the child in these cases seems to be limited to supervision of the parental care or to the providing of alternatives. What so far remains almost completely unexplored is the image of the parent in the mind of the injured child.

Reciprocal Rejection: Children's Fantasies About Parents

Children are accepting and rejecting towards their parents. Abnormal degrees of rejection from children may come at the point when parents no longer sustain the image of perfection, and yet either they or the child refuses to part with the idealization. The qualities of goodness or badness may be perceived separately by the child, and each quality projected on to one parent. One parent then appears as all good and the other as all bad. Later, when grown up, many individuals may begin to feel that perhaps they did an injustice to the parent who was rejected. Occasionally a child accepts all the badness of the parents as his or her own, and, where there has been insufficient contact perceives the lack of communication as a barrier between them and feels responsible for creating it.

Fairy stories incorporate some of the familiar themes which recur transitorily in most people's minds. The child who no longer fulfils the parents' image becomes the changeling substituted by fairies. Children who find it hard to believe in their fleeting exalted fantasies cannot believe that these imperfect men and women can be their real parents. Was not the son or daughter of some king stolen away and placed in an ordinary home? At no situation of life are people entirely exempted from these fantasies. There is always a higher position which could have been one's own.

Lady Elizabeth in *The Confidential Clerk* by T. S. Eliot stated

Do you know, Colby, when I was a child
I had three obsessions, and I never told anyone....

The first was, that I was very ugly
And didn't know it. Then, that I was feeble-minded
And didn't know it. Finally
That I was a foundling, and didn't know it....
I refused to believe
That my father could have been an ordinary earl!
And I couldn't believe that my mother *was* my mother.
These were foolish fancies. I was a silly girl.

10

Acceptance:
the Basis of Infant Care

IN THE discussion of rejection it was emphasized that rejection is seldom complete. Where rejection processes are expressed, there is usually an accompaniment of some degree of the opposite processes which we may call acceptance.

Bonding

The word "attachment" which includes the notion of "bonding" has been applied to the reciprocal processes between parent and child which are the basis of acceptance. Bowlby[1] has taken this theme, adapting theoretical schemata "elaborated partly from psychoanalysis and partly from ethology. He utilizes the object-relations approach to psychoanalysis and the pathogenic potential of loss." On this foundation he put forward the view that infants who have successfully formed an attachment may, when adult, go to the ends of the earth, but never become lost souls.

Any activity which is directed towards the care of the child implies some degree of acceptance, and there are unexpressed feelings of acceptance even when the evidence is hard to find. Ordinarily we might judge the level of acceptance by different kinds of provision, and these can be summarized as material needs and non-material needs. The material needs are those upon which life depends: food, clothing, shelter, protection from injury and disease, and treatment and care for any injuries or illnesses which might occur. Without these provisions no child could survive.

Raising the Standards of Material Care

Within living memory the rejected child was likely to be neglected with regard to these provisions, and both neglect and ignorance as to the best methods for providing for the material needs were factors in the higher infant mortality of the last century. Higher general standards of material provision, which are associated with the higher standards of living, have reduced mortality and morbidity, and rejection

---

[1] J. Bowlby, *Attachment and Loss*, Volume 1 *Attachment*, The Hogarth Press and the Institute of Psychoanalysis, 1969.

is more likely now to become evident as deprivation with regard to the non-material needs of children.

Physical abuse has, however, by no means disappeared, and is discussed under the headings of non-accidental injury, or child abuse.[2]

We now emphasize the emotional needs of children, but we can only afford to do this when we can take it for granted that the material needs are met.[3] We must never lose sight of the fact that physical care is the basis of life. At the beginning of this century the infant mortality rate in the U.K., which is the number of babies in each 1000 who die before reaching their first birthday, was 160. Infant mortality varied between town and town, and between different social classes in the same town. Suprisingly, it still does.

Infant Mortality, Handicap and Medical Services

In 1976, the infant mortality rate for England as a whole was 14.20, for Scotland 15, for Wales 13.6. Perinatal mortality, which represents the number of still births and the deaths before the age of one week per thousand total births, is another index of the effects of environmental factors and obstetric care. In 1976, figures for England, Scotland and Wales respectively were 17.6, 18 and 19. The total figures conceal the immense disparity between (say) Orkney, infant mortality rate 8, perinatal 4, and Wolverhampton, where the figures respectively were 20.5 and 23.5. It is interesting to add that the shock of learning the high figure in Wolverhampton led to the appointment of additional infant welfare staff, with a consequent immediate reduction in this figure.

The conditions which lead to an avoidable loss of infant life also can lead to severe mental and physical handicap in survivors. James Loring and Mary Holland of the Spastics Society have called attention to the figures of child-bearing experiences in different countries in relation to the aetiology of handicapping conditions in children.[4] They state that we can learn from French perinatal programmes, in which the payment of an antenatal allowance is conditional on attendance at antenatal clinics. The French have attempted to measure the financial cost of saving a life "free from handicap".

The much higher infant mortality rate at the turn of the century was a consequence of lack of knowledge and, sometimes, of a failure to apply existing knowledge. It became recognized that more babies died amongst the poor and in the large towns than amongst the wealthy and less crowded communities.

---

[2] J. Court, The Mother Who Injures Her Child, *Social Work Service*, December 1973; C. H. Kempe, *et al.*, The Battered Child Syndrome, *Journal of the American Medical Association*, No. 1, 1963, pp. 17–24.

[3] In the financial stringency at the present time of writing, there is a deliberate erosion of provision by the state of benefits which were originally introduced in order to guarantee minimum standards of health and welfare. It is currently held by some of those in authority that children are so sufficiently well cared for in their homes as to make it unnecessary to provide school meals, subsidized or unsubsidized. We consider that the abolition of such services is not without danger to a significant proportion of the child population.

[4] J. Loring and M. Holland, *The prevention of cerebral palsy: the basic facts*, The Spastics Society, 1978.

The Layman as Pioneer

As in many other social reforms, the pioneer spirits were individuals in private or public life who began to arouse the social conscience of the community with regard to the unnecessary death of young babies. Gradually, as a result of the work of these individuals in this and other countries, public services were built up with a statutory basis to deal with the problem. One example was the Mayor of the town of Huddersfield in the year 1903, Alderman Benjamin Broadbent, who earned the nickname of "Baby Broadbent" because of his work in the publicizing of ideas on infant care. He was inspired by Dr Moore, the Medical Officer of Health for the town. Being a rich man, he offered a gold sovereign to every baby born in his own parish during his year of mayoralty, but this was not to be given on the date of birth but on the first birthday. During that year the infant mortality went down by half! It would appear that a sovereign could buy a baby's life in the year 1903, but this would not be quite the truth. The gift was part of the publicity on infant care which was conveyed to the parents of young babies by the medical staff of the Health Department. The town adopted a scheme for notifications of birth in order to assist in the visiting of homes in which the babies were born. This was instituted on a voluntary basis at first and the scheme was taken up by other municipalities, and later was applied compulsorily to the country as a whole.

Earlier efforts at provision for needs of infants included a scheme which was the forerunner of the Health Visitor who in some countries is called the Public Health Nurse. In Salford, Lancashire, in 1862, a Ladies' Committee was formed to employ "honest working women" to visit and teach mothercraft in the homes of young infants. In rural Buckinghamshire, in 1890, a Dr. De'Ath instituted a training scheme for such visitors.

Maternal and child health services, the staffs of which include medical officers and health visitors, are now an established feature of the local authority health services in all parts of the country. Community health services of various kinds became built up by the drawing together of provisions of vastly different origin as well as by the establishing of entirely new projects.[5]

The improving standards of infant care have been most effective with regard to the preservation of life and the prevention of physical illness. It is sometimes said that many of the children whose lives have been saved, survive merely to suffer emotional neglect or, in some cases, children with some physical or other handicap may survive to a life which is limited by those handicaps. If so, it pushes the frontier of our work a little further out, and we must continue to attempt to raise the level of living for those children whose lives are handicapped in any way.[6]

Non-Material Needs

Beyond the physical factors which allow survival, there are non-material needs for which provision should be made. These can be set out under the headings of *love,*

[5] Since 1974, the organization of these services is the responsibility of Area Health Boards.
[6] Cicely D. Williams, *Lancet,* I, 345 (1964), points out the absurdity of the idea of "survival of the fittest" in communities with high infant mortality. The conditions which kill off the weakest also cause chronic sickness in those who survive.

opportunities of expression appropriate to the child's individual capacity, and *standards*.

The *love* of which we have spoken is given to a child as a right and not as a reward for being a particular kind of child or for a particular kind of behaviour. When we speak of the mother's love for the child, we can recognize the general potential of mothering (or parental feeling) which is present in all human beings. There is an appeal which any infant has which calls up something in all human beings but with various degrees of intensity. That perhaps is the starting point. Some additional feelings are released by specific responses or activities of the child which are referred to in the term "bonding". There is a further component which comes from the satisfying of the maternal image or fantasy which the mother has had of her child before the confinement, and sometimes even as a young girl before her marriage. The existence of the child partly embodies the image or fantasy, but the process of the confinement and the feeding of the baby at the breast may give the mother a new experience for which her fantasies have given her no preparation.

The *opportunities for expression* of a child's capacity should be those which are appropriate to the reality of the child, i.e. of a particular age, level of ability and the culture which is approved in the generation in which the child lives. The image may include factors which relate to the parents' concept of their own childhood which took place in a culture which has since been the subject of change resulting from rapid technical progress.

The opportunities or outlets for the child's activity apply to the child's physical, intellectual and emotional life.

Physically there is the need for freedom of movement which will allow for the development of muscular skill. The young infant is relatively more active than the older child and has lesser capacity for sitting still or for being quiet. As the infant develops, the emphasis on physical activity will depend on the total range of ability, and upon the valuation of some activities in a particular setting.

The *intellectual* life includes formal education in school and also the learning that accompanies all other activities and interests. There are problems when the child's intellectual capacity is higher or lower than that of the parents or of the rest of the family. The imposition on the child of levels that are inappropriate may lead to intellectual failure and, at the same time, may cause injury to emotional development.

In *emotional* life the child needs freedom to express feelings in relation to the individuals closely associated by family ties. The young infant is closer to awareness of the conflicts of love and hate than the older individual who has learnt what can be said to be socially acceptable.

The *standards* referred to are the moral or religious framework which is provided first within the family and then within the community. A child may be made to feel that actions within this framework are approved, and that beyond it they call for censure.

The framework which is provided in the first place becomes absorbed into the personality and needs to be appropriate to the age of the child and to the general culture. The framework should not be so restrictive that the child is inevitably bound to go beyond it.

All the above provisions should be at an appropriate level. The child should not be expected to respond or to perform in a manner beyond his or her capacity, and the capacity is the personal quality which may differ from that of other children of the same age. A child who is pressed to perform beyond his or her own level, or kept back from activities within his or her capacity, may accept the inappropriate demands of others and build them into internal standards. The child may thus continue to apply them long after those who initiated the process have ceased to be part of his or her life. This applies also to standards of morality. The capacity to absorb abstract standards, in the form of principles which can be generalized, is not present in children before a certain age. It is damaging to give even the *right* standards at the *wrong* time. The right standards are those which are observable in practice. No matter how good the standards may seem to be, they will prove wrong if it should be inevitable that they will be transgressed. Standards should not be too rigidly applied even when they are appropriate. Children need the comfort of knowing that it is not the end of the world if they do something which their parents and they both agree is wrong. They may even need the comfort of knowing that they can do wrong and that the parents can check them.

Relativity of Levels of Provision

All these provisions—the right kind of love, and the right kind of opportunities and the right kind of standards—vary somewhat with cultural changes. No child ever gets the ideal provision in all these categories. Rejection is relative and so is acceptance. The general provision for children today is at a higher level than it was a generation ago. It is true that there are still children who are grossly deprived of the appropriate love, opportunities and standards, but, on the whole, there is a higher standard of living and a higher standard of loving. Thus, parents of today might consider themselves to have been deprived as children in comparison with children of their own.

Cycles of economic recession and boom produce generation after generation of children who grow up in a different economic climate from the one their parents knew. Parents who grew up in the depression of the 1930s had children who became grown up in the "never-had-it-so-good" years. Now as parents themselves, some of *their* children have to face the consequences of the inflation of the eighties. Economic changes are quickly reflected in changes in the birth rate.

Each generation has to adapt to the fluctuating levels of provision, and to be able to set appropriate standards in the place of those which were "normal" when they themselves were young.

There has also been a "generation gap" of moral and cultural values. The two World Wars, and their aftermaths, seemed to mark out periods of drastic change which sharply separated the generations. We have the impression, however, that in recent decades the adult generations of parents and grandparents hold more in common than their respective predecessors did. The sharpest contemporary generation gap seems to be the one that separates the adolescent culture from both childhood and adulthood.

Valuing Deprivation

Some parents may look back with affection upon aspects of deprivation which no longer exist. Those who have become successful through their own efforts, and who are amongst those responsible for raising the general standard of living, may have found their driving force in some of the difficult circumstances of their childhood. They may thus wish to give the benefit of their early deprivation to their own children and to other children. They deplore the higher standards of consumption, and feel that the defects of character which they see in the younger generation are due to a lessened regard for money and for what money buys. Such parents may even begrudge their children the standard of living which they themselves are at present enjoying, recollecting that they were not able to have some things at the age at which they come automatically to their children.

All parents show something of this if they tell their children that they ought to be grateful for what they get in food, toys and pocket money, because they themselves did not have them as children.

Looking Back in Anger

Other adults who recollected the distress of their families looked back in anger at the authority and social system which allowed their parents to suffer. Their resentment continued and remained directed at individuals who represented "the establishment" in a world which had changed in some respects but which seemed to remain the same in others. They were unable to forgive those who did not seem to suffer in childhood, or who did not suffer in the same way as themselves.

Vicarious Reparation

Some families are trapped in a cycle of continuing deprivation and even those who escape from early severe economic hardship may not escape consequences in later life. Some wish to make up for what they themselves missed by giving to their children what they themselves would like to have had—even when some particular article may be of no special interest to a child nurtured in plenty. Such a parent may be puzzled by lack of response from the child, but something is also missing in the act of giving. If parents can release themselves from the task of making reparation for their own personal deprivations, the gift to the child gains a value in its own right. Any gain to the giver comes from the satisfaction from a gift that is given to the reality of a child, and not to the residue of the child in the adult. Reparation is thus an unexpected, and perhaps unconscious, consequence of the appropriateness of what is offered and received.

Finding a Balance: Building up Family Standards

All these processes may occur to a marked and predominant extent in some individuals, and they also occur at times and to a lesser extent in all of us. A large number of people, however, carry the scars of their deprivation fairly comfortably. They can look back with compassion at some of the hardships that they and their parents suffered, and remember also that these were endured because the family accepted the hardship as a necessity and not as a virtue in itself. There are those who are able to give freely what seems to be appropriate to their present standard of living and the standards of the time.

Prevalent standards can provide special problems. Material standards have risen rapidly and, in some cases, fallen rapidly, and some parents have not acquired any certainty of the appropriateness of the amount of money and other material satisfactions for their children. Times of hardship give people the certainty of knowing what they can and cannot afford.

Where a parent feels it is wrong or overindulgent to give money and goods at the same level as other families in the neighbourhood, it may be a perfectly reasonable viewpoint. The difficulty is to convey that viewpoint to a child as part of the standards which the family as a whole can share. It is no use saying, about some purchase of which parents disapprove, that we "cannot afford it". Often, in such cases, the child has taken money for frivolous purchases like those of schoolmates from the uncounted small change in father's pocket or mother's handbag. Sometimes this has gone on for months or years before accidental discovery of the theft. The point is that the parents said they could not afford it, and then *did* afford it, and they did not even know.

Children are more likely to accept individual family standards as their own when the reasons for them are shared with them, and when they have an appropriate degree of participation in the making and changing of the family standards.

The Spoilt Child

We should include a word about the spoiling of children. A spoilt child is usually one who is hated by other children, by the parents of other children, and even by his or her own parents. Spoilt children are thought of as having everything they want. It would be more correct to say that a spoilt child is one who has everything *asked for* as a substitute for other levels of attention. Goods are given instead of love. It is not surprising, therefore, that what is asked for, and what is given, never satisfies. These children ask for what they see. If it is a toy, they do not play with it. If it is food, they leave it on the plate. At times something is refused but the child has only to storm and rage to alter the parents' decision. Parents feel wrong when they give, and wrong when they deny. Such children are deprived children. Deprived of love, deprived of the appropriate level of outlets, they are also deprived of standards.

Some children are indulged out of love and not out of apathy or inability to give standards, and the results of such indulgence are less harmful if the parents do not think of it as indulgence but regard it as a pleasure to them as well as to their child.

To summarize, acceptance is consideration for the child, as a living individual who is not a miniature adult but a complete person of his or her own age and stage. Rejection is the preference of the parents' image of what a child should be to the reality of the child. The problem is that the fantasy competes with the reality. Parents reject themselves as well as their children because they have an unrealistic fantasy of performance which they impose upon themselves in addition to that which they impose upon their children.

Aiming at Perfection

Parents may wish to make exactly the *right* provision for the children, and the danger is that they will feel entitled to perfect children in return. They try to give them what is outlined above—exactly the right kind of love, the right kind of outlets and the right kind of standards. They try to give them the right kind of food (whatever happens to be the current selection of proteins, carbohydrates, fats and vitamins). Sometimes in the anxiety to give the right amount and kind of food, it is forced down the child's throat. The child has to read the right kind of books from the start, enjoy the right kind of entertainment, and the standards imposed must include the right kind of manners. One must confess that it is impossible for parents to do right, and perhaps they should not try all that hard. They should be content merely to do their best!

The anxiety to achieve perfection can be part of a general wish of parents to be approved themselves, and, if they derive their approval from their cultural activities, they will seek confirmation of their status from their children's activities and achievements.

A newspaper account of a Christmas pantomime included a description of audience reaction, and quoted a conversation overheard between two families with children on their way out of the theatre. One mother said to the child of her neighbour, "What part of it did you like best?" and before the child could reply, her mother said, "*We* liked the ballet best." It would have been a lowering of status to have enjoyed the vulgarity of the dames.

This anxiety about perfection is played upon by advertisers of children's food preparations, clothing and detergents. Goods are advertised as those used for children by "mothers who care". A beautiful example of this kind of advertising appeared some time ago in *The New Yorker*. The picture showed a child of perhaps 6 or 7 years old standing in a circle of his toys. He is carrying a space helmet, is holding a space gun, a rifle and a machine gun. His belt contained a dagger and a sword. The toys around him included a train, wagons, cars, toy boat, armoured cars. His mother is sitting and his father kneeling at the boy's feet, the mother holding a toy aeroplane. Yet there is an anxious look on these parents' faces and above is the caption "What do you mean—we are neglecting the child?" Below are the words "Neglect? This child of ours? Why, he has everything—everything we can give him for his health and happiness! But has he? Without realizing it you may be neglecting one of the most precious, most meaningful events of your child's growth—his appreciation of great music. He ought to have had a Child's Library of Musical Masterpieces."

Perfection is unattainable; cultural aims are infinite. The most important thing about acceptance is the acceptance of human limitations and the preparedness to do our ordinary best.

Making up for deficiencies

Degrees of deprivation are a factor in disturbances of the thoughts, feelings and behaviour of children. Sometimes such a disturbance is considered to be due to some single damaging experience, but more frequently a long-standing deprivation is responsible. Consequently one can prescribe the supply of the missing provision as the cure. It is surprising how frequently popular remedies, which are recommended for behaviour disturbances or delinquency, can fit into one of the three levels of provision that have been described. Some people say as their regular prescription "Give them love", others say "Give them outlets and opportunities—Youth Clubs, hobbies, special classes", others say "Give them discipline—punish them hard." None of these remedies is effective when given alone. Love is not enough; it needs a background of outlets and a discipline which is appropriate. The best opportunities are useless without the love that is the respect for the individual and a framework within which the young person can recognize the community to which he or she belongs. Punishment is ineffective except against a background which accepts with affection the individual's personality and which gives a recognition of the need to develop and express the self.

Personality is a living organic whole, and the needs must be recognized in their entirety.

11

Deprivation, Privation and Provision:
Separation and Union

WE SPEAK of normal development and depict a series of stages in which, with their inherent capacities and potentialities, receive provisions that are necessary to take them on to each succeeding stage. The word "normal" can mean the average which is observed, or it may imply ideal standards by which we judge the imperfect actualities of the lives of each individual. To some extent normality is relative, as the standards by which health is judged have a tendency to rise.

Deprivation and Privation

Strictly speaking the word *deprivation* is used to mean the taking away of something which we have once had, and another word, *privation*, is used for the absence, from the beginning, of something which may be essential (or perhaps merely important) for normal development.

What we are now going to discuss is not the level of privation at which a whole population suffers a high infant mortality—where there is insufficient food for a nation and where endemic disease constantly threatens health and life. It is more the denial of the prevalent standards amid comparative plenty. At the levels of provision where survival is generally taken for granted, the different *aspects* of provision are given a differing importance. At a personal, and sometimes, at a social-class level, the relativity of privation and deprivation has constantly to be kept in mind, whether one is discussing a single case, or the characteristics of a social group.

In every community, and in some communities more than others, there are many individuals for whom the provisions are far below the standards which are called normal under any criteria.

Separation

Physical deprivation is recognized in malnutrition even to the extent of failure to survive (see Chapter 9). The cases include those for whom food is simply not available in the disasters of famine and the more general failure of food production to meet a population's needs, down to the individual cases where food is available and withheld from a child by inadequate or punitive parents. Amongst the forms of child abuse, deliberate starvation features along with physical battering.

The *emotional* needs have been discussed earlier in terms of relationships with other individuals, particularly the mother. The most important emotional deprivation is any interference with the child/parent relationship. The importance of the mothering relationship in the development of the child was emphasised by Bowlby in his monograph, *Maternal Care and Mental Health*, published in 1951 by the World Health Organization, which had the declared aim of calling attention to the part played by deprivation of maternal care in the aetiology of mental and social disorders. The word deprivation has now become firmly associated with the idea of separation from the mother. The word arouses strong feelings: some think of separation as the basis of all psycho- and socio-pathology, others seem to be at pains to prove that maternal care is an unnecessary process in the upbringing of a child. Some seem even to go so far as to think of mothering in the first place as a pathogenic process, and readily resort to enforced separation of the child from the family as a favourite therapeutic procedure!

The acceptance of Bowlby's thesis was widespread but not universal. Some observers rightly called attention to the nurturing process in which a father also has a role; to the extended family with multiple mothering; to the professionalized mothering in a variety of organizations, such as the Kibbutzim in Israel; to supplementary mothering by a succession of adults in private homes where, in addition to the natural mother, there are nurses or au pair girls; and to the day nurseries and child minders and grandmothers for another social class.

Maternal Presence

It is remarkable that something so basic as the importance of the physical presence of the mother in infant nurturing should be hailed as a modern discovery, and yet Bowlby's formulations have had a sensational impact. It was Bowlby who described harmful effects of separation from the mother, and, after emphasising the damage to personality attributed to separation, he went on to the study of the processes by which attachments are formed. He is notable for a much quoted phrase: "... mother love in infancy and childhood is as important for mental health as are vitamins and proteins for physical health."[1] His work has influenced public policy, for example with regard to the rights of mothers to keep contact with any children admitted to hospital. At a practical level, however, Pamela Hawthorn[2] made a comparison between the "Stated Policy" and the "Observed Policy" in nine paediatric wards. In only one of these wards was the principle of "resident mothers" encouraged, and here the determining factor was the personal influence of the ward

[1] J. Bowlby, *Maternal Care and Mental Health*, WHO, 1951.
[2] P. J. Hawthorn, *Nurse, I Want My Mummy*. Royal College of Nursing, 1974.

sister, even though the public policy formulated by the Platt Report was officially recognized.

What is surprising is the heat of argument as to the validity of Bowlby's thesis. There has been frank disbelief from hospital staff that the absence of the mother makes a difference to the child. There has been protest from mothers who felt that they were being bludgeoned into 24 hours a day and 365 days a year of uninterrupted contact with an infant. There has been protest from fathers who felt excluded from a role in parenthood. Finally, there has been protest from professional workers when they saw havoc created by unstable mothers on hapless infants.

Even worse was the cynical use of Bowlby's thesis that the biological mother is best, when some public authorities were reluctant to find adequate resources for residential care in cases where mothering had blatantly broken down, or where the mother was a participant in "child abuse".

The study of this issue must take into account the fact that any choice that the mother makes is bound to have some adverse as well as beneficial effects. To go out to work and leave her child to the care of others is a deprivation of her own mothering potential; to isolate herself from the working world is a personal and social deprivation of another category. Naomi Richman has shown that the incidence of depression in mothers is highest amongst those who remain at home.[3]

The study of the effects of separation have to be supplemented by the examination of the kind of care available outside the home. Considerable numbers of children have to have substitute care for a variety of reasons. The late Simon Yudkin, working from his clinical base as a paediatrician, brought out this fact from a constructive viewpoint in order to improve the standard of care in these circumstances. He and Anthea Holme[4] made detailed studies of child care in fatherless families and where the mother worked outside the home. They pointed out that the phenomenon was not new. Ever since the industrial revolution, a high proportion of mothers with dependent children have been compelled by economic necessity to take jobs outside their homes. Others went out to work by choice. For a long time middle-class mothers did not have a choice. There were few suitable occupations open to them, and women teachers had to resign their posts on marriage.

Effects of Separation on Mothers

Yudkin and Holme came to the conclusion that the need for such care would grow, for three reasons: a greater equality in marriage; a longer working life after the reproductive period, with a consequential involvement in professional career structures; and, finally, financial pressure relating to the desire for a higher standard of provision for children. They spoke of the compromise that mothers have to make between the choice of remaining in their own homes, and following employment which has a satisfaction of its own. They were concerned about a neglected

---

[3] N. Richman, Depression in Mothers of Preschool Children, *J. Child Psychol. and Psychiat.* Vol. 17, 1976, pp. 75–8.

[4] S. Yudkin and A. Holme, *Working Mothers and their Children*, Michael Joseph, 1963.

factor—the effect on the *mother* of separation from the child. Looking outwards towards the community, they called for more effective supervision of child-minders. A large number of children of working mothers do, in fact, remain completely unsupervised in empty homes without even child-minders.

It is still necessary, therefore, to take, as our starting point, Bowlby's account of the mothering process, stressing the physical presence of the biological mother, and for us then to go on to all the supplementary processes and contributions to infant care from the father, siblings, other relatives, and all the professional and substitute care which comes in subtle ways to the population generally, and, more explicitly, as a professional service, to those with special needs.

The biggest stumbling block which Bowlby's theories have raised is that of the notion of the irreversibility of the effects of separation. A whole range of disrupted families have, in fact, to make do with separated lives; and the child-caring profession, now merged with other social services, who provide residential care for deprived children, are obliged to start where Bowlby seems to leave off. For them it has to be an article of faith that reparation is possible, and that life can go on even where devastating experiences have occurred.

Depression in Infancy

Bowlby has given an insight which provides a clinical model for the recognition of deprivation, and a pattern for treatment, which can be encapsulated in the formula: separation = mourning = depression.

Experienced professional observers have been (and some still are) blind to the manifestations of depression in the infant and young child. The clinical syndrome of depression is readily recognized in the adult as a possible threat to life (although those who surmount the experience may reach new levels in the life that is preserved).

Depression which occurs unnoticed in infancy can be reactivated in subsequent stages of development, and the theme is made more complicated by the occurrence of depressive processes in successive stages of normal development during the transitional phases.

The healthy outcome of these normal experiences of depression, to which Winnicott[5] called attention, is no comfort to those whose early depression is so severe that full recovery does not, in fact, take place.

Irreversibility is truly a fact of life. Time itself is irreversible. What has occurred has occurred. To assume that the effects of bad experiences are erasable does an injustice to the distress of the occasion. This is not to say that bad experiences may not be surmounted by subsequent events. Moreover as Clarke and Clarke[6] point out, early bad experiences are often followed by equally bad subsequent experiences, making it difficult to disentangle cause and effect. At a practical level, it is necessary to concentrate on the task of providing the best service available to those who have suffered.

[5] D. W. Winnicott, The Depressive Position in Normal Emotional Development, in *Through Paediatrics to Psycho-Analysis*, The Hogarth Press, 1975.

[6] Clarke, A. M. and Clarke, A. D. B. (Eds.) *Early Experience: Myths and Evidence*, Open Books, 1976.

We cannot leave this theme without referring to the multitudinous voices in support of, and in opposition to, the ideas attached to Bowlby's name. Michael Rutter[7] has summarized the massive literature and records of theoretical and experimental studies in order to provide a balanced view of the features of Bowlby's formulation which have become accepted and also of the necessary modifications. He quotes a large body of animal evidence on the effects of early life experiences, and the smaller number of well controlled human studies. He states that these latter studies, "... have amply demonstrated that early life experiences may have serious and lasting effects on development. This conclusion of Bowlby's which was regarded as very controversial twenty years ago is now generally accepted as true."[8]

Degree of Interaction with Mother Figure

Ainsworth[9] had previously stated that it is not the physical presence of the mother that counts, but the amount and quality of the interaction that takes place between mother and baby. Summarizing, she postulated three major sorts of condition in which deprivation may occur:

(1) Insufficient care or interaction with a mother figure when the child is separated from his mother and placed in an institution or hospital.
(2) Insufficient care or interaction when in the care of the mother or mother substitute (due to her illness or inadequacy).
(3) Inability of the child to react with a mother figure even when one is present and willing—a condition which is due to previous breaches or interactions.

This is an important and comprehensive statement, and takes into account the deprivation that can take place within an apparently normal home as well as in foster homes and institutions.

The restatement of the concept of deprivation is given point by a casual contribution made by Bowlby of a discussion reported in *The Determinants of Infant Behaviour*[10]—"The moral of all this is that we should never just say 'deprived' about a baby, but 'deprived of what, at what time and in what conditions'."

New Postulations I
Complementarity of Separation and Union

It is therefore proposed to make some postulations with regard to the necessary provisions of maternal or parental relationships, the general environmental and social requirements and, in addition, to make some further comments on the interactions within the family. It is a fallacy to look upon separation as a single and once-for-all process, and likewise to seek its effects in the child alone. Separation is merely one part of a double process and is an essential element of every human

[7] M. Rutter, *Maternal Deprivation Reassessed*, Penguin, 1972.
[8] Ibid. p. 121.
[9] M. D. Ainsworth, *The Effects of Maternal Deprivation*, Public Health Papers No. 14, WHO, Geneva, 1962.
[10] B. Foss (Ed.). Methuen, London, 1951.

relationship. To unite with another and yet to seek to become a separate identity is the two-sided process of living together. Everyone begins in physical union with a mother. The capacity to separate increases, and, in the development of each individual, it is necessary for the capacity for separation to have appropriate expression—appropriate to each stage. Complete separation never occurs. We seek reunions and new unions. It is a disorder of development if we fail to emerge as separate individuals, but it is equally abnormal to separate too completely. Thus, in studying the basic theme of separation and union, we must not attach value judgements to the processes themselves. We must not say that separation and dependence are good or bad in themselves. It is a question of how much, and when. *We must learn to recognize the complementarity of separation and union in normal family relationships before we can proceed to define those relationships which are disordered and in need of help.*

The Family as a Functional Unit

We must also postulate the functions of the family as the promoter of the mental health of its members. We can do this under three headings:

(1) The satisfaction of adult (male and female) sexual needs.
(2) The procreation and the care of the young.
(3) The transmission of the culture.

The three functions are interconnected, and each participant shares in transactions and interactions, giving and receiving, belonging together and moving apart.

Psychiatric and sociological literature is singularly lacking in the study of the urge in human beings to find partners and to have children. There is much attention to the pathology of interaction and there is often the impression that having a child is the incidental or even accidental result of the sexual relationships which are sought independently of reproduction. Even the term "reproduction" is abstract and takes no account of the longing for the physical presence of a child as a person taking flesh and blood from the parents and giving them a new and independent life.

The topic of loneliness has been left to the Bible and the poets, although we must recall Fairbairn's contribution to psychodynamics was to say that instincts need "objects" and not satisfaction (see p. 39). We could substitute the word "persons" for objects.

The family itself has no point of beginning. A child is born to parents who have pre-existing complicated family involvements to which is added the new relationship with each other and with the child that they are going to have. The child is a fantasy—welcome or unwelcome—before it is a reality. Even in their own childhood, the parents had pictured themselves somehow in their own parents' role. Both the mother and the father of a child have some kind of image of the child that they are going to have, and of the part that they will play in his or her life. The image may have no relation to the real child, and the tragedy for some children—and some parents—is that it is hard to give up the image for the reality. Sometimes a real child moves more quickly towards a separate identity than the imaginary child, but, in the case of a handicapped child, the dependent state may be retained at levels beyond those which the resources of the parents can support.

We must remember that the "nuclear" family, which seemed to have emerged out of a more complex network during the last fifty years or so, is no longer the norm, if indeed it ever was over any large areas of the world. We have, on the one hand, the extended families which still exist in Asian and also in many indigenous cultures; on the other hand, the increasingly common phenomenon of the one-parent family, where the one parent may these days sometimes be the father.

There are also "artificial" families, either where groups of adults have chosen to live together, perhaps under the label of a "commune", and those families which are created by the remarriage of divorced parents, either or both of whom may bring with them children from their previous marriage(s). In the communal arrangement, it can be very reassuring for a child to have a number of adults to form relationships with, but equally disturbing if the composition of the household does not keep relatively stable. Where divorced parents have remarried and a child is *not* the parent's own child, then the parenting role is so much the more difficult to assume satisfactorily for either parent or child. These difficulties may be compounded if a child is born of the new marriage.[11]

New Postulations II
Definition of Deprivation in Terms of Provision
Which is Lacking

The provisions made within the family or the community setting can be expressed as (see Chapters 1 and 8) *environmental*—referring to material provisions; *personal*—referring to the organic or mental aspects of the individual; or *interpersonal* with reference to relationships with significant individuals. These three categories of description of needs and provisions are not mutually exclusive. Any problem or disorder can be described in terms of any or all of them. Moreover, provision can never be complete, and deprivation of some degree is universal. Deprivation is only of value as a diagnosis when there is some awareness of lack of fulfilment of need, and where that awareness leads to some abnormal feeling or behaviour.

Discussion of the nature of the deprivation is a form of diagnosis, and should be the basis of a decision for treatment or intervention. Help can only be given if a problem can be presented within, or translated into, the terms which are relevant to the techniques and resources of the agency which has been consulted. Help is sought from medical, social and educational services for the effects of deprivation, and sometimes it is a matter of chance rather than of abstract principles as to which particular service is consulted.

Illustrative Cases

The problems set out below, which were referred to child guidance clinics, are quoted as examples where there was the possibility of different viewpoints, and

[11] B. Maddox, *Half-Parent: Living with Other People's Children*, Deutsch, 1975.

where satisfactory consultations needed action and cooperation of different agencies. Some conclusions are drawn from these cases but, more important still, fresh questions have to be posed regarding the basic principles of professional help.

First case. Michael was referred at the age of 5 for a behaviour problem at home and at school. The family doctor's letter stated: "Only one teacher is capable of handling him, and, as a result of this, she has spent two weeks recovering from an attack of asthma." Michael was not allowed to stay at school for school dinners, and the mother complained that *she* hadn't time to go backwards and forwards for him at midday. When she took him out shopping with her, he kicked and screamed or wandered away, and was then picked up at a distance by the police. A brief account of the history and conclusions is given in a section of the psychiatric report[12] to the family doctor.

> "Both parents were born abroad. The mother had a disturbed childhood and came to England at the age of 15. She met her husband on a return visit to her home and they married and settled in England. When Michael was 3 *weeks* old they went back to her home country; he was ill on the journey and was admitted to hospital. A series of hospital admissions followed. For a while he was in the care of the maternal grandmother, and for part of this time the mother was again in England. There were still a number of journeys backwards and forwards, and the second child was born at the grandmother's home. Michael's most serious illness was an infection with cerebral symptoms and paralysis. He was given penicillin and streptomycin and recovered completely....
>
> "In my view the behaviour problem is that of a child with an unorganized personality. He has had no consistently present parent figure, and he has been exposed to different standards, and sometimes he has had a complete absence of standards. It seems probable that conditions have been more stable during the last year than previously, and I feel that he is beginning to show some degree of integration.
>
> "Having missed parental contact when in hospital, there are some stages in his development in which he is lacking, and he needs, for the time being, the kind of attention from the parents that would normally be given to a much younger child."

Perhaps that report was a shade optimistic. He was admitted to an observation class consisting of five or six children, under an individual teacher, in which the children presented problems of educational or clinical diagnosis. Several months later the psychiatrist made the following note:

"The problem of precise diagnosis remains undecided but the possibilities include:

> First, brain damage following the cerebral infection.
> Secondly, subnormality.
> Thirdly, emotional maladjustment associated with the repeated separations from the parents.

---

[12] Some details of reports are omitted or deliberately altered.

Fourthly, deficiency in the incorporation of social controls due to the instability and inconsistency of parental attitudes."

He added that these diagnoses were not mutually exclusive, and that the educational problem was more a behavioural one than a cognitive one. The child's behaviour continued to be difficult even within the small observation class. Arrangements were made through his family doctor for him to be admitted to hospital for physical observation. An X-ray of the skull, electroencephelogram and air encephelogram were all carried out and were all normal. A combined report from the neurologist and psychiatrist attached to the hospital stated, "He gives the impression of being a brain-damaged child even apart from the history being in favour of this." He was transferred to a psychiatric bed but his behaviour in the ward led to his rapid discharge! After his return home he was found to be uncontrollable in the observation class, except for short periods, and the suggestion was made that he should attend for mornings only. The mother commented "Of what use is that to *me*?"

A psychological assessment of his ability gave him an I.Q. of 73 on the Stanford Binet scale, and the psychologist found him to be amenable enough in an individual setting during the limited time of the test. In another interview he showed imaginative constructive ability with building bricks, making complicated symmetrical structures in each of which he introduced all the bricks that were at his disposal.

What would be the diagnosis here? Deprivation of mothering? Inappropriate mothering? Inherent defect? Brain damage due to infective processes? And, speaking of the diagnosis, what passes for diagnosis may be merely an association of words. "Overactive" is translated into "hyperkinesis". "Hyperkinesis" becomes a precise diagnosis, equated with brain damage. This "diagnosis" is sometimes made on the evidence of a history of some injury or infection, even if there are no objective signs of actual damage. If there is neither history nor evidence of any damage to brain tissue, the diagnosis is "*minimal* brain damage"!

After "diagnosis" what is the appropriate treatment? Should the boy be admitted to a psychiatric in-patient unit, and, if so, how long should he remain there? Was his need more that of primary experiences of which he had been deprived? This problem had aspects that were (1) social and educational, (2) individual and clinical, (3) interpersonal and familial.

The suggested solution was the transfer to a residential school for educationally subnormal pupils, where, it was hoped, home and school in one process would have some of the maturational effects which we would seek from therapy. He would return home during school holidays, but it would have to be recognized that the parents would continue to be unable to contribute to the developmental or therapeutic processes—although they are well able to organize their own lives in a manner which appeared satisfactory to themselves and their acquaintances.

Second case. Maureen also was referred to a child guidance clinic at the age of 5 years—she was the third child and only girl in a family of five children. It was stated that she was undersized and not talking.

At the age of 3 years she had been admitted into the paediatric ward of a general hospital in a stage of extreme emaciation. She gained weight on an ordinary diet and without treatment, and it was inferred that the emaciation was due to neglect of feeding. On her discharge she was referred by the paediatrician to a specialized clinic for psychiatric investigation, and his report included the following paragraph:

"My first interest was trying to find out the nature of the relationship between the mother and the child which could lead to the child reaching such a desperate physical state without the mother kicking up more fuss about having the child seen; that is, I got the impression of an unusual lack of concern on the mother's part."

After a diagnostic interview two years later at the child guidance clinic the psychiatric report included the following passages:

"There are many anomalous features in this case. Maureen is undersized, looking more like a 3-year-old child than her chronological age of 5 years. She is the middle one of five children and the only girl, and, from the descriptions given by the mother, the others are all normal.

"Maureen is described by the mother as 'backward' and having no initiative. She is 'well behaved', never runs about, and never shows affection.

"During her interview with me, Maureen played silently with toys and, although she made no open response to my participation, she followed some of my movements later.

"The mother stated that at home Maureen mostly plays with toy cars and has a wheel-barrow and a doll's pram. She places the cars on top of one another as if they were bricks. She uses the doll's pram as a general purpose vehicle and not for her dolls, and, although she has dolls, she never plays with them and she never cuddles a soft toy. Her play is mostly with the toys of the two younger children, whom she follows around.

"She has only a few words with which to communicate with her parents, saying 'Mum', 'Dad' and 'sweets', and she recognizes the bell of the icecream van. She probably speaks to her brothers more than to her mother and father.

"At one stage in the history, it had been implied that her feeding was neglected to such an extent that she became emaciated, but, according to the history given by the mother today, it seemed that the mother fed her with a great deal of perseverance in the face of refusal to accept food. The mother states that Maureen now eats very well but still has to be fed. There remains, however, as has been previously noted, a strange lack of contact between Maureen and her mother. This may centre on the fact that Maureen, although born at home, was taken straight into hospital because she only weighed 4 lb 4 oz. She remained there for six weeks until her weight was 5 or 6 lb.

"I should be inclined to explain the present state of affairs on the assumption that the mother has herself a low level of capacity for the mothering process and for the responses that develop successively at critical periods during the early stages of the infant–mother relationship. It may be that the child also has some inherent defects which have affected her capacity to respond in a way that normally reinforces the mothering reaction."

This girl, too, was admitted to the observation class and some progress was made, albeit slowly. The child acquired a small vocabulary and made contacts with the teacher and with other children.

During further interviews, the mother seemed to be on the defensive against possible criticism, and her comments all implied that if there was any blame, it was on the child—"She never stops eating, yet she *refuses* to grow."

Growing was, indeed, so slow that the possibility of some endocrine abnormality which might lead to dwarfism began to be considered. A conference, with the family doctor, school medical officer, the teacher at the observation class, along with the clinic staff, reached the conclusion that further physical examination was necessary. Investigations included tests for ACTH assimilation, anterior pituitary function, and an air encephalogram was carried out to reveal the presence of any structural defects within the skull. All proved negative. Hard objective facts to explain this child's condition were absent, but some explanatory assumptions could be made with regard to the possible aetiology and pathology.

This child had certainly suffered nutritional deprivation. Was she deficient in supplies or in her utilization of them? Was it possible that the mother was an individual with a less than average capacity for mothering, and that special circumstances created a different relationship between her and the child from that with other members of the family?

Could we assume that mothering in general has three components? The *first* is the general potential of care and concern that every individual has for the young and helpless. This is present in men as well as in women, and in children with regard to younger children. The *second* component is the bonding which was originally studied by ethologists as part of the tie between the young and the mother in animals and human beings. Was this process missing in this case, at first because of Maureen's prematurity and stay in hospital, and later because of physical retardation? The other four children received a degree of mothering, but Maureen seemed to be excluded almost as if she had never been accepted as her mother's child.

The *third* component in mothering is the learned technique which can be picked up by observation of others and which can be professionalized by planned teaching. In this particular case, where the mother's capacity for mothering seemed to be low, it might be limited to the primitive built-in responses which did not receive the signals for their release.

Third case. This is one where the complaint came entirely from the school. Robin was seven years of age and of above average intelligence. Complaints had been made about him when he was 6 years old, and more recently the Headmaster stated "Robin is quite beyond control in the classroom; when he is criticized at all, he resents this so much that he lashes out and kicks his desk. He puts up his fists as though to attack the teacher, and puts out his tongue at him and generally disturbs the class. There is no alternative but to exclude this boy from school."

His mother thought that this was a storm in a teacup. He is no trouble at home "except that he is enuretic". At the age of 4 years he was in hospital for three months "to have his legs straightened" and afterwards had to wear splints. The mother feels that he may have been indulged at home afterwards because of this.

The phrase "indulgence" had been used elsewhere about this boy, implying that he got a higher level of provision than the average child. This might be true if we take into account only the interaction in which a parent responds to the child's demands for some gift, for some privilege, or to be excused from some duty. We have, however, considered in an earlier chapter provisions as including *standards* which provide a required framework of essential behaviour. Indulgence in this sense is deprivation of that framework.

Robin was never subjected to social controls within his family; and school with its rules, was a new and strange experience. His aggressive response suggested an attempt on his part to enter into an interaction with the teacher at an adult level—a fantasy life in which he inflated himself to adult size. This is the essence of the oedipal situation which, when it occurs at an earlier stage, and is resolved, leaves behind the foundations of the superego.

Here, the *social diagnosis* was behaviour problem; the *individual diagnosis*, unre-solved oedipal situation; the *interpersonal diagnosis*, uncertainty of role.

But what of the teachers' participation?

Life in school involves acceptance of an ideology in which there are reciprocal roles of child and teacher. The acceptance of each others' roles makes it possible for one teacher to control many pupils. Transference is at first to the impersonal role of the teacher rather than to the actual person, and the transference is based upon expectation, or an image, of the teacher, which has already become elaborated as part of the superego structure.

If the child is deficient in these images, the teacher has to fall back on the resources of his or her own personality. It becomes necessary to contain the im-mediate situation and to become the source of the first introjection of controls. This is a slow process and is part of the growth of personality of the child which should have taken place in earlier years of infancy. But teachers, and any other adults concerned, may at times respond with the immature part of their own personality. Adults may fear their own unresolved oedipal features. Every adult feels at times to be a small inadequate child, who has to blow the self up to grown-up size to do an adult job. Teachers, therefore, like parents, need support and reassurance. They should not be made to feel more inadequate by criticism of failure or mismanage-ment. They need help with the problem of the child, and support for their own role.

The child's therapeutic needs in this case could not be supplied by the procedure frequently described as "free play". It was necessary to provide a kind of freedom which is contained within a framework of control that is possible of acceptance. The solution offered was part-time attendance at a remedial class with a teacher who was able to give individual attention along with freedom of activity that was legitimized within a framework of a special kind of school life. Here the therapy remained within the educational system. There was no further need of the services of the clinic and the boy continued to attend the ordinary school for the major part of each week.

Comment might be made on the fact that although enuresis was mentioned by the mother, no attempt was made to treat that condition. It had not been presented by the parent as a problem, and it is doubtful whether psychotherapy would have been effective in the absence of concern about this aspect of the problem. The enuresis could be regarded as just another indication of the immature part of the boy's personality which was being fostered by his mother in an attempt to make up for what they had *both* missed when he was in hospital.

Essential Provisions: The Deprived Child and Deprived Parent

We are now ready to make some general statements on deprivation of the provisions which are essential for the development of personality.

(1) Mothering depends upon the three factors or components—(i) the general potential for care, (ii) the ethologically studied bonding processes, and (iii) professionalization or learned techniques.

(2) A child will suffer deprivation of some of these factors if physically separated from the mother (or mother substitute!).

(3) There can be defects in the mothering *process* even in the presence of mother, or mother figure, if there is some barrier to the mothering process.

A mother may be inadequate as a result of a temporary depressive illness after the confinement, or through physical illness or more permanent mental or social subnormality. There are mothers who can manage to cope with two or three, or perhaps four children, but whose capacity gives out with the birth of another child. A woman who is a mother has other roles as well. She has the care of other children in the family, she is the wife of her husband, she may have a role in her extended family, social obligations and occupational responsibilities. She is a person in her own right, and has her physical illnesses and mental disturbances, and her day-to-day problems. There are times when something has to give way. Dr. Hoffmeyer of the Mothers' Aid Centre in Copenhagen[13] used the phrase "mothering insufficiency" which is an operational rather than a clinical diagnosis.

(4) The family process does not depend upon the mother alone. There are the interactions directly with the father or the indirect effects of his support of the mother, or his competing demands upon her. There is the equally complex interaction with brothers and sisters or other members of the extended family.

(5) Barriers in the child may prevent the receiving of a mothering process which is available. Physical, sensory or mental handicaps can lead to a failure of the child to perceive or to respond to the care.

(6) Deprivation in the child causes deprivation in the parents. The parenting process is one in which the parent undergoes development of personality as well as the child. If the child is separated from the parent, even if sufficient care is given elsewhere for the child's developmental needs, the parent is deprived of the processes which are normally set going by the changing responses of the child. The parent/child relationship is undeveloped. Some responses from the child *initiate* processes in the parent, and some responses *reinforce* them and maintain them; and the further responses which come from the child, as the child grows, can *inhibit* some aspects of the tie and therefore allow separation to occur when dependency is no longer appropriate. A retarded child does not give the first initiating signals, and

---

[13] H. Hoffmeyer, *The Feminine Role and Motherhood*, WHO Seminar, Athens, 1962, Mimeographed working paper EURO.206 2/WP6.

may be "rejected" because those responses are not present. The child who does not give the latter signals may be "over-protected" because these inhibiting signals are delayed.

Deprivations, separations, and physical, sensory or mental handicaps are not static conditions. They may multiply their own ill effects. For example, a mentally handicapped child starts with a lower potential for development. The handicap prevents the receiving of some of the personal interchange that is offered, and he or she may not therefore develop even up to the level of the potential. Next, failure to reach the expected normal stages at appropriate times robs the mother of the rewards that come in the ordinary way from a child who benefits from her attention. We can recall that Maureen's mother felt that her child *refused* to grow.

(7) Separation can be a deprivation, but it is also a deprivation to deny the child levels of independence and individuality that are appropriate to each age or stage of development.

(8) A further level of deprivation could be called *cultural deprivation*. Intellectual development depends upon experience of the surroundings and of the various objects encountered. A child needs to learn the textures of materials and the names of things.

It has been suggested above that the experience of deprivation is relative to the general standards which are available, and which become the norm in a particular epoch or country. It had been mentioned earlier, too, that parents can feel deprivation in comparison with their own children who are experiencing a higher standard of living than that of a previous generation.

The Deprived Clinician

The recollection of a personal deprivation can affect others as well as parents. We can speak of the deprived clinician who, with the recollection of his or her own unsatisfied needs, identifies with the child and becomes hostile to the parents, to other professional workers, and to the community as a whole.

We can apply ethological findings to professional motivation, as well as to the tie between mother and child.

It has been observed when studying the behaviour of the female rat and her young that there is a "retrieving" phenomenon. The mother brings back any of her progeny which stray from the shelter of her body. When, experimentally, an adult mouse is substituted for an infant rat, the mother spends so much of her time and energy retrieving the actively mobile mouse that her own offspring may die.

The hedge sparrow feeds the cuckoo that ousts the natural offspring from the nest. Once, at a social gathering, the hostess described how she had been the witness of the whole course of the upbringing of a cuckoo in a nest in her garden. She described how busily the hedge sparrow brought food to the cuckoo which eventually grew bigger than the foster mother. There seemed to be something in the cuckoo's cry that drove the hedge sparrow to work at a frantic rate. At one point other hedge sparrows gathered around the nest. One of the guests present asked "What were the other hedge sparrows doing?" A psychiatrist amongst the guests intervened and said, "Those were the social workers!" What was intended as a touch of humour revealed a poignant truth. The cry of distress calls out an effort to give beyond one's resources. Social workers are among the professionals who accept the call to deal with the insoluble. They suffer even when the one who calls for help seems insatiable and yet manages to thrive. Worse, they carry the guilt when victims of the family or of society (the battered child or the aged recluse) actually dies.

Relativity of Deprivation

Let us return to the concept of the relativity of deprivation.

Grandparents of the present generation were almost all deprived in comparison with the children of today. There is a higher standard of living and a higher standard of care which is demanded now as the minimum. Some adults of today were deprived even by the standards of their own generation during the unequal hardships of industrial depression.

Deprivation of material needs is not inevitably pathogenic. In some homes a loving and united family surmounts the difficulties.

The unity of a loving family is not a simple or static process. Provision has to be made for the achievement of separate identity. Satisfactory families are the ones from which it is easiest to separate and re-unite. The simultaneous nature of the drive towards union and separation means that at times one aspect is hidden. There is no need to look for hidden processes when everything goes satisfactorily. When there are disturbances in family relationships, we need to study the family inter-action as well as what goes on in the single individuals.

Professional work advances into the areas where new discontents are becoming apparent. For some disturbances it is enough to deal with the individual; for others we need to know more about the structure of the family in health and illness.

When we come to consider the prevention of disturbance, we need to know more about the structure of society itself, and the transactions between the individual, the family and society as a whole.

The growing areas of medical, social and nursing work are areas of uncertainty. Scientific knowledge is always limited and relative, at any one time and place.

Without the feeling that somewhere there exists some permanent lines of reference to contain and guide us, we lose sense of purpose and of direction. Uncertainty becomes the basis of growth when it proceeds from a central core of faith, and when acknowledgement of our doubts leads to the search for more knowledge.

Care-taking professions owe their existence to a belief that human progress is possible and that people can help one another through their interaction.

The feelings that lead to our caring for the young can extend to the caring for mankind in general. The energy expressed in conflict within an individual, and which also exists between individuals and between groups, can also be the source of adventure and creativity. We can recognize good and bad in their expression, but the underlying process is neither good nor bad. We cannot improve our nature by seeking to eradicate from ourselves that which might *become* bad.

We must recognize the inevitability and the universality of the conflicts that exist in ourselves and our organizations, knowing that we have, at the same time, the urge to find harmony within ourselves, with our neighbours, and with as much of the universe as we can comprehend.

12

Play and the Pre-school Child

IN EARLIER chapters, we have discussed the stages of psychosexual development and some aspects of the relationship of child and parents. The physical and intellectual growth need to be taken into account simultaneously. Moral development adds another dimension to which we shall make brief reference.

The Physical Matrix of Living Activity

The physical aspect of development has its stages with lines of demarcation between them. The toddler is a different being from the child who is, as yet, unable to walk. For the stages of intellectual growth, we have selected the account given by Piaget.[1] His stages represent the increasingly complex organization of perception and performance.

The physical appearance of a child changes in the second and third year, and the relatively large-headed baby or infant is succeeded by a well-proportioned little person with a more recognizable individual personality. The human infant is born at an immature stage in the active life of the individual as compared with the young of other mammals and, therefore, there is a longer period of infantile dependence to be spent outside the womb.

Some mammals are capable of standing and moving independently, and finding their own way to the mother's nipple within minutes of birth. In these cases, infancy is short, but the mature animal does not differ much from the infant except in size and agility. The human infant starts at a more dependent stage and yet is able later to reach heights of thought and understanding that seem unparalleled in the animal kingdom.

The most significant difference between the human being and other animals is the size of the brain relative to other tissues. Of all the body organs, the brain of the human infant is nearest at birth to its full size and, therefore, the head is larger in proportion. Perhaps birth can be delayed no further, as otherwise the head would be too large to pass through the pelvis of the mother. Birth thus takes place at a stage where the body is immature and where capacity for physical activity and movement is low. The dependence in infancy, prolonged to some extent into childhood and adolescence, allows for the personal transmission of the skills and knowledge of the immediate family and of the culture of the race and, at the same time, allows for the individual response of each new personality to that culture.

[1] J. Piaget and B. Inhelder, *The Psychology of the Child*, Routledge and Kegan Paul, 1969.

108

Physical growth is rapid. The performance of co-ordinated movements increases in complexity with the growing mastery of the self and the environment. It is a surprising fact that half the adult height is reached at approximately one and three-quarter years in girls and two years in boys. Intellectual growth is represented by the mastery of language and, with a rapidly growing vocabulary, language becomes a factor in the child's growth. During the emotional development, there is a conflict between acceptance of an imposed role and the search by the child for a personal identity. The child imitates members of the family as a token of identification with them, and shows negativism in emphasis of individuality.

Values are attached to actions. Some parents approve only those of a child's actions which they themselves have initiated. Unanticipated actions may then be taken as opposition to them, and, therefore, bad. The same theme will occur in both education and therapy, viz. the recognition of the responsibility of the teacher or therapist for introducing some desirable aims, while acknowledging the possibility of results which go beyond anything that they may have envisaged.

For the landmarks and chronological steps in a wide variety of accomplishments the reader is referred to Chapter 4. It is our purpose, however, to discuss the process through which these developmental stages are reached. Play is an activity which serves as a medium through which the individual develops.

The Nature of Play

Plays occurs throughout life from infancy to old age, but it is associated particularly with childhood. Play is the opposite of work for the adult, and of lessons for the child. In the industrial north of England, a man is said to play (or laik) when he is away from work, even if this is due to unemployment or an industrial dispute.

Playfully, one could say that men have leisure, children play, but women (even with our changing sex roles) seem to retain the responsibility for the routine of family life. When play is organized, as in playing cricket, anyone who does not take it seriously is said to be "playing" at it.   Play as a leisure activity is difficult to define, as some individuals choose as their relaxation the work that others carry out for a living. A business or professional man may be a weekend farmer and perhaps carry out heavy work, or go sailing and master the technicalities of seamanship almost as competently as a regular seaman. On a wider scale, the householder, after a week's work in a factory, office, or professional practice, may spend long hours working in the garden or making equipment for the home. Some may find relaxation in inactivity, but in this case there must be a readiness to face the thoughts which come unbidden when the attention is not directed on to some specific focus. Perhaps some people choose deliberately not to "play" in their so-called leisure hours for fear that these thoughts might be unwelcome; and some people occupy their leisure from their primary occupation in activities that are, in effect, alternative occupations.

Here we enter the dimension of time: "bound" time and "free" time[2], and there are those who immediately proceed to find fresh ties to activities in any time that is

---

[2] See J. Henry, *Pathways to Madness*, Jonathan Cape, 1972, pp. 14–15.

free. It may be allocated to paid occupations, an additional evening job, or finding a share in the "black" economy of earnings that are unrecorded and untaxed.

There are certain factors of all play activity which have been expressed as theories, descriptions, or interpretive statements. Every statement carries some personal scale of value by which play is judged.

(1) Play is *non-adaptive behaviour* and is not directly aimed at essential tasks. Perhaps it is for that reason that many people are intolerant of play because the activity is without an approved end-product.

Non-adaptive behaviour can be an elaboration of essential activities which have a biological or cultural value. This starts with the infant at the breast when the infant loses the nipple and finds it again, by accident. Deliberately the infant lets the nipple go, deliberately to seek it again, and the activity is built up into a game which is enjoyable. There may be a sharp reminder from the mother when the game goes on too long, to get on with the serious business of feeding. The conflict of interest between play and work begins early in life!

(2) Play has been looked upon as a *recapitulation of the history of the activities of the race*. Children's games have been noted from time to time to have a similarity to primitive man's adult activity. As a general theory this is discredited, but it is a fact that some children's games contain set rituals which resemble primitive religious rites.

(3) *Symbolization* is a feature of play when an object is allowed to represent ideas or other objects. Children develop their imagination in their play with simple objects, allowing them to serve for a variety of purposes. The manufactured toy has a clearer purpose, and the meanings are apparently predetermined by the manufacturer. The simple empty cotton reel on a string trailed behind a child can represent a car, a train or a person. Symbolization allows for ambiguity. In this sense it resembles wit or humour which is the artificial bringing together of incongruous meanings, and which permits the revelation or release of meanings which usually have to be hidden. The obsessional child or adult cannot tolerate the existence of more than one meaning at a time. Such an individual wishes to know the right meaning or use of each object, and that is a way of avoiding the possibility of co-existing ideas which are in conflict with one another.

It is the symbolic quality of play that is used by therapists who look for the representations (in symbolic form) of unconscious thoughts and wishes. In this sense play allows for the revelation of the aspect of mental life which is not ordinarily accessible to consciousness.

The Functions of Play

The purpose served in the personal life of the individual can be

(1) *An activity in its own right*. Play has enjoyments and satisfactions that need no other justification.

(2) *Recapitulatory*. Children often repeat, in play, activities or events of the previous day whether these have been satisfactory or unsatisfactory. Thus children are able to absorb these activities into their minds. The play becomes an external representation of the recollections of the activity, and serves as a focus for the

integration of the ideas into the personality. In this sense, play has the same functions as some of our dreams, our art products, or our personal efforts to commit thoughts with pen to paper. When we have given body to our thoughts in movements or language, we can deal with them as if they were fresh objects of mental stimulation or inspiration; and we can not only re-absorb them but also use them as starting points for the development of fresh ideas.

(3) *Anticipatory*. People practise activities in games, and play at what is in store for them in the future. Pre-school children play at going to school, or at adult occupations or recreations. A child plays at and lives the life of a milkman, a bus conductor, a housewife, a nurse or a handyman. At an early stage children begin to separate the role of the two sexes with regard to different occupations, but there is some overlap. A boy may want to help mother to cook or to clean, and a girl may help a father with his carpenter's tools. This play at the adult occupation is very little help to the parent who has to carry out the real activities. If the fantasy role of the child is rejected, the immediate gain of freedom from the help that is a hindrance, is at the cost of having later to rebuke the child for having no wish to take responsibility for a share of the household chores.

(4) *Reparative*. Anxiety-inducing activities may be deliberately reproduced in the safer setting of play, in order that the child might be able to come to terms with them. During World War II children played at being bombed. Today in Northern Ireland we have a reminder that in conflict-torn regions and countries, children play at the roles of opposing forces. Children who have been inoculated or immunized against infectious illnesses may play with imaginary needles at giving pricks to themselves and others.

(5) *Communication*. Although play can be solitary, it more often needs another individual and becomes part of the medium of communication with other children or with adults.

Play thus serves an activity which permits the development of personality through use of the child's mental and physical capacity in learning and in socialization.

Some of the aspects are *integrative* in a natural and spontaneous way. All these aspects may serve as a medium for therapy. Margaret Loewenfeld[3] describes play in general terms as "the expression of the child's relation to the whole of life."

The same author says, "No theory of play is possible which does not cover the whole of the child's relationship to life. Play is therefore taken as applying to all activities in children which are spontaneous and self-generated, that are ends in themselves and that are unrelated to lessons or to the normal physiological needs."

Learning Through Play

It will be seen that children learn through play, and that play is an important component of school life. Because of this, some workers have attempted to compare the success rate in the learning of some particular performance through play with that of learning through direct instructions. This seems to us to misunderstand the whole nature and significance of play. Formal instruction is probably the best way

[3] *Play in Childhood*, Gollancz, 1935. Reprinted 1965.

of teaching what has already been formulated by teachers (or the teachers' teachers). Play on the other hand allows us to enter into some of the byways of thought and understanding. One process gets one directly from point A to point B; the other allows one to explore the surrounding country.

Discussion of play is carried into the "difference–deficiency" debate. The argument is between the idea that every social environment has its own values, valid for those who belong to that environment (and not be tampered with by the schools) as against the idea that certain values and experiences (such as that of play) are vital to "normal" social and emotional development.

Those who advocate both play and formal instruction, recognizing their different contributions to development, avoid this polarization. The argument, however, contains some implications as to the role of educational intervention into the social-class values and attitudes that children bring to the school. Completely undirected play would preserve unaltered the background ideas of the home culture. For some people this would be a desirable aim. In a society where "middle class" values predominate in the academic world and the organization of community life, the teacher has to make a moral choice on whether to intrude or not by formal instruction into a culture which if unaltered, would seem to leave its children with some disadvantages.

We take the view that play should be seen in the context of the variety of provision which is necessary for child development, and not as an ideologically based exclusive theory of education.[4]

Appropriate Levels of Play

There is a need for adults to accept the child's play at the level which is appropriate to the stage of the child, and not to impose the adult image of what activities should be. In the early stages, words are inadequate and the child needs materials of play in order to express mental intake and output. The touch, the smell, the taste and manipulation of materials are all part of the search for realization (making real as against fantasy) of the self and the outside world. The first objects of play are the products of the child's own body or the objects introduced into the body through the mouth. The child can play with the nipple, or the teat on the bottle, and with the regurgitation of food. Play with saliva takes place long before learning to play with soap bubbles. Through play the child learns first the similarities and then the differences between body products and external objects. Sometimes a special importance is attached to particular objects which serve as a borderland between the self and the external world. A bit of blanket or paper or some small article or specially selected toy can be preserved by a child for a considerable time. Winnicott[5] gives the name "transitional object" to articles used by a child which are kept as close personal property and used by the child as intermediate between the idea of what is

---

[4] See J. Piaget, *Play, Dreams and Imitations of Childhood*, Heinemann, 1951; B. Tizard, Play, the child's way of learning, in *Biology of Play* (edited by B. Tizard and P. Harvey) Heinemann, 1977.
[5] Transitional Objects and Transitional Phenomena, *Int. J. Psycho-Anal.* **35** (1953); also in D. W. Winnicott, *Through Paediatrics to Psycho-analysis*, The Hogarth Press, 1975.

the body and the idea of what is outside it. The phrase "security blanket" used by Charles M. Schutz in his "Peanuts" strip has passed into the American idiom.

There is a gradual moulding of perceptions of external objects and external events into the idea of space and time. Play serves to organize this into the mind. Piaget has reminded us that new facts are assimilated into existing "schemata" or patterns of thought. Nobody can benefit by the presentation of facts or statements that are completely unrelated to ideas which are already present. Play serves to provide these schemata and forms a bridge between family experience and the outside world. In that sense it is related to education.

Nevertheless, there is some resistance to the idea of gaining of experience through anything as pleasant as play. It is true that children, as well as needing to be free, need to be directed at least part of the time. Even though the child first plays with food and enjoys that play, and the mother enjoys the enjoyment, she brings the child back into the formal and necessary activity in a way which is accepted. At each stage, the child needs a framework; and also needs freedom to explore, within, and a little beyond, that framework.

Toys as a Possession

Mass production and cheap (often plastic) materials have made available a large number of toys, well within the scope of "pocket-money". Many children, consequently, have so many toys that they cannot actually remember how many, or precisely what, they own. In previous generations, when toys were less available and more precious, children in the poorest families would have to find alternative ways of having "play things", because they would not own toys as such.

Thus, the cost of toys is an important feature of the economics of family life. Sometimes toys are bought on sight, on every shopping expedition, and are regarded as destructible and replaceable. In other cases, they are bought only for Christmas, birthdays, or other special occasions. Yet again, and even now, shortage of money, and a forward look to an adult future, may lead to a complete embargo on anything with a non-utilitarian purpose.

Most children manage to build up a distinction between what can legitimately be used up, and replaced, (e.g. crayons or fibre-tip pens) and what should endure as lasting possessions (perhaps teddy bears or tricycles). Some toys fall in between. It will depend on circumstances (emotional and financial) whether or not it is a tragedy if a doll or soft toy is left on the bus.

If toys are bought to represent the unlimited generosity of the parents, they are more likely to be thought of as consumable and therefore to be destroyed.

Another factor is the child's own sense of possession. In some families "sharing" is given a high moral value, and children, whose parents would not dream of lending out their own cherished possessions, are expected to share even their "best" toys with siblings and visitors. It is also possible that sheer lack of living space may make it difficult for a child to have any toy as an individual possession, kept apart from the common family stock.

Toys, then, become the means by which the economic milieu becomes apparent to the child, and they provide a focus for the child's comparison of his or her position with that of other children. Play space, the number of toys, and the conditions in which they are used, all become part of the children's images of themselves in relation to other children. The particular ethos of the distinctions that are made between play and work, consumption and durability, reflects the differing values of various families and communities.

We can summarize by saying that play is the activity which gives stimulus to the child's mastery of physical skills, the developing intellect, and emotional relationships. It precedes the kind of formal learning that we call education, and continues through childhood into adulthood. It is a method of absorbing total experience in the period of life before a child is able to deal with the more formal abstractions that become the tools of later intellectual and social development.

Moral Development

Recently, attention has been given to moral aspects of social and intellectual life, introducing the notion that social interaction is rule-governed conduct.

Piaget has studied the development of rule keeping and rule making in the games that children play. He infers that at about the same time that the principle of conservation is acquired, rules cease to be external, imposed and unchangeable. It becomes possible for the child to share in the rule making, and to take responsibility for rule keeping.

The argument remains as to whether this development can be explained simply as a process of maturation, or whether there is a possibility of the structured teaching of moral values. This then raises the question of what these values should be. Moral education has often been interpreted as teaching children to be good at moral reasoning, rather than to be morally good. We take the view that an intellectual approach to morality leaves out both the inherent value judgements and the emotional satisfactions of participating in something which can be held to be "right".

Another question is whether moral education be a curriculum subject, or whether its teaching be a feature of every communication, including those which are incidental to play activity.

These issues, to which we offer no answer, also omit the unconscious and irrational element which pervades the concept of superego development, referring in a psychoanalytical framework, to the same theme.

Fantasy, Imagination and Creativity

We should add a little about the games and make-believe which are a feature of the young child's life, and which leave a residue in the fantasy of older children and adults. There is a link between the game of pretending and dreaming, but children learn to make distinctions between reality and pretence, and in this sense the process is different from that of dreams.

Sometimes the child's illusions seem to be adopted deliberately in an effort to keep a private world free from intrusion by adults. Some children have an imaginary companion, a fantasy child or animal, and through this companion are able to retain some life space into which no adult dare intrude. It is exasperating to the parent, and many parents are greatly disturbed by the child's fantasies of strange events and scenes which are described in great detail. The parents are concerned about the virtue of truthfulness and the vice of falsehood, and perhaps they are also concerned about the existence of such a private world in the child's mind which they cannot really share.

Is it surprising that the child should have this private world when parents have their own world and talk to each other about affairs which are not supposed to be understandable by the child?

Some fantasies the child accepts ready-made from the adult, and the parent is more tolerant and may even create and cherish the childlike illusions which are traditional, such as the existence of Father Christmas and the "tooth fairy". For the most part we relinquish our fantasies voluntarily, and the child learns to maintain an equilibrium between a private world and what one learns to perceive as reality. We learn to recognize reality in the image of our parents' perceptions as they are presented to us. We learn about ourselves from the way that adults treat us. Our identity becomes secure when we are treated with respect, and in this we can agree with George Bernard Shaw who allowed it to be said in the play *Pygmalion* that the definition of a lady is one who is treated as a lady.

Unhealthy development of personality could be the product of a child's perception of the self with the eyes of the adult who does not value the life of childhood, and who judges the child's behaviour on the model of a scaled-down adult.

L. K. Frank emphasised the creative quality of the ever-changing roles of masculine and feminine that the child could adopt and abandon when not yet finally committed.[6] Play is tentative, a child through play can relate the self to the past and then reorientate the self into the present. Experiences are recapitulated, assimilated into new perceptions, allowing advances into the future. Perhaps this is what Winnicott meant when he stated that part of the mother's job is to help the child "to catch hold of time".

[6] L. K. Frank, Therapeutic Play Techniques, *Amer. J. Orthopsychiat.* (1945).

13

Social Problems of Education

Compulsion

Universal and compulsory education in Great Britain began with the 1870 Education Act. Previously, education had been organized on a voluntary basis. Many important grammar schools existed, and, in addition, the churches and various charity schools provided a wider range of education for poor children. There remained at that time a considerable section of the population which was illiterate because of the lack of opportunity to learn.

The impetus for a universal educational system for the nation came, in the nineteenth century, through a mixture of reforming and economic factors. There was the idealistic aim to provide for the whole population the advantages which one group had previously secured by their own choice and their own efforts. At a less altruistic level, the industrial revolution had provided a need for a more educated work force. At the same time, the widening of the franchise led to the demand from radical elements for an opportunity, through education, to narrow existing financial and social inequalities.

There was also the hope that poverty and disease, which were thought to be due to ignorance, could be eliminated by a generally improved education.

The 1870 Education Act created School Boards which were given the power to levy rates, provide buildings and employ teachers. Subsequent acts made education compulsory from the age of five up to a school-leaving age, originally eleven years, gradually increasing until, in 1918, it was fourteen years.

Compulsion rested upon the parent to ensure that the child received satisfactory education, and it became the duty of the Local Education Authority (LEA) to enforce the obligation, if necessary by legal procedures.

Local Authority schools which covered the whole range of education up to the school-leaving age were designated "Elementary Schools". Many LEAs also established "Secondary Schools" on the pattern of the existing grammar schools, for a selected group of children over the age of eleven years.

Progress Towards Secondary Education

The lengthening of the period of compulsory school attendance up to the age of fourteen years, from the previous limit of the age of eleven years, created an anomaly in that the children in the upper ranges of the all-age elementary schools

116

overlapped in age those who had found their way to the new secondary schools or to the grammar schools. Progressive educationalists began the agitation to provide secondary education for all, and for making a complete separation of education into primary and secondary with a break at the age of eleven years. (This followed the grammar school, though not the public school, pattern).

In the years between the First and Second World Wars, the Hadow Report of 1926, and the Spens Report of 1938, made recommendations for different categories of secondary education to cater for varying "aptitudes and abilities". Selection should be made on intelligence level, and to some extent attainment, but the aim was to achieve "parity of esteem" for the different kinds of secondary school.

These reports received uneven implementation by the various LEAs. Some took up enthusiastically the idea of secondary education for the whole of their school populations; others restricted secondary provision to a favoured few.

Selective Education

Three forms of secondary schools emerged: secondary grammar, on the pattern of the traditional prestigious grammar school; technical high schools (sparsely represented), intended for pupils of the same high level of intelligence as those in the grammar schools, but with technical rather than academic aptitudes; and secondary modern schools for the unselected remainder. Where secondary provision was not made for the whole school population, the unselected children remained in the elementary school.

Parity of esteem was somewhat illusory, and there was no mistaking the rank order.

In the earlier years of the twentieth century, admission to the grammar type of school, even when established and administered by the LEA, was largely through fee-paying. However, selection by "educational ability" grew rapidly in some areas, and a number of outstanding Local Authorities established the principle of one hundred percent "special places" awarded on the results of selection procedures, including intelligence tests, applied to the whole school population at the age of eleven years. In those areas, the ability to pay fees was no longer an entitlement to a Local Authority grammar school place. Thus, at that stage, selection by intelligence seemed to be a democratic advance.

The idea of the predictive value of intelligence tests was taken up and promoted by a number of educational psychologists (notably Cyril Burt of the former L.C.C.). The use of these tests, together with attainment tests, extended the provision of the grammar-school type of education to large numbers of working-class children, through what became known as the "Scholarship Examination". Secondary grammar schools became the pathway through which many working-class children reached universities and the professional classes.[1]

This selective system acknowledged the elitist character of the secondary grammar schools, and values have been attached to this type of education which are still the focus of controversy.

[1] The validity of Burt's work, and, indeed, his personal integrity, have recently been called into question. What remains is his influence on the development of education.

The 1944 Education Act firmly established the principle of free secondary education for all; it made provision for special education for children with certain handicaps; and it extended the age of compulsory education. Provision was made in the Act for a school-leaving age of sixteen years. In the short term, the extension was from fourteen to fifteen; and the second stage, known as ROSLA (Raising of the School-Leaving Age) was, after several postponements, finally implemented in 1972.

With the implementation of the 1944 Act, the separation of primary from secondary education gradually became universal, and, within secondary education, the selective system became the predominant one for the next twenty years.

The primary stage was divided into infant (5–7 years) and junior (7–11 years) levels, sometimes with separate infant and junior schools, and sometimes with two departments in the same primary school.

In contrast with the system of selective secondary schools, and perhaps as a reaction to the inequalities which that system deliberately preserves, there has been a powerful and successful movement for comprehensive secondary education. At the moment of writing seventy-five per cent of pupils of secondary-school age receive their education in comprehensive schools. The impetus for this movement came from dissatisfaction with the image of the secondary modern schools which catered for the (approximately) seventy per cent of pupils "rejected" by the selection procedures, in which success was equated with admission to a grammar type of school. Many comprehensive schools, however, still use selective procedures *within* the school.

Comprehensive Education

Comprehensive education became the established Labour Government policy in 1965, and became more generally implemented against rather uneven opposition. The then Labour Government embodied the policy for universal comprehensive secondary education in the 1976 Education Act, which for the first time actually *required* LEAs to bring all their secondary schools into the comprehensive system. Many complied, and some seemed to drag their feet, hoping that a change of government would make the final arrangements unnecessary. A very few openly defied the policy, even in the courts. At the time of writing, the Conservative government has declared its intention to repeal the 1976 Education Act. The aim of equalization of opportunity is notionally accepted, but many parents, of all social classes, still aim at securing the unequal advantages for their children that were provided by the grammar schools and by some schools in the private sector of education.

Independent grammar schools and privately organized boarding and public schools remain a small but important part of the educational provision of the country, and their ex-pupils continue to fill a large proportion of the posts in the higher ranges of Government and the Civil Service.

At their best, comprehensive schools enrich the educational provision for *all* their pupils; at their worst, those who are socially disadvantaged in their homes remain equally disadvantaged in those schools where the curriculum does not take account of variations of culture and capacity. These latter schools may fail to capture the imagination of children from homes where the values of academic education are not an integral part of the self-image and aspirations. Amongst this group, children who would have been selected and transferred to grammar-school life can remain overlooked; consequently, they receive neither the academic education of the grammar school, nor those benefits which comprehensive education offers to those who can respond easily to its more stimulating features.

Let us recognize the complexity of the issue, even to the extent that many pupils of working-class origin achieved outstanding success through the grammar schools at the price of alienation from their parental home. Education itself can alienate, no matter how it is organized. Wherever the values of the home and the school are not shared, or when the respective cultures develop in different directions, it is inevitable that the child will become alienated from the home or the school, or both.

Influence of School on Achievement and Behaviour

It had become a dominant assumption that home background was the overwhelming factor in determining whether or not a child would be "successful" in school. A recent study conducted under the leadership of Professor Rutter[2] demonstrates convincingly that (regardless of home background) differences in academic progress, attendance rates, and in the behaviour of pupils inside the schools and delinquency outside, were all far greater between one school and another than had ever been publicly acknowledged. Many parents, however, have been in no doubt about the beneficial or other influences that are due to particular schools.

Clegg and Megson[3] had earlier concerned themselves with the problems of "distressed" children, and pointed out that these problems can affect as much as fifteen per cent of the school population. The problems are not only those of so-called problem homes. Children who need special help at school because of difficulties they face at home come from all social classes, are of all levels of intelligence and are among the pupils of every kind of school. No existing or conceivable remedial service could cope with this high proportion of children. The only hope is through the education system, and school must be the place where these children can find an environment that provides a healthy and compensating influence on their development.

The implication of the Rutter study is that it is in the capacity of the school to do just this, through the organization within the school, the expectations of the teachers that they *can* succeed with all (or nearly all) children, and the personal models of behaviour which the teachers themselves offer to the children. A simple matter like the teacher's consistent unpunctuality will obviously affect the behaviour standards of a whole class of children.

Varying Patterns of Education

Simultaneously with the growing impetus for comprehensive education, the pattern of primary and secondary education was being challenged.

[2] M. Rutter *et al.*, *Fifteen Thousand Hours: Secondary Schools and their Effect on Children*, Open Books, 1979.

[3] A. Clegg and B. Megson, *Children in Distress*, Penguin, 1968.

It was no longer taken for granted that the age of eleven should be the age of transfer to secondary education. Some felt that children of this age were not yet ready for the specialization of the secondary school; others felt that adolescents (now recognized as being in a separate stage of development between childhood and adulthood) should be catered for in a distinctive way.

Thus there has arisen a proliferation of types of educational institutions, all catering for different age ranges.

The new category of middle schools takes children from the age of eight or nine up to twelve or thirteen years. Junior and senior high schools cater respectively for the ages of eleven to thirteen years, and fourteen to the eighteen (or nineteen) year upper limits. In these patterns, one can see reflections of the preparatory and public school age ranges.

In addition, there are sixth-form colleges which take the sixteen to nineteen range of a whole group of decapitated secondary schools. There are also further education colleges, where young people can continue their education after the age of sixteen, either full time, or on day-release courses from work. These frequently provide a second chance, to gain qualifications for entry into some technical occupation or to proceed to higher education, for those who have been unsuccessful during their years of compulsory State education.

Post World War II Government Reports

We cannot leave the question of education as a social provision without mentioning the reports of post World War II government committees such as those of Newsom and Plowden. Though their direct influence on educational provision has been limited, they were notable for their use of social data as a basis for deciding on criteria for educational provision.

The Newsom Report (1963) on Secondary Education, while not questioning the principle of the secondary modern schools, showed clearly that "disadvantaged" children were only too likely to end up in "disadvantaged" schools.

The Plowden Report (1967) on Primary Education, recommended that certain localities should be designated as "Educational Priority Areas" according to specific criteria of social disadvantage. In the implementation, some *schools* (rather than localities) were so designated, and given extra funding for facilities to cater for their large proportion of socially disadvantaged children. The criteria included: overcrowded housing; high levels of unemployment; single-parent families; delinquency; heavy calls upon the social services; and a large immigrant proportion of the population.

Special Education

Children with physical or mental handicaps, of different kinds and severity, should have had these handicaps identified in their first year of life, either in their homes by Health Visitors, or through attendance at Child Health Clinics. Some of these children receive continued observation and treatment at multi-disciplinary assessment centres. Medical and Social Services should assist the families with problems of the child's development, and with preparation for school life. Such services, lavishly provided in some localities, are sadly deficient in others.

The 1944 Act introduced the idea of "special educational treatment" either in ordinary or in special schools for children who suffer from disabilities of body or mind. Previously the only categories of handicap to be specially recognized were those of the educationally subnormal, the physically handicapped, the blind, the deaf and the epileptic. Six new categories were added in the Handicapped Pupils and School Health Service Regulations of 1945. Amongst these was the category of maladjusted pupils. This was not only a recognition of emotional disorders in children, but it also provided the authorization for the setting up of Child Guidance Clinics. These have a function in the "ascertainment" of maladjustment. The consequence may be either transfer to some special school for treatment as an educational process, or the result may be the offer of treatment within the clinic, on a multi-disciplinary basis and involving the whole family.[4]

The reorganization of the Health Services (implemented in 1974) which integrated the Hospital Service, the Public Health Service (including School Health) and General Practice, provided opportunities for the comprehensive care of children in their families, but it interrupted (or even reversed) some of the progress in the School Health Services of outstanding local authorities.

Further developments have been recommended in the Court Report,[5] which at the time of writing has provided stimulus for discussion, but there has been very little in the way of implementation.

Educational provision in special centres and special schools may run alongside nursery-school provision, day nurseries and play groups. Pre-school medical examinations, and school medical examinations in the first year of school life are supposed to cover the whole of the child population.

Community Child Health Services are also intended to cover the whole child population, but family practitioners may carry a responsibility for some of the care.

Responsibility for special provision for handicapped children has passed somewhat randomly, for different purposes, to one or other of the Health, the Education or the Social Services. The aim is to provide a coordinated service, but there always remains pressure to contain as many children as possible within the main stream of the educational system.

On purely educational grounds, there has, for a long time, been a division into those who can be educated in the ordinary schools, and those who require special schools or special classes. Some of the more severely handicapped children require residential care.

The largest group of handicapped children is of those called educationally subnormal (E.S.N.). These usually receive recognition when the child passes from the infant school (where the main experience is in the manipulation of materials and ideas) to the junior school, (where attention is directed to formal learning).

[4] See J. H. Kahn and J. P. Nursten, *Unwillingly to School*, Pergamon Press, 3rd Ed. 1980, Chapter 5; and *Report of the Committee on Maladjusted Children*, HMSO, 1955 (The Underwood Report).
[5] *Fit for the Future: The Report of the Committee on Child Health Services*, (Chairman: Professor S. D. M. Court), HMSO Cmnd 6684, 1976.

The concept of educational subnormality is, in contrast with the identification of physical, sensory and emotional handicaps, an almost entirely educational distinction. The implications, and some of the identification procedures, include social and medical factors, but these relate to a level of performance in school, and are not the equivalent of a clinical diagnosis.

There is a certain amount of formality in the procedure for the ascertainment of educational subnormality. It includes an assessment by an educational psychologist, a medical examination and observations from the teaching staff. The social dimension is provided by the health visitor, or a social worker from the Social Service Department. These various contributions are usually discussed at a conference of all these parties under the aegis of, and with the final responsibility of, the Education Authority.

Pervading all this comprehensive procedure is the idea of differential intelligence levels which can be recognized by testing.

Purely on the level of I.Q., the E.S.N. group of children are often considered to be those in the range between 50 and 70. In practice, a large number of children with I.Q.s down to 60, and sometimes a little below, are able to remain profitably in the ordinary school; and some with an I.Q. over 70 need the special facilities of the E.S.N. school.

Severe Mental Handicap: Heterogeneous Group

Amongst the children with an I.Q. of under 50, there are a number who differ from the majority in no other respect than the low intelligence level. They represent the lower end of the normal distribution curve. In addition to these, however, there are children whose low intellectual ability and performance is the result of congenital physical abnormalities, or chromosome anomalies—such as mongolism (or Down's Syndrome)—and there is a further group in which the mental handicap is the result of irreversible damage to the central nervous system as a result of complications during pregnancy and the perinatal period. Some of these complications are themselves resultant of factors associated with social class groupings.[6] Severe pre-eclamptic toxaemia, low birth weight, form a complex which is related to the stresses which impinge more heavily on mothers with a starting point of lower than average physical state of health and who receive less than optimum standard of obstetric care.

Thus children who are called severely subnormal, in the terms of the 1959 Mental Health Act, do not form a homogeneous category. Up to recent years however, such children were excluded from the educational system, either because they could not benefit from schooling or because their presence was disturbing to other children. Many health departments of local authorities made provision for the day-care of these children. At first the units were called Occupational Centres because the idea was to relieve the burden which the child's handicap placed upon the parent, and at the same time, to find some activity for the children. The idea of occupation

[6] H. G. Birch *et al.*, *Mental Subnormality in the Community*, Williams & Wilkins, Baltimore, U.S.A., 1970.

gave way to the idea of social training—hence the name "Training Centres"—but in some localities emphasis was placed not on the incapacity which the child suffered from the mental defect but on the capacities which remained and could be developed. It became an assumption that some intellectual growth was possible along with the physical growth, even though this would be at a slower rate than that in the average child. It was also recognized that there would be emotional distress in the child and in the family because of the strain of expectations which were either too high or too low for the child's capacity.

Some modern purpose-built training centres[7] incorporated, in the architectural structure, provision for intellectual growth by means of teaching of the nursery school type, increasing slowly in complexity at each age range; provision for emotional growth through play, creative activities and psychotherapy; in addition, those who needed it were given physiotherapy, speech therapy and general medical care. The basic concept was not that of formal "educability" but of "developability"—a concept which is equally pertinent to activities in ordinary schools.

Education of the Handicapped: The Need for Multi-Disciplinary Services

Experience of the progress which had become possible in these training centres under the organization of Health Departments gave the Education Department the confidence to take back into its system the responsibility for the education of the entire group of mentally handicapped children, whether educationally subnormal (E.S.N.) or severely subnormal (S.S.N.). The transfer of responsibility from Health Departments to Education Departments formally took place on 1st April, 1971.

This transfer has had important social consequences in the uniting of the whole child population as requiring educational provision. It is to be hoped, however, that there will be no illusion that teaching alone will give every child the resources for optimum development. Some forms of mental handicap are the result of social deprivation, some of physical abnormality, and in all of them there is the need to consider the interaction of the physical environment, the social and family background, and the child's individual constitutional and developmental history.[8] Even within the educational system there is the need for specialized and multi-disciplinary assessment and reassessment. The same considerations apply in the E.S.N. school and in the special schools for sensory and physical handicap.

The idea of "ineducability" has been officially removed from regulations and statute. Given a change in expectations, many children have been found to gain in knowledge and skills against all the odds.

Sadly, some children will always remain unreachable, and, in practice, ways are found (such as being on hospital waiting lists, or being excluded, suspended, or even withdrawn from school) of keeping them outside the formal educational process.

---

[7] J. H. Kahn, The Newham Community Mental Health Services, in *New Aspects of the Mental Health Services* (edited by H. Freeman and J. Farndale) Pergamon Press, 1967, pp 579–80.
[8] J. H. Kahn and J. Redman in *Social Work*, Jan. 1969.

Special Education v. Integration

Many people are loath to admit such wide variations in the ability of children, and argue either that it is bad for children to realize they have a lower ability than the average, by being separated, or, alternatively, that it is good for children of higher intelligence to have the children of lower-grade intelligence with them, as part of the building of their characters.

The same theme arises with children who are physically handicapped.

The Warnock Report[9] firmly recommended the integration of handicapped children into the ordinary schools. A necessary corollary was a recommendation that initial teacher training should include themes that were developed as part of the post-qualification studies which now exist for work in special schools.

The Warnock Committee thought that all intending teachers should have the opportunity to gain a sufficient understanding of the needs and abilities of both normal and handicapped children; the observational skills necessary to recognize special needs; and the knowledge of where and how to get special help.

In-service courses were also recommended to develop the same understanding, skills and knowledge for practising teachers.

Some teacher training institutions had already developed courses along these lines, and the publication of the Report should stimulate others to do so.

The aim of integration of handicapped pupils into the ordinary educational system is to avoid the social handicap of segregation. We should, at the same time, recognize the equal disadvantage when a handicapped child at an ordinary school is treated "normally", and therefore expected to "cope" without special help. Integration may well come to mean ignoring the handicap, in a good cause!

It is a praiseworthy aim to get rid of a stigmatizing label, but if the label is the entitlement to a good and appropriate school life, the stigma disappears. The very diversity of official schools and homes for handicapped pupils should indicate an accumulation of knowledge and skills. A list is given below of the categories of special provision used by Local Education Authorities:

Blind pupils	Maladjusted pupils
Partially sighted	Delicate pupils
Deaf pupils	Physically handicapped
Partially hearing	Speech defect
Educationally subnormal	Hospital special school
Severely subnormal	Mentally handicapped
Epileptic pupils	Severely mentally handicapped
	Profoundly mentally handicapped

It does not seem credible that the experience embodied in these establishments can be distributed without loss over the whole range of ordinary schools.

Social Interaction of School and Home

There are differences in social interaction between families and schools in different areas. In predominantly middle-class areas the educational aims of the school

[9] *Special Educational Needs: The Report of the Committee of Enquiry into the Education of Handicapped Children and Young People* (Chairman: Mrs H. M. Warnock) 1978.

are fully accepted by the parents, sometimes even to the extent of reproducing at home the same kind of educational pressure as exists within the school.

Even in the private sector of education there are preparatory schools and grammar schools where selection becomes more and more geared to the measurement of intelligence. Many middle-class parents begin to fear that social mobility can be downwards as well as upwards, and that unless the child can be groomed for academic education from an early stage, he or she will be subsequently barred from entry into the channels that lead to professional training. Some middle-class children are subjected to homework after school, and special coaching, from the very moment of school entry. School ceases to be a social experience because the children are competitors and not playmates. Even children of high intelligence are subjected to these pressures in order to keep level with the advantages given to other children, and the result often is lower rather than higher performance because of the strain imposed when the reward of success is to have even higher standards of success demanded.

There is a special problem in metropolitan and large urban areas where there is a uniform concentration of working-class occupation over an extensive area. The ideology of the teachers (whatever their original class) is middle class. Approval goes to the attitudes and types of performance which are acceptable in middle-class areas, and the teacher is frequently hostile to the working-class culture.

Children in "disadvantaged" areas suffer if it is taken for granted by their teachers that, inherently, they have a low level of intelligence.

Alternatively, the teachers may, as an article of political faith, consciously decide not to impose through education a different culture from that of the child's home background. Consequently they may not do any teaching at all! This is an educational philosophy which by no means gains support from working-class parents whose assumed culture is intended to be preserved, nor is it representative of the majority of schools.

Equality of Ability or of Opportunity

There are many who refuse to believe that there is any difference in the intellectual potentiality of the normal range of children. It can be a matter of political belief that all men are equal in ability. Any differences in adult performance would then be due to the withholding of opportunities, or the differences in experiences which are dependent upon financial provisions or on social class. If it should occur that, even with equality of provision, some children still show differing responses to education, those who believe in inherent equality must also conclude that either those who fail do not avail themselves of the opportunity, and are at fault, or that they have suffered some disease which prevents them from doing so.

If it is not assumed that all children have equal ability (whatever the causes) then there is conflict as to how equality of opportunity should be achieved.

There are those who believe that to introduce any greater "equality" into the system would be to force everyone to suffer the same experiences, and therefore to ignore special needs of pupils at every level of ability.

Few people however actually want all children to be exactly equal in all aspects of their education. Rather, they press for greater equality in the sense that they see specific inequalities (e.g. in provision in different areas) as injustices which should be removed. The comprehensive system has been seen, rightly or wrongly, as removing social inequalities.

Education and the Mentally Handicapped Child

Philosophy of education, and the philosophy of treatment of mental retardation, both depend upon the prevailing culture or political belief. We have referred to middle-class parents who press the child in a belief that hard work will bring any child up to the level demanded for academic education. There are also those who believe that concentration on schoolwork will raise the mentally retarded child up to average performance. Luria, who has enlarged our perceptions on the function of speech in the development of personality, has written about the mentally retarded child in Russia,[10] and, in doing so, he gives incidentally some enlightenment on the educational aims in the schools of that country. His is an environmental philosophy, and the schoolchildren he studies are expected never "to direct their behaviour or use their knowledge to carry out some task other than the one prescribed".

Communication of language to a child is thought of as being in terms of commands and prohibitions—"Do this" and "Don't do that". This is the *regulating* function of speech.

> "The child of school age finds himself in circumstances where he needs to study according to a strict programme prescribed by the teacher. This means that the child must not behave in accordance with the dictates of his personal motives and needs, but must carry out the orders of the teacher, and follow his spoken instructions all the time. He must remain within the limits set by the instructions given him, and must not allow his attention to wander on to the irrelevant things. Psychologically speaking this means that all the motives behind the activities of the child who has just attained school age must be reorganized, so that the basic motive influencing behaviour during lesson time must become 'the directions of the teacher'."

The child who rebels against this routine, or who fails to show ability to concentrate, becomes regarded as one who has suffered some serious brain pathology during early uterine life.

Equality or Uniqueness

It would be easy to find fault with the underlying concepts of much of Luria's writings, and yet our own educational philosophy is far from uniform either in its presentation or acceptance.

The modern educationalist in this country is committed to a theory of uniqueness rather than equality of the individual, and to the practice of helping each child to express the self at his or her own particular level of ability. This involves

[10] Prof. A. H. Luria, *The Mentally Retarded Child*, Pergamon Press, 1963.

differentials in expectations, and acceptance of variations in routine progress. There are arrangements for different schools for children with different levels of ability or different degrees of handicap. There may be different educational streams within the same age range, and different rates of progress are possible in different groups even within the same class. The teacher becomes concerned with the personal life of the child, and with the social interactions of children as well as with the level of scholastic attainment. Sensitivity to the wider variations between children, and to the changing response of an individual child makes more demands on the teacher than a philosophy which assumes that the teacher gives a constant amount of information, which the children absorb in various proportions according to their co-operativeness, diligence and voluntary concentration on the work.

Where freedom is given to children to find their own level of response, new levels of creativity may be reached. Teaching can become a joint adventure between children and teacher in which, at times, both parties reach some point of understanding at the same moment. But this freedom needs a framework, and the child needs the imposition of some standards in the school in the same way that they are needed at home.

It should be possible to postulate concepts about points of *social* change which appear either as catastrophic upheavals or as stepping stones to a new and better era.

The development of *professional* concepts brings about points of change which are alternatively crisis events or stepping stones, similar to the way-stations in *personal* development. Old certainties and adjustments are destroyed before the new ones are able to give their satisfactions; and there are regrets for the advantages that came from old methods. The greatest anxiety exists when old practices are given up before the new ones have been comprehended, and disappointments are greatest when methods are changed while retaining the desire for the results which were believed to come from the former practice.

Children in present-day schools may appear more self-confident and self-assertive, and may approach the adult with a feeling of social equality. The respect for rules has to be a much more subtle process, and it is likely to break down when there is an attempt to enforce it by methods which were appropriate to a more subdued generation.

The time comes when concentration on scholastic work is possible as a voluntary effort of the child, and the attitude to work will depend upon the acceptance by the child of the ideology of the school. A framework of compulsion is necessary. It is a reassurance to the child to know that at times there is no option but to work. But compulsion itself is a process in which the child *gives* authority to the teacher and, in more abstract terms, to the community. It is rule by consent.

There is a need to build a bridge between the culture of the home and the culture of the school. In the home there should be respect for the process of education, and, in the school, respect for the separate culture of the home locality. Where the two cultures are not in contact, the child rebels in one place or the other, or in both. Sometimes a gap in the cultures exists because parents who recollect their own strict upbringing at home and in school with affection, look upon modern educational methods with suspicion.

There may be other cases where school and home together lag behind the prevailing culture of the outside world, and where the children form a rebellious group deriving an ideology from the wealth of stimulation of the mass media.

Rapid technical change and rapid change of culture produce uncertainty until new techniques and adaptations become more coherent.

14

Primary Education

Infant School (the Child from 5 to 7 Years)

This period is marked out culturally as the age of infant-school attendance. Physically it is a period of rapid growth. (There is such a period again in early adolescence.) In the years 5 to 7, there is a maturing of some of the structures in the central nervous system, and this can be recognized by changes in recordings on an electroencephalogram. The maturation in structure is accompanied by maturation in function, and it is at about this time that there is development in the capacity of the child to adapt to external conditions, and to see the outside world more nearly as it appears to others, and less as a part of personal fantasies. The child develops a greater capacity for directed thinking. In Piaget's formulations there is recognition of new levels of mental development which have now become possible.

Culturally Determined Activities

School attendance begins arbitrarily in Great Britain at the age of 5 years and, although in many countries in Europe school entry comes later, most children are ready for the break from home life at this age. The rate of development physically, intellectually and emotionally varies, and, although a child's life should be considered as a whole, the different aspects do not always develop in step with one another.

The role of the child in society varies with the culture, and it alters along with technical changes in the background of community life. In some primitive cultures, adult activities are simple enough for the child to be able to enter into them at a comparatively early age. The gender role becomes distinct from the beginning; the boys helping the men in the search for food, hunting, fishing, trapping and even in their fighting; the girls helping the women with the cooking, washing and with the caring for the younger children. With industrialization, the child became valuable in economic terms, and children were introduced into factories at much the same age as when formerly they would have been of help in the house. During the nineteenth century, the economic value of the child in poorer homes was the prime factor, and their lives were expendable. Even in homes where there was more regard to the value of children in their own right, there was still a social distinction between children and their parents. In the middle-class home there could be three levels of provision in food, clothing and accommodation—the best for the parents, a grade lower for the children and a still lower grade for servants! It was not merely a

129

selection out of the food which was available in the house—three different qualities of food were deliberately purchased. This was the "adult-centred" or "employer-centred" world.

The present-day home is "child-centred" rather than adult-centred, and often it is the children who receive the highest quality and more expensive items.

The physique of children today shows an improvement over that of children born a generation ago.[1] Children of today are taller and healthier than their grandparents were at the same age. There is an improvement in general health; better hygiene and diet lead to a greater resistance to infections in general, and there is increased immunity to specific diseases as a result of inoculation for diphtheria, whooping cough, tetanus, measles and poliomyelitis. There are also tests for susceptibility to tuberculosis.

Some of these procedures carry a degree of risk even to the extent of brain damage. With regard to whooping cough for example, it is left to individual judgement whether to accept susceptibility to a possibly serious disease as against a possible dangerous consequence from the means to prevent it. The anxieties which stem from this risk have led some parents to refuse all immunizing procedures.

Transference to the Teacher

The needs of the growing intellect at this period are met by the beginnings of school life, but, at this stage in particular, education is not a matter of intellect alone. The wholeness of body and mind is reflected in the practice of the modern infant school which is a place where children play, eat, drink, go to the lavatory, wash their hands, dress and undress, and learn new levels of control of body processes. These activities are the learning of new skills and are also part of the child's emotional life. Infant school is the first experience that most children may have of life away from home, although a few may have had previous attendance at a day nursery or nursery school.

The emotional aspect of the change to school implies the capacity to separate from the mother. There have been progressive stages in the child's life; the exclusiveness of the tie between the mother and child is broken into when relationships develop with the father and with brothers and sisters. Family life has begun. The child now extends the range of contacts and relationships to include other individuals in the neighbourhood and more remote family. School is more definitely a life in the outside world.

Some children may not be ready for the separation, and sometimes the parents may not be ready. The parents have had control of the child's environment, and the child has had a close relationship with both parents. Even the relationships with siblings are closely bound up with relationships to the parents—every child thinks

[1] "Cosy myth that all is now well." In spite of the general improvement, Dr. Harriett Wilson stated that there are still some 500,000 children in Britain who live below the minimum standards laid down by the Ministry of Social Security. *The Times*, 19th Dec., 1966. Recent surveys still confirm this point. The numbers of children in poor economic conditions are fewer, but of those who live in below-standard conditions, the proportion who die in infancy remains the same. Improved medical services alone are not sufficient to combat the increased morbidity and mortality that are the consequence of economic and social deprivation.

of brothers and sisters in relation to the part that they play in the life with parents. The normal resolution of the oedipal situation permits the child to accept a life as equal with children of the same age.

Some part of the child's fantasy relationships with parents remains, and some of it becomes transferred to the teacher when the child begins school life. The teacher inherits the role formerly attributed to parents. The magical qualities which children believe are possessed by parents, and which can be used sometimes for their benefit, and sometimes against them, disappear when the child begins to see parents more realistically as fallible human beings where goodness and badness can exist in the same person. The child also relinquishes any wishes for magical powers, and is grateful that parents can survive bad thoughts as well as responding to good ones. The teacher at this stage succeeds to some traces of the child's primitive image of the parents. The teacher knows everything and seems to be able to see right into the child's mind.

Teachers are also figures in their own right who allow the child to develop new levels of relationships with an adult, and from whom the child absorbs qualities which add to their own personality. Some of these qualities are taken in unconsciously through the process which has been called introjection, and there is also the process of a more conscious identification by a child with the qualities of a teacher who is admired and maybe loved.

Rules and Restrictions

At the time of school entry, the parents and the child alike need to be ready to allow some transfer of the relationships which had previously been confined to the home setting. School entry implies a life with a large number of other children, as equals, whose rights have to be respected. It is therefore a limitation of the child's demand for undivided adult attention. It includes a certain amount of observance of rules, and children need some preparation in advance for the acceptance of restrictions on their demands for immediate personal gratification. Normally this preparation has been provided within the home in doses that the child has been able to tolerate.

Children who have never had a reasonable restriction of activity may find school intolerable. Others are unable to make the transfer from relationship with a parent to relationship with the teacher because child and parent are so closely dependent upon one another that separation would cause distress to both parties.

Separation from the mother at some stages of the child's life has been discussed from the point of view of the damage caused to the child's emotional development, but there are stages where the capacity to separate is the indication of progress. Some children make such rapid progress that they are ready to separate from the mother to the school at an earlier stage than 5 years of age. Separation could be a part of further progress from a home which has been a good home. Other children need placement at some kind of nursery school or day nursery as a substitute for a home which is unsatisfactory and where progress has *not* been made, either because the mother is not there, or because her capacity to supply the child's needs is too limited.

These two different kinds of needs and purposes may be served in a single nursery school or day nursery, and it is necessary to distinguish between the two purposes. In one case, the school or nursery is an extension of the home; in the other, it is a substitute for it.

Infant school is a transitional process between a life representing a home and the more directed educational type of establishment represented by the schools which the child will attend later. The infant school introduces limitations of behaviour in a form which is acceptable and which is within the capacity of the child to tolerate. It legitimises some of the natural outlets of expression of the child's physical, intellectual and emotional life, and sharpens interest in the surroundings.

Social Learning in Groups

Part of the purpose of the infant school is to bring the child into social relationships with other children. This aim affects even the arrangement of the furniture in the school. At times, the children sit at small tables where a group, around the table, can share a task or work independently. At other times, children may form a half-circle facing the teacher, and on many occasions there is a going to and fro around the room with complex and changing participation of different groupings. In these arrangements it is assumed that when children are talking to each other they are being good. The more traditional placement of children in parallel rows, all facing the teacher, was for the purpose of maintaining a relationship of each separate child directly with the teacher and not of the children with one another. The children who are side to side or front to back have difficulty in communication with one another, except by interrupting the allotted task. Talking to one another is bad. It was assumed that the main purpose of the school was the absorption of knowledge and no thought was given during school time to the idea of setting patterns for the formation of social relationships with equals. The formal pattern imposed some strain on the teacher in keeping order, but the aim was clear. The informal arrangement demands flexibility from the teacher in order to be able to accept and utilize unexpected responses in both work and play activity. It also brings unexpected pleasures.

Formal learning has its place, and there are developmental steps in the child of readiness to read, to make abstractions of ideas and to form concepts. The stage of readiness has been linked with the structural maturities referred to above, and which are recognised physiologically by electrical changes in the activities of the central nervous system. These steps can also be recognized by psychologists who work on the lines of Piaget.[2] They occur at different ages in different children, and we cannot force these new areas of comprehension before the child is ready.

Jerome Bruner[3] has taken the idea of sequential stages of mental development and linked them with a theory of instruction with some practical consequences for education. His idea is that it is possible to lay foundations in the earlier stages for

[2] J. Piaget, *The Child's Conception of Number*, 1952; *The Child's Construction of Reality*, 1955. Routledge and Kegan Paul.

[3] J. S. Bruner, *Towards a Theory of Instruction*, Norton, New York, 1966.

complex and abstract modes of thought which will appear much later in the child's development. This has been called the Spiral Curriculum.

Words, Symbols and Mental Concepts

Language is an instrument of mental progress.[4] Words are the tools of communication, and they are also the material which permit our mental processes to grow. The power to keep in mind a mental representation of objects which are not within the range of vision depends upon words. Words stand as *symbols* for objects, and later as symbols for more complex ideas. We build up concepts with words and numbers, and even the simplest mathematical concepts are more complex than they at first appear. We can say that one and one make two, but this is a complicated process of abstraction! One pint of milk can be added to another pint of milk and that makes two pints. The addition actually has taken place. We have one apple, and another apple, and then we have two apples, but the apples have not been added to one another. The addition has been done in our minds. If we have an apple and a pear and say we have two pieces of fruit we have first to abstract the quality of the unity of each piece, and also to abstract the quality that they have in common of both being a fruit. It is some considerable time before children reach the step when these mental manipulations have any real meaning, and these steps cannot be hurried. At the proper time these complex processes are taken for granted and the means by which we reach them are forgotten.

Children with a poor verbal background may become retarded in their development, and there are some children who are unable to speak even at the time of school entry. It is possible that children need some kind of "normal" linguistic provisions in the home, without which they will be linguistically "deprived". Some children come from homes where the parents themselves have an impoverished vocabulary. A problem of West Indian children who come from homes where a patois is spoken, valid within their own language community, is that their speech may be taken as "incorrect" by speakers of "standard" English. Another problem group comes from highly articulate parents who have not realized the necessity of constant and close linguistic communication with the child at the child's own level. Some children again, have suffered a succession of au pairs or child minders each bringing different languages, idiom, or vocabularies, into the home. In each case there is a lack of continuity in language provision, within the home itself, or between the home and the school.

The issue is complex in the extreme because what is restriction to some children is enrichment to others. An additional language can give rise to additional thoughts—as long as there is freedom to pass from one system to another, and enlarge the number of meanings of individual words in both.

The same theme occurs where there is a regional dialect which seems to separate some individuals from a larger community, and yet others attach the highest value

---

[4] B. Bernstein, Aspects of language and learning in the genesis of the social process, *J. of Child Psychol. and Psychiat.* (1961); F. D. Flower, *Language and Education*, Longmans, London, 1966; A. T. Ravenette, *Dimensions of Reading Difficulties*, Pergamon Press, 1968.

to preserving the power of expression that dialect users can extract from different shades of meaning attached to a single word.

Bilingualism is a transient feature of immigrant communities, but exists in permanent form, for example in some parts of Wales. In countries where there is more than one "official" language there have been studies on the subject of the effect on personality.[5]

Personality and Identity

It is necessary to recognize that a child differs from an adult and is not a small edition of an adult. Children should be judged by standards that apply to childhood, and, just as the standards of adult life cannot be scaled down to form a measure for the child's performance, it would be equally inappropriate to scale up the mental life of a child and expect it to represent the mental life of an adult. The normal mental life of a small child contains such a high proportion of fantasy that it would be diagnostic of insanity if it occurred in an adult, and yet this level of fantasy *is* normal for the child.

We must also remember to consider the child not only as having a different kind of existence from the adult, but also a personality which is in the process of formation and change, and with its own special vulnerabilities. Our picture of the child's personality needs to be considered, not in isolation, but in relationship to other children of the same age at the same stage of development, and also in relationship to the culture, subculture or "multi-culture".

Children need to develop a sense of identity, to know their own names and to feel a sense of separateness as well as of belonging, to have possessions, to have a sense of being which is gained by the communication to them of the image that other people have of them. They begin to respect themselves when adults show respect and concern for their separateness. Then and then only, do they learn to respect the separate identity, the personality, the possessions and the rights of other children.

A conscious sense of morality is gained gradually as distinct from the irrational prohibitions that form part of the superego. Children begin to observe the rules because the rules now appear to be rational and capable of being observed.

There is a problem at home and at school of children who defy and ignore rules. At home the children who have these problems usually have parents who are either very strict or who have no rules at all. Some parents make a line of demarcation around the child's permitted conduct, and the circle is so small that it is inevitable that the child's normal activities should pass beyond the permitted area. Having, in *normal* activities, gone beyond the boundary set by parents, there is then no further boundary to prevent the child from passing into areas of conduct which are considered abnormal by general agreement. Thus the child of overstrict parents shows *no discrimination in misbehaviour*!

Parents who offer their children no rules at all can neither expect obedience nor that the child's behaviour will be governed by inner controls. Peace can be bought

[5] W. E. Lambert, A Social Psychology of Bilingualism, *Journal of Social Issues*, No. 23, 1967; J. P. Soffietti, Bilingualism and Biculturalism: *Journal of Educational Psychology*, No. 46, 1955; DES Survey 14, *The Continuing Needs of Immigrants*, 1972.

from time to time by giving in to whatever the child demands. This is sometimes thought of as giving the children what they want, but such children have no means of knowing what they want. They can only guess at what they are expected to demand and they do their best to demand it.

Expectations and Images of School and Teacher

The majority of children have some image of school life and of the teacher's role before attending school. They learn about it from their brothers and sisters or from the children of their neighbours, and they play at school before they actually attend. An "only" child who also has little contact with other children does not get a coherent picture of school in advance and is rather less prepared. Most children, however, have a picture of what to expect. The image of the teacher and of school life helps the teachers to maintain their own role. A large class is kept under control by a single teacher partly because of the child's adaptation to an expected role; the school becomes part of the child's culture. If the child has not included the school in the culture that has so far been absorbed, the teacher has to cope without the help of the normal child's ready acceptance to school life. The teacher then has to depend upon his or her personality and gets no assistance from the professional role. Granted variations in individual capacity, it is not surprising that some teachers find it more difficult than others in dealing with the exceptionally unruly child.

The child who has not yet absorbed inner restrictions, and the child with inappropriate ones, are equally outside the normal range. The child with unresolved oedipal anxieties, who still inflates the self in fantasy, attempts to deal with adults at an equal level of rivalry, and threatens teachers who themselves might have residues of childish anxieties. Most people at times feel that they are still small children acting the part of grown-ups, and they are afraid of being found out. Most adults have feelings of inadequacy which make them vulnerable, at times, to threats. The adult is partly protected by the general acceptance of adult status, and the professional person has the additional safeguard of the recognition of professional standing. It is very disturbing when an adult's professional status is challenged even by a small child. The danger of relying too exclusively on the status of the role is that there is nothing that remains but exclusion for those children who challenge that role.

Parents sometimes wish for a school to have complete success in restricting a child who has been overactive at home; yet if the permitted range has been too narrow, and the child's normal activity has become abnormal by definition, then in time it becomes abnormal in reality. Such children fear the different framework within the school as much as they defy it. School represents the authority of the community and consequently these children exclude themselves from identification with the community. They have now become antisocial.

Freedom Within a Framework

Teachers who can accept such problems have to rely more on personal resources and need a wide concept of the educational process. They become able to think of education as serving intellectual, emotional and social needs in one combination, and are able to allow the child to achieve satisfaction in a wider and changing range of activities. Art, music and poetry have long been recognized as giving access to the child's *feelings* rather than to *intellect*, and thus help the child's emotional development. The ability of a teacher to change the nature of the activity of a class from moment to moment can help to legitimatize the activity of some children in cases where it would become an open and successful challenge to the teacher if an attempt were made to enforce the continuance of a set programme.

Challenges which do occur may be dealt with at times by force of character or physical force, but such challenges also lead to division between those who conform and those who do not. Sometimes, those who do not conform are merely excluded. Some teachers and other professional workers interpret the contemporary change from completely repressive control as meaning that discipline is no longer necessary or advisable. They offer freedom from discipline and hope that order will spontaneously emerge! They find chaos instead. A framework is necessary even if it is a less restrictive one than was formerly applied. There is a level of freedom which allows the child to develop creatively in the realms of movement, learning, and joining in social activities, and every stage is a new adventure. Children develop more quickly if each one can go at the pace which is appropriate for each stage of maturation of body and mind. A class of small children are all at different stages of development and, although they can have many joint activities, uniformity should never be looked for.

Freedom needs restriction at the point where a child asks for restraint. It is as if a bargain is made: "I will let go if you will keep me safe." The teacher needs to be able to anticipate the point of danger and to be able to bring the child back within acceptable boundaries before he or she has gone too far.

A time comes when concentration on formal learning and conscious thought are within the range of the child's mental structure but, even then, the child needs permission at times a regress to earlier patterns.

The Child from 7 to 11 (Junior School)

At the age of 7 years, school life begins to take a greater importance in the total experience of children. They are more ready for formal aspects of learning, but the newer concepts of education look upon the learning process as an aspect of total experience in which the emotional life is as important as the purely intellectual.

The period is one where physical growth continues but not as rapidly as at the earlier stages. Physical skills increase and these derive as much from the informal activity of children playing together as from formal physical education.

The Secret Life of Childhood

The emotional life, too, becomes more bound up with brothers and sisters and with classmates than with adults, and the social life of children of this age begins to develop as something apart. Perhaps there is less information about the mental life of children of this age than of any other age. They have become partly released from the boundaries of home, and they are beginning to have their secret games. There is a folklore that appears to be transmitted from one generation of children to another, yet leaving little recollection in the minds of the adults whom they eventually become.

Examination has been made of the verses[6] that children repeat and the games that they play, and interesting facts about the rapid spread of these activities over widely scattered areas of the country have been discovered. Work has also been done on the child's creativity in poetry[7] and other art forms[8] and on the part played by these creations on the development of the child's personality.

The greater verbal freedom of present-day children (or at least of some of them) seems to have led to a readiness to communicate the secrets of playground life to parents and teachers. Fights and squabbles may be reported with no suggestion of "tale telling" and so are playground rhymes and jokes—even those which involve traditional playground scatology. The lavatory language of parents (kept secret from the children, just as the children's was kept secret from parents) has become a common speech.

In the so-called latency period, the sexuality of boys and girls has many forms of expression in language and body activity, but, in most cases, groups of boys and groups of girls evolve their sexual rituals separately from one another.

Child Health and School Life

The school life becomes representative of all aspects of personality. The School Health Service (now reorganized under Area Health Authorities) is concerned with the physical and mental health of children and the making sure of provision for any treatment which is found to be necessary. Hearing and sight are checked; meals and clothing can be provided free on the grounds that children need to be in good health and well fed and clothed in order to benefit from education.

Variations in Ability

The learning process begins to reveal variations in ability. Junior-school teachers have the difficult task of providing work at appropriate levels of difficulty for every child, over all the areas of the curriculum. In many schools, children are sorted out into groups of different ability levels, probably on the basis of reading, mathematical and verbal reasoning tests. In large schools, children may be "streamed" into different classes, though this practice is much less common in the junior school than it was formerly.

Some teachers retain the whole class as a mixed-ability group, and endeavour to set work for each child individually.

Whatever method of organization is used, the ideal of educating all children to the limit of their potential is unlikely to be realized. Teachers can at best "try to do better"!

[6] Opie, I. O. and P. O. *Lore and Language of Schoolchildren*, Clarendon Press, 1959.
[7] Marjorie L. Hourd, *Coming into Their Own*, Heinemann, 1959.
[8] Herbert Read, *Education through Art*, Faber & Faber, 1943.

H.G.D.P.—F

In Chapter 2, we adopted a working definition of intelligence as "the capacity to extract the relevant information, in order to draw conclusions when dealing with a problem, for a purpose."

Measurement of intelligence is more controversial. For example, there are assumptions that the distribution of intelligence in a large population follows the regular pattern which is observed in the presentation of data regarding qualities which have a chance distribution. The name "normal distribution curve" implies that there is something natural about the range of a particular quality in any given population. It is easy to see, however, that with a quality like height the shape of the curve will alter when the modal height reached by members of the population as a whole has increased. Even national stereotypes of qualities like height alter, and presumably, so would the shape of the curve representing the actual distribution of qualities. The distribution of intelligence has for a couple of generations been assumed to be governed by unassailable statistical laws, codified in patterns of the Gaussian (normal distribution) curve. We reproduce such a curve (p. 139) and acknowledge the fact that it has been a power for good in the recognition of the differential needs of children at different levels of ability. "Ability" however is used in many senses, some of which include immediate levels of attainment, and some which imply an inherent, unalterable, genetically determined quality.

It is this latter sense which is sometimes used nihilistically as a reason for continuing to hold low expectations of large groups of children who already come under some categorization, in terms of race, social class or regional culture. It is in this context that intelligence testing has become the subject of controversy.

We would hold that the concept of intelligence levels is not to be discarded lightly, and, without making generalizations, there can be a value in determining the level at which intelligence finds expression at any one phase of development in individual children, both for educational and therapeutic purposes.

The pattern of selection for grammar schools, which still exist in a few LEAs and in the private sector of education, has leaned heavily on the use of intelligence testing. The figure on p. 139 gives the idealized pattern of distribution of intelligence, which still remains in mind both in the identification of candidates for higher education, and for the identification of those with degrees of mental handicap selected for special education.

Much theory and dogma with regard to intelligence testing has had to be discarded. Most psychologists are now disenchanted with the idea that the test results have a predictive value, as it has been made abundantly clear that some of their educational uses created "self-fulfilling prophecies" either to the advantage or detriment of pupils.

Flight from Testing

For this reason, a number of educational psychologists have become dissatisfied with traditional practice.[9] Work with individual children in schools has become burdensome, because every child who is referred to an educational psychologist is

[9] See e.g. Bill Gillman (Ed), *Reconstructing Educational Psychology*, Croom Helm, London, 1978.

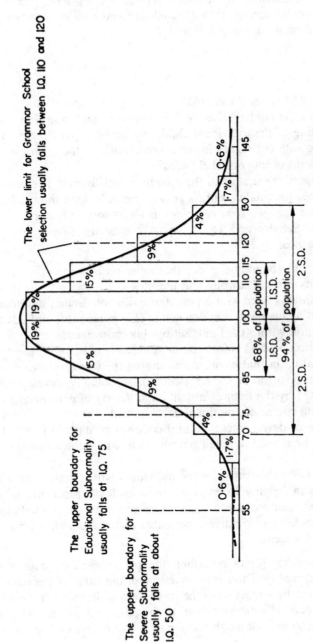

Fig. 1. Theoretical distribution of intelligence in the population (but see footnote on page 14).

the representative of a large but unknown proportion of the child population. Consequently, there appears to be a stampede away from work with individual children into diverse activities: to provide a service to the teaching staff; to make a contract with particular schools to modify educational policy; or to act as consultants to the educational service as a whole.

Continuing Roles

We ourselves would prefer the alternative view of other educational psychologists that there is a valuable contribution in the descriptive and interpretive content of psychological testing of the individual child, and that the psychologist has a continuing role, along with colleagues in other professions, in the diagnosis and treatment of the problems of individual children.

Education is one of the factors in the growth of intelligence. The original potential may be an inherited quality, but its growth depends upon the total experiences of the child. In this, the *quality* of education is an important factor.

H. Mayman, R. Schafer and D. Rapaport[10] offer the following propositions concerning intelligence:

(1) It is necessary to abandon the idea that a person is born with a fixed "intelligence" that remains constant throughout life.

(2) Every individual is born with a potentiality for intellectual development that may be referred to as his natural endowment. This potentiality unfolds through a process of maturation within the limits set by this endowment.

(3) This maturation process is fostered or restricted by the wealth or poverty of intellectual stimulation in that environment during the formative years.

(4) This maturation process is one aspect of personality development and is fostered or restricted by the timing, intensity and variety of emotional stimulation, and by the resulting course of emotional development.

(5) In the course of development, natural endowment differentiates into various functions that can be tapped by intelligence tests in which these functions underlie achievement.

(6) Formal education that provides the individual with systematically presented ideas plays a role in helping to enlarge the individual's repertoire of facts and relationships to be organized into a frame of reference for the assimilation of new experiences and moulding of creative experiences within the limits of his emotional receptivity and endowment.

There are many other topics regarding the part played by education in the development of personality. There is the question of the value of the relationship of the child with the teacher, apart from the mechanics of learning the kind of information usually associated with education. In the junior school the child, as a rule, has one class teacher and, although there may be an occasional specialist teacher

---

[10] *An Introduction to Projective Techniques* (edited by H. Anderson and G. Anderson) Prentice-Hall, New York, 1951, pp. xxiv–72 and p. 547. *Interpretation of the Wechsler-Bellevue Intelligence Scale in Personality Appraisal*, Chapter 19, pp. 541–80.

for physical education or some other subject, most of the child's time in school is spent with the class teacher. In many cases where children have unsatisfactory home or family life, the teacher is the one consistent and stable influence.

Some children may miss a consistency of relationship with a teacher by reason of the social mobility of parents who move from district to district as a result of promotion.

The teacher's consistency may be something that the child values, but school at this stage becomes a place where rules exist, and the child who comes from a home where all rules are changeable on appeal may resent and fear the representative of a more inflexible system. Some children thus fear their teacher who represents obligations for which they have not been prepared. Others may seek the attention and the love of the teacher as a continuation of that of their parents, or as something which they have not yet had.

Emerging into a Community

School is larger than a family and is a miniature community. Symptoms of emotional disturbance may be considered to be related to school life simply because that is the area where new and important activities of the child are taking place. The emotional life becomes more concerned with siblings and with class mates rather than with adults. Although parents and teachers remain important figures within a child's mental life, the main interaction, however, often is with others around the same age. Life has become less bound up with early fantasies about adults, and by this time the oedipal situation should have become resolved.

In some circumstances the infantile involvement with fantasy representations of the parents remains at a fairly high level, and this is more likely to occur when the parents themselves find a value in the involvement of their child in their conflicts. There are special cases where there is no opportunity for the resolution of the conflict. Where parents become separated and the child remains with one, or where one parent dies, or is absent for long periods, a high intensity of relationship with the child can be sought by the remaining parent as a substitute for the missing partner. The child is expected both to supply the emotional needs of a parent at an adult level and, at the same time, to remain an obedient small child, and be protected from undesired influences outside the home.

Some families have a self-enclosed life either by choice or force of circumstances. Parents who have to move from town to town may find it difficult to form satisfying relationships with neighbours and friends; and so do their children. If the roots of emotional involvement are torn up several times, no fresh ones will be laid down. The child may develop easy but superficial relationships at school, and even with friends in the neighbourhood; but the deeper emotional ties remain exclusively within the immediate family.

The danger of such close-knit family life is that the hostile component of the developing feelings is restricted to home consumption along with the affectionate component. Emotional life is lived at too intense a rate, and parents and children sometimes find themselves damaging to one another.

Other families build up a life which is centred on their material possessions, and this applies particularly to a generation of parents who derived satisfaction from the acquisition of the furniture and equipment as a result of their own efforts, and at a higher level than that which existed in their home of origin. Evenings are spent around the television set, and the weekends in outings in the family car. In such homes the mental life seems to be entirely restricted to preoccupation with objects and with ideas, and there is an undervaluation of emotional fulfilment at a normal childish level.

New Values in Home Life

In recent social history there have been some reversals of values. There are vast estates in prosperous industrial areas where families have refurbished their homes in "contemporary" style, making all-through living rooms, that have no place for a toy, and no natural space for a child to do homework. Paradoxically, at the same time, many of the traditionally house-proud middle classes have found a value in somewhat controlled chaos in their homes in order to give what they feel is appropriate freedom and space for their children's activities in their growing years.

Whatever aspect of home making is emphasized, the value of the inverse is inevitably left out.

It is difficult for parents who feel that they are making such rich provision for their children to face the criticism that they are leaving something out.

The same kind of problem exists when families live in a social setting which is not in accordance with the family standard. The children whose parents live on the premises of a corner shop in a "slum" district (and there are many slums which have not yet given way to new housing projects) suffer from the expectation that their parents have a higher standard of behaviour than is expected from the children around. The habits of thrift which are necessary to maintain the small business may seem less desirable to the child than the extravagance of the feckless people who live near.

Conflict and Coherence

The tripartite nature of the child's life—home, school and community—becomes important, and the personality becomes best integrated when there is some coherence in these factors. Most children can manage to adapt to a double life, where home and school represent different cultures, (unless the cultures are in *active* conflict with one another), but it is more difficult if they are faced with yet a third life, where the culture of the neighbourhood is also separate.

15

The Secondary-School Child

ANTHROPOLOGISTS who study primitive societies in the belief that those cultures are less complex and more rigidly uniform that our own are sometimes impressed by the precise role which individuals in those cultures have at each stage in their lives. It has been thought that the expectation of a particular status at each stage of life gives the individuals an advantage in that they know clearly the boundaries of each stage. It would seem, however, that the life of children in this country has been divided in a like fashion by the different stages of school life.

Biological and Cultural Boundaries in Life of Child

The phases of personality development include many that are biologically determined, and the boundary lines recognized by psychoanalysts and described in Chapter 3 include early stages in infancy where there is dominance of sensations in successively different areas of the body. The Oedipal Situation follows that in which the genital sensations predominate, and then comes a latency period.

The next stage is that of puberty. Puberty, however, begins at different ages in different children, and there is also variation in the average age of commencement in children of different countries and in different epochs in the same country. In the last 60 years in Great Britain the average age of the menarche in girls has been lowered from approximately 15 years to under 13 years.[1] The figure of 13 years is the average of wide variations ranging from 10 years and under,[2] to instances where the onset of menstruation is delayed beyond the age of 15 years.

Reference has already been made to the nature of secondary school education. Since the 1944 Education Act there has been an almost complete separation between primary education (infants and junior schools) and the secondary schools. The primary schools are sometimes "streamed" but in general are unspecialized.

Comprehensive Schools: New Ideas or Ideology

Comprehensive schooling has become partly a political issue, but this should not obscure the educational factors, and there are dangers that these latter factors can be diverted by giving the label of "comprehensive school" to a grouping of different

[1] J. M. Tanner, *Growth at Adolescence*, Blackwell Scientific Publications, 1962.
[2] Provision has had to be made for the disposal of sanitary towels in girls' toilets of primary schools.

143

secondary schools in separate buildings with separate educational policy. When comprehensive schools are newly created with a single large building, or in a group of buildings on the same campus, it still has to be decided whether divisions of different types of education should exist for children of different abilities. There are some comprehensive schools in which the classes are unstreamed and these are often at their most successful when the change from streaming is accompanied by a change from the set lesson within a set syllabus. Children of different ability benefit from cooperative contact with one another if they are freed from the 45-minute working period in which each child attempts to follow identical instructions from the teacher, and where this is substituted by joint tasks and projects with teams of teachers. In the latter, work space spills over from classroom to classroom, to central hall and to specialized workshops.

It cannot be emphasized too strongly that there is no virtue in a change of name of type of school if there is not simultaneously a change in the educational policy and practice.

New Beginnings, New Problems

There are problems in the transfer from junior to secondary school, whatever category the secondary school might be, and these problems are similar to those of school entry. The child who enters the infant school leaves the confines of the home, and goes into a wider world. The new area of living, which occupies so much of waking life, is frightening to some children, and some of them show their distress for a day or two, or a week or two, before settling down to school life. Others have a longer period of distress. By and large the child's personality grows to the school and the school shrinks in size as he or she becomes familiar with it. Class-mates become identifiable, and each year there is a class teacher who is responsible for the greater part of the teaching and the supervision of behaviour. There may be one or two specialist teachers in the primary school, but each class has one teacher whom the children look upon as their own.

The contemporary secondary school of any type is likely to be larger than the primary school, in order to justify expensive equipment and spacious playing fields by a spread of the cost over a large number of children. Pupils are drawn from several primary schools, and, to the newcomers, the older children look to be as tall and as powerful as the teachers.

The large yearly intake means that there are a larger number of classes for each year group. There are more specialist teachers taking each class for one subject only and, therefore, the rules which formerly were carried to the child in the person of the class teacher are now no longer attached to any particular individual. Rules are known to exist, and the consequence of breaking them seems to be dire, but the child is less clear as to what the rules are about. No wonder that many children entering secondary school have a recurrence of the anxiety that they first felt at the time of entry into the infant or junior school. They are now leaving the school which had become as familiar as their home, and passing on to something frightening and unknown.

Middle schools and junior high schools (where these have been provided) are smaller, and their pupils are more likely to feel part of a recognizable community. The teaching methods tend to preserve the approach often used in the top classes of primary schools viz: a system where one teacher is responsible for a large part of the curriculum, while some subjects are taken by specialist teachers.

Against these advantages, there is the disadvantage for the pupils that they face another transition point at 13 or 14; and for specialist teachers that they are deprived of access to advanced work with fifth and sixth forms, with a possible loss of prestige and personal esteem.

For most children, settling down in the new school can be as easy and as brief a process as if the first school entry. For other children, however, the transfer becomes one of the factors in school refusal.[3]

The segregation of children into different secondary schools carries a social problem. Children become separated from their friends by going to different schools or widely different sections of the same school.

Diversity in Stages of Growth

Even when attempts are made to minimize the differing experience allotted within the educational system to different children by the secondary-school stage, nature has provided a new and widening range of inequalities. For some the entry into the secondary school is the beginning of puberty. A few children have not achieved this biological stage by the school-leaving age of 16 years. There is the inequality between girls and boys in which, at the beginning, girls have an advantage of almost two years. For many it is a period of rapid physical growth, the secondary-school period enclosing the "adolescent spurt". Girls have their peak rate of growth between 12 and 13 and have achieved maximum height (plus or minus 13 months) at $16\frac{1}{4}$ years. Boys, whose peak rate of growth is later and occurs between 14 and 15 years, are able to overtake girls as regards height and do not achieve mature stature until $17\frac{3}{4}$ years (plus or minus 10 months).[4]

The social class differences are likely to affect the general response to education and the time of school leaving, and there are a variety of factors related to home neighbourhood, family circumstances and attendance at particular schools, which can increase expectation of becoming delinquent.

School, School-Leaving and Afterwards

At some stage, pupils in secondary schools are divided up according to a judgement of their capacity for a subsequent higher education. Some are expected to leave at the statutory age of sixteen, with or without one of two possible kinds of examination qualifications: G.C.E. "O" levels or C.S.E. A proportion of the pupils who take examinations stay on at school for "A" level examinations, and of these

---

[3] J. H. Kahn and J. P. Nursten, *Am. J. Orthopsychiatry* **32**, 708 (1962).

[4] See Tables 1 and 2, pp. 156, 157.

there is a further selection of those who continue to some kind of higher education.[5]

In many cases, the decision for a continuing education is made early in secondary school, either in the home, or in the school, or in both. In other cases, the decision rests on chance factors related to the initiative of parents, the personal interests of teachers, the distinctive organization of particular schools, and on changes in public policy. For instance, in the first year of implementation of ROSLA (Raising of the School-Leaving Age), the number of all children leaving school with no examination qualification whatever (i.e. not even one C.S.E.) dropped dramatically from 40 per cent to 20 per cent.

Comprehensive education largely remains more of an ideal (or ideology) than a reality. Sorting out begins early. Some schools stream children on entry on the basis of their primary school reports. In these schools, the syllabuses, and later the curriculum, tend to be different for the different streams. Others have mixed-ability classes for the first two or three years; but many of these put children into "sets", according to their attainment, for individual subjects, especially for Mathematics and Languages. Mixed-ability teaching makes heavy demands on the teacher, in the organization and evaluation of the children's work, and presents problems of discipline. Where it is enthusiastically believed in, it produces examination results that compare well with those from streamed classes, but its benefits seem to be more social than educational.[6]

In the fourth and fifth years, children will take options, which may or may not lead to examination qualifications. The options will probably be presented in groupings of subjects, from which only one group may be chosen. It can, for instance, be impossible to combine Physics and Woodwork. At this stage, parents will usually be offered an interview, and children "counselled" into a "suitable" choice of options. In mixed schools, there is a tendency for girls to "choose" subjects like Home Economics and Biology rather than Mathematics and Physics.

Children may be placed into "O" level or C.S.E. streams, with no opportunity for themselves or their parents to query the decisions. When the "O" level hurdle has been passed or failed, entry into the Sixth Form may be strictly on the basis of minimum examination qualifications, and pupils must follow "A" level courses prescribed by their previous attainments. Some schools, however, allow virtually unrestricted entry into the Sixth Form, allowing a second chance at "O" levels, and even CSEs, or perhaps a first chance for late developers.

How much parents are aware of the many selections which take place, and the possible consequences for the child's adult life, will depend very much on their own social and educational background. The "articulate" parents will be able to query decisions in terms that are acceptable to the schools. For those who are not even aware that decisions *can* be queried, choices are made by default.

---

[5] At the time of writing, there is much discussion of the possibilities of a common examination for all children at 16, and of the replacement of G.C.E. "O" and "A" levels by "N" (normal) and "F" (further) levels. The aim is to reduce early specialization, while still offering some studies in depth in the Sixth Form.

[6] See Hunter Davis, *The Creighton Report*, Hamish Hamilton 1976.

Burden of Fulfilment

Those pupils who from the start are expected to have their sights directed to some kind of higher education, have to face immediate burdens for a long-term fulfilment. There are examinations ahead, and a good deal more is expected in the way of homework. There is an expectation that these pupils have their own motivation for school work. This is difficult to maintain without the kind of support and valuation of education which is usually taken for granted in the middle-class section of the community.

If children from homes hostile to the values of education find their way into academic streams, they either have to accept the ethos of the school (with the consequence of possible alienation from the home background) or, by rejecting the school's values, place themselves in peer groups which are likely to be seen as "anti-school" by both children and teachers.[7]

Economic Consideration

A separation takes place at the statutory school-leaving age, where some young people find occupation (or gain the status of being unemployed) while others continue at school. The former have high wages (or receive unemployment pay, or supplementary benefit) which they do not necessarily pass on as contributions to the home finance. Also, in the evenings and weekends, their time is at their own disposal.

Those who remain at school, have less time, and less money, of their own. They may feel they are a financial burden to their parents, who are expected to provide school uniforms and the money for extracurricular interests. This can only be sustained by those (parents and children alike) who can forgo immediate satisfaction.[8] Moreover, those who choose the academic route can no longer count on an ultimate financial advantage—the rapidly shifting balance between pay levels in industry (at the shop floor and in management) and in the various professions, makes it difficult to calculate in advance where financial advantage may eventually lie.

Those to whom academic work has a self-evident value may feel that these considerations do not apply. It is too much, however, to expect that this high valuation of work satisfaction should be shared by all. In recent years the "caring" professions have officially shown themselves to be conscious of comparisons of pay vis-à-vis other occupations, and have ceased to be content merely with an image of dedication to a job.

Problems of Discipline

The later years of secondary school life bring problems of discipline. Teachers control their classes by the consent and acceptance by the pupils of their role and

[7] Jackson and Marsden, *Education and the Working Class*, Pelican, 1966.
[8] Educational grants go some of the way towards meeting this problem, but, in common with other discretionary grants, these may be withdrawn in periods of financial stringency.

status, and, to a large extent, this is given. At all stages of school life, however, there are some children who have derived no sense of identification with school life. These children, who have no reason to accept the general standards of the school, place themselves outside the ordinary observance of the teacher's instructions. In dealing with them, teachers are deprived of the support which originally comes from the child's deference to their impersonal role. They now have to fall back upon the resources of their own personality, and, in this case, have either to help the child to incorporate something entirely new into their personality, or to exclude them from the class.

This problem becomes intensified in the last years of the secondary school if the education should seem to be irrelevant to the young person's life. It becomes almost an impossibility for a teacher to control a class of unwilling pupils when they are equals in size. Where adolescent boys and girls would accept discipline in a factory from someone who is teaching them a job which they want to learn, the remedy for the problem might seem at first sight to be a return to earlier school leaving. A better remedy would be to modify the educational process in such a way that the children of average, and lower than average, intellectual capacity can be accepted at their own level, and be provided with educational aims that were not originally formulated for another category of children.

Mutual rejection of standards as regards school and home is less likely to happen when the teacher can take a part in community activities of the locality of the school, and where teachers have not separated their own selves from the ideology of their home of origin during the process of education. Respect for different ideologies is more possible when there is contact and continuity. The problem of division of culture between home and school becomes even more complicated at this stage when, with the beginning of adolescence, the young people develop a culture of their own.

Need for New Curricula

One wonders how far progress has been made in the provision of appropriate curricula for the needs of young people at different ages, different levels of intelligence, and in different social settings, and to what extent the educational process can be created anew as a joint adventure during every contact between teacher and pupil.

Margaret Miles, writing in 1963 in anticipation of ROSLA, stated:[9] "It is now apparent that the smallness of the proportion of boys and girls formerly considered capable of advanced work was due not to lack of talent but the lack of opportunity." She adds, however, that there are disturbing aspects which have already become evident, and that in this case:

"When all young people of 11 to 15 or 16 are together in the same sort of school they are expected to conform to a code which formerly applied only to about one-fifth of them. The pupils at the pre-1944 secondary schools were, as we have seen, all 'willing' pupils, but the pupils in the post-1944 secondary schools

[9] *Bulletin of the British Psychological Society*, July, 1963.

are there for the most part because they have got to be. The majority are glad of the opportunity, but there is bound to be a minority of boys and girls who reject the school uniform and all it stands for, are longing to leave, refuse to do homework and so on. A very small percentage of these unwilling secondary school pupils make demands and cause anxiety out of all proportion to their numbers..."

We cannot escape the obligation to provide the best education for all children of all levels of intelligence and all kinds of social background. To do this means that the teachers will be facing demands of an unprecedented nature. The educational provision which they have been trained to give becomes inappropriate, and the type of education that must replace it has yet to be created. Teachers need to have some renewal from professional training sources and, in addition, they will need support from the professional staff of the School Psychological Service and Child Guidance Clinic for the problems that are inevitable.

Crises

School entry, change of school, and school leaving are episodes which mark the transition between developmental stages or levels of functioning. These may appear as crisis events. When the outcome is favourable the episodes mark the attainment of new levels of capacity. Adverse effects, however, may appear as regression to earlier levels.

Failures of school attendance are discussed elsewhere under the heading "School Phobia" or "School Refusal".[10]

The lengthening of school life for the whole population has created new problems which are related to the issue of compulsion. From the earliest years of universal education it was considered necessary to enforce participation in a service provided for the benefit of the child population. Although, in most cases, school attendance is now a willing acceptance of provision offered by the community for its individual members, there are many instances when the whole force of the law has had to be brought to bear upon those who would otherwise refuse participation. If children truant, or if the parents withdraw them from school attendance, prosecution can take place; and in the last resort the child can be taken from its parents into the care of the local authority which presumably will ensure school attendance. Illness is an "excuse," and some forms of school refusal fit into a medical or psychiatric framework which allows for treatment to be offered. Thus, a child not attending school must either be ill or breaking the law. The few exceptions are those where the parents are making some adequate alternative arrangements for the child's education.

Limits to Power of Compulsion

The extension of universal education into adolescent years was intended to give the total population the benefits that some of the more favoured sections of the community had been able to obtain privately or through willing and joint partici-

[10] J. H. Kahn and J. P. Nursten, *Unwillingly to School*, 3rd ed., Pergamon Press, 1980.

pation with the local education authority. Those who continued their education into the later teenage years were a volunteer minority. The school could create a framework of its own choice for those pupils, and any who did not fit into that framework could remove themselves or be removed. When this kind of educational provision was made generally available, it became necessary to recognize that there are practical limits to compulsion. If a boy or girl of 15 or 16 years rebels against school life, and does not attend, there should be more alternatives than to be categorized either as delinquent or ill. The dilemma of those representing the community is real, because it may be felt that those who are most in need of opportunities to mature in an educational setting may be the very ones who would wish to withdraw early into an external world of work and pleasure in circumstances where they could become exploited or join the exploiters.

Educational Misfits

It is no use harking back nostalgically to the years of earlier school leaving, even for young people who have achieved an apparent maturity which makes school attendance seem incongruous. Such maturities may be precarious, and some such pupils, disruptive as they may be, are vulnerable sexually and in their relationship to the law.

Numbers are so great, that Education Authorities have been compelled to make special provision at secondary-school stage for those who opt out or who are disruptive.

The ILEA, for example, allocated the sum of £1,600,000 in 1978 for "positive rather than negative educational solutions" although, they stated, "it may still be necessary for schools to suspend some of the most disruptive pupils."[11]

"Educational Guidance Centres" have been provided for each geographical division, well staffed, and intended for pupils who have opted out. "Support Units" (a name chosen in preference to "Disruptive Centres"!) are distributed less uniformly, and depend upon local initiative, and on head teachers' perception of need. Money, staffing and accommodation have been allocated, (and, sometimes, actually provided!) but what remains to be seen is whether there is any relevant theory, and practical skill, for the understanding of the problems and for the tasks involved.

Alongside this official provision, there is a free-school movement (not quite amounting to "de-schooling") in which there are more flexible school hours and curriculum, and which draw from the neighbouring culture. In some cases parents find the funds for the teachers and materials, and some have been given official recognition and support by the Local Education Authority.[12]

Images of the Pupil Role

The next chapter will deal with adolescence, but it is unrealistic to separate consideration of school life from the personal and social issues of the adolescent stage.

[11] ILEA Report to Education Committee Schools Subcommittee, 1979.
[12] E. Midwinter, *Education and the Community*, Allen and Unwin, 1975.

The traditional image of the pupil role is that of acceptance of the rules of school and of the curriculum. Those who rebelled against either of these were looked upon as presenting problems to be dealt with individually, either by treatment or by measures intended to enforce the rules. Even "opting out" was thought of in terms of personal history.

When a large number of pupils share a neighbourhood or peer-group common culture, individual measures are not only likely to be unsuccessful, they are inappropriate. These problems have always existed, but the new feature in the lengthening of school life is that pupils may identify themselves with an external adolescent culture, and some have gone beyond that and have competently entered an adult world.

Some post-school young people "drop-out" from a social system with which they refuse to identify. Some, who pass on to further education, or find jobs, carry their rebellion, powerfully, into their student or occupational life.

What is new is the *effective* rebellion of pupils in ordinary schools—even if it appears to be more a matter of individuals than of organizations. There is now a problem of considerable size, of boys and girls, from the earliest years of secondary school, where some are disruptive, some merely absent themselves, and some find themselves in personal turmoil and confusion. The problem is both individual and collective. It is a problem for teachers who cannot reach something which does not appear to be a problem to the pupil; it is a problem to parents who see a child deviating from "normal" pathways to stable adulthood, which they themselves had never questioned; and it is a problem for the Education Authority (and the community) which has the responsibility for providing education and which has an obligation to make it compulsory up to the age of 16.

It may be of comfort to know that some children opt out and then find their own way back to education in their late teens, early twenties or even later.

For many, however, there is no road back; and some, for whom even a coherent subculture is no protection, are personal casualties.

16

Adolescence

ADOLESCENCE is the interval between childhood and adult life. There are biological, social and cultural boundaries between the two stages. Puberty is the biological dividing line; cultural and social aspects of adolescence refer to the status and role of the young person in society.

Transitional Stage: Social Implications

In countries or cultures where the technical aspects of living are comparatively simple, puberty signals an abrupt passing from childhood to adult life. The transition may be marked by some initiation ceremony of varying degrees of importance. There is no in-between period. After the ceremony, the young person has the full privileges and obligations of manhood or womanhood. Those who "fail" the initiation tests are doomed to remain children and not marry. In some other cultures there are a succession of in-between stages, each with a well defined role. It can be an advantage for young people to know exactly what is expected of them at each stage, but those who are deviant and whose progress either has been retarded or has taken a different direction, are unable to fill expectations. They may find no place at all in their community.

Lengthening of Preparatory Stages for Adult Role

In cultures characterized by more complicated technical processes of living, there is a need for longer preparation for adult life. With each advance of available knowledge, occupations become more specialized and need longer training. There is therefore a tendency towards a lengthening of the period between the stage when the child has reached adult capacities and that in which the ability or permission to put those capacities into operation.

Puberty comes at a definite point in the life of each individual, although the time varies from one individual to another. It is the stage when the sexual organs in the male and female begin to carry fertile cells, one of which can unite with a corresponding cell from the reproductive organs of a member of the opposite sex.

The period of adolescence includes the various social and cultural changes, and the boundaries are uncertain because the different functions of adult life require

152

different qualities. The laws and customs which regulate the various aspects of living activities have developed independently of one another. It is not permissible in the U.K. to marry before the age of 16, whatever the age might be when procreation can begin. Marriage has obligations over and above the procreation of children. It is assumed that children need a family, and that the parents of children need to have sufficient maturity to take on family responsibility.

The Family Law Reform Act of 1969 brought the age of majority down from 21 to 18 years. Young people have the vote, the capacity to enter into agreements involving financial obligations, and the freedom to marry without having to seek parental consent, at the age of 18.

With regard to the criminal law, there have been considerable alterations in the age at which young people are answerable to the courts for their offences. The changes were foreshadowed in the White Paper of 1968 *Children in Trouble* (Command 3601) and were embodied in the Children and Young Persons Act, 1969. The Children's Act of 1975 added some restrictions on removal from care. The age of criminal responsibility remains at the age of 10 and in this respect there is no change from the Children and Young Persons Act, 1963, notwithstanding that the Ingleby Report, on which this Act was based, had recommended the raising of the age of criminal liability to 12 years. There is, however, a change to the effect that children between the age of 10 and 14 will not be subject to prosecution but at the time of writing this section has not been brought into operation. Up to the age of 14, children can be brought before the court under "Care Proceedings" and, over the age of 14, under "Criminal Proceedings". Further details of the current legislation are to be found in the Home Office *Guide to the Children and Young Persons Act, 1969*, and more detailed interpretations of the present position with regard to care proceedings are given by Watson[1] and by Feldman[2].

The most radical change is that no person may be charged with an offence, except homicide, "by reason of having done or omitted while he was a child", i.e. under the age of 14 years. At intervals, the age at which the child will be excluded from criminal jurisdiction will be raised to the twelfth birthday and then successively to the thirteenth and fourteenth birthdays. In effect, a good deal of the responsibility of children who formerly would have been regarded as offenders has been transferred to the Social Work Departments of local authorities, either through supervision orders or care orders. It will have to be seen whether committal to care with placing in "Community Homes" will be regarded by the public as being different from former placement in remand homes or approved schools.

Although the name "Approved School" has disappeared, "Community Homes", "Community Schools" and "Assessment Centres" still carry some of the old image, and little has been done to implement the intention to remove the differentiation between offenders and those in need of care as a beneficial provision. From another viewpoint, there has been criticism from the Bench that the Juvenile Court has no further power over a young person who continues to offend after already having been placed in care.

[1] J. Watson, *The Juvenile Court, 1970*, Shaw & Sons.
[2] L. Feldman, *Care Proceedings*, Oyez, 1978.

Occupational Marks of Maturity

Entry into occupational life depends upon the degree of training necessary for a particular job. In some cases, the work itself is the training, and we should not ignore the fact that some so-called unskilled jobs require the acquisition of a great deal of scarcely verbalized instruction ("Steady there, Bill!"). In other cases there is a formal apprenticeship, after which the individual ranks as a skilled worker, who, in later years, speaks with pride of the period of training. Others again continue their education throughout adolescence and early adult life, preparing for traditional professional jobs, or for some occupations which have not yet fully come into existence. At one time, maximum skill was acquired early in occupational life, and promotion merely marked extensions of responsibility. Now, the learning process, formerly an adolescent experience, continues in many occupations into adult life. For occupational purposes, transition from adolescence to adulthood varies according to the image of the job.

Changing Fashions

The uncertainty of the functional boundaries of adolescence is matched by an alteration of the custom of marking out periods of life by the assumption of different styles of clothing. Earlier in this century a young girl would "put up" her hair at about the age of 18 years to signify that her girlhood or adolescence was over, and that womanhood had begun. A young boy indicated his manhood by wearing long trousers for the first time.

At the present time, women's hairstyles bridge the decades, but there may be some styles which teenage girls may adopt collectively to assert a coherence in the social life of adolescents as a special group—more than children, and consciously separate from the adult population. Adult fashions are adapted for the adolescent mass market, and, conversely, the experimental creations that come from the adolescent's own culture penetrate the world of high fashion.

Yet, still within this changing scene, there are some subtle indications of what is appropriate to children, to adolescents and to adults.

Maturational Sequence

Physical and sexual aspects of maturation have variations from individual to individual; and, on average, girls mature earlier than boys. The accompanying tables (pp. 156, 157) show that the reaching of a particular chronological age, between, say, 9 and 18 years, in itself gives no indication of the details of maturation to be expected.

Physical Growth

Physically, adolescence is a period of rapid growth which is sometimes associated with enormous appetite. Some girls try to curb their appetite, and "diet" because of the fear of becoming too fat. Sometimes this is because they seem to wish to delay their physical development and remain child-like. Some girls become self-conscious about the development of their breasts, and acquire a stoop which conceals them. There are others, however, for whom the mature figure cannot come too soon.

Obesity is a health problem in itself at all ages, and recent studies have postulated a relationship between the number of fat cells which become established during infancy, and the tendency to obesity throughout adult life. There are psychological aspects of obesity connected with the part that feeding plays in emotional satisfaction in the mind of the feeder and the fed. Some people eat when they are anxious, and some when they are depressed. To some, eating represents the goodness of maternal care.

There is yet another aspect of the effect of the shape of the fat deposits on the human frame, viz. the relationship to sexuality. Female sexuality is given emphasis in illustrations which focus on breasts and buttocks. However, the stereotype of what is considered to be sexually attractive is *either* fatness *or* thinness, and varies from country to country, and from generation to generation within the same country.

There is a more hidden connection of body shape with fantasies regarding pregnancy. The condition known as "anorexia nervosa" (refusal of food to the point of actual starvation) has serious physical consequences, sometimes fatal. This may be an outcome of fears regarding the nature of sexual identity.

Menstruation; Seminal Emissions

Physical growth includes the maturation of primary sexual organs, which are the testicles in the boy and the ovaries in the girl. Secondary sexual characteristics include the growth of hair around the genital organs and under the armpits in both sexes, and on the chest and face in young boys. There are changes in the shape of the breasts and hips in girls; in young boys the tone of the voice alters along with visible changes in the shape of the larynx.

All these changes may be welcomed by some adolescents who look upon them as a sign of maturity, but many are unprepared for a change which needs the acquisition of a new image of the self. The rapid physical growth gives a young person a body with which he or she is unfamiliar. The long limbs need a new kind of posture or balance; and, therefore, young people often appear to be ungainly, not knowing what to do with their arms and legs. Young girls are sometimes disturbed by the growing protuberance under the nipples, and many a girl is taken to the family doctor in the belief that there is some tumour developing when one breast develops a little in advance of the other. The boy whose voice is changing may be taken by surprise by the unfamiliar noise which comes from somewhere in his body, and his voice may alternate unpredictably between high-pitched and gruff sounds.

Sexual capacity can be a source of pride or anxiety.

When a girl reaches puberty the ovaries begin to discharge fertile egg cells. One passes each month from an ovary, which is within the abdominal cavity, through one of the channels, called Fallopian tubes, which are at either side of the uterus or womb. Meanwhile the lining of the uterus develops an increased blood supply and enlarges in preparation for the supplies that would be necessary if the egg cell

TABLE 1
Normal Maturational Sequence in Boys

Phase	Appearance of sexual characteristics	Average ages	Age range*
Childhood through pre-adolescence	*Testes* and *Penis* have not grown since infancy; no *Pubic Hair*; growth in *Height* constant. No spurt.	—	—
Early- A D	*Testes* begin to increase in size; *Scrotum* grows, skin reddens and becomes coarser; *Penis* follows with growth in length and circumference; no true *Pubic Hair*, may have down.	12–13 years	10–15 years
Mid- O L E S C E	*Pubic Hair*—pigmented, coarse and straight at base of penis becoming progressively more curled and profuse, forming at first an inverse triangle and subsequently extends up to embilicas; *Axillary Hair* starts after pubic hair; *Penis* and *Testes* continue growing; *Scrotum* becomes larger, pigmented and sculptured; marked spurt of growth in *Height*, with maximum increment about time pubic hair first develops and decelerates by time fully established; *Prostate and seminal vesicles* mature, spontaneous or induced *Emissions* follow but *Spermatozoa* inadequate in number and motility (adolescent sterility); *Voice* begins to change as *Larynx* enlarges.	13–16 years	11–18 years
Late- N C E	*Facial* and *Body Hair* appear and spread; *Pubic* and *Axillary Hair* become denser; *Voice* deepens; *Testes* and *Penis* continue to grow; *Emission*—has adequate number of motile *Spermatozoa* for fertility. Growth in *Height* gradually decelerates, 98% mature stature by 17¾ yrs ± 10 mo; Indentation of frontal *Hair Line*.	16–18 years	14–20 years
Post-adolescence to adult	Mature—full development of *Primary* and *Secondary* sex characteristics; *Muscles* and *Hirsutism* may continue increasing.	onset 18–20 years	onset 16–21 years

* Normal range was accepted as (80% of cases) 1st to 9th decile.

should become fertilized by spermatoza from the male. When fertilization does not take place this preparatory lining is shed, and this is menstruation.

Menstruation can occur to some girls without previous warning, and may give rise to alarm, the loss of blood causing a fear that some internal part has been damaged. A girl without sexual knowledge is not without sexual thoughts; and feelings of guilt are attached the process of menstruation. Such a girl, who tells her mother anxiously about the flow of blood, is likely to have a mother who is still, even at that stage, unable to give her any satisfactory explanation. Quite frequently the response of the mother is in these exact words "This will happen once a month, and now you must keep away from boys." The lack of explanation increases the fears, and peculiar fantasies may be built up regarding the relationships between the

TABLE 2
Normal Maturational Sequence in Girls

Phase		Appearance of sexual characteristics	Average ages	Age range*
Childhood through pre-adolescence		No *Pubic Hair*; Breasts are flat; *Growth* in height is constant, no spurt.	—	—
Early-	A D	Rounding of *Hips*; *Breasts* and nipples are elevated to form *Bud* stage; no true *Pubic Hair*, may have down.	10–11 years	9–14 years
Mid-	O L E S C E	*Pubic Hair*—pigmented, coarse, straight primarily along labia but progressively curled and spreads over mons and becomes profuse with an inverse triangular pattern; *Axillary Hair* starts after pubic hair; marked *Growth* spurt with maximum *Height* increment 18 months before menarche; *Menarche*—Labia becomes enlarged, *Vaginal Secretion* becomes acid; *Breast*—areola and nipple elevated to form primary breast.	11–14 years	10–16 years
Late-	N C E	*Axillary Hair* in moderate quantity; *Pubic Hair* fully developed; *Breasts*, fill out forming adult type configuration; *Menstruation* well established; *Growth* in height is decelerated, ceases at $16\frac{1}{4} \pm 13$ mo.	14–16 years	13–18 years
Post-adolescence to adult		Further growth of *Axillary Hair*; *Breasts* fully developed.	onset 16–18 years	onset 15–19 years

* Normal range was accepted as (80% of cases) 1st to 9th decile.

two sexes. There may be a dread of the most ordinary contact in games or at dances.

Even in sophisticated circles, menstruation is thought of as an inconvenience (the curse). With a literature of its own, it is not only regarded as the focus of fantasies and folklore, but also as an expression of the self.[3]

Most girls, however, have been prepared well in advance, and are able to look forward to menstruation, with pride, as a badge of womanhood.

The boy has two testicles in a bag called the scrotum close to the penis. During the course of an individual's embryonic development the testicles are within the abdomen in a place comparable with that of the ovaries in the girl. During intra-uterine growth of the infant male, or sometimes later, the testicles descend from the abdominal cavity into the scrotum, but after descent each is still connected by a

[3] P. Shuttle and P. Redgrave, *The Wise Wound: Menstruation and Everywoman*, Gollancz, 1978.

tube which has accompanied the testicles through a channel (inguinal canal) in the groin, and these tubes link up at the level of the prostate gland at the base of the bladder with the urethra which is the passage carrying the urine from the bladder through the penis. Thus the passage through the penis carries urine during the emptying of the bladder, and semen which is produced by the testicles. Ejaculation occurs as a result of sexual excitation, and this is usually preceded by erection of the penis which gives the firmness that allows the penis to penetrate into the female passage (vagina) when sexual intercourse takes place. With the emission of semen the erection usually subsides.

Apart from sexual intercourse, emissions of semen can occur as a result of manual stimulation of the penis (masturbation), or as a result of fantasies. These may occur spontaneously in dreams, or sometimes they may be deliberately stimulated by the choice of erotic reading material, erotic pictures, or by recollections of previous experiences. An emission gives relief to sexual tension and is pleasurable.

Sometimes one or both testicles fails to descend, and this may call for medical or surgical treatment. Once again it is necessary to call attention to unfounded fears that an anomaly is connected with sexual "transgression" such as masturbation.

Sexual activity in both sexes follows a pattern of awareness of a need which is accompanied by tension and the seeking of relief for that tension. Even in the satisfaction of the need there is, however, an overwhelming quality about the experience. Sensations that are unusually intense are often associated with anxiety. Satisfaction ordinarily relieves the anxiety, but sometimes the anxiety outlasts the physical relief. This is a pattern which has been previously noted in the intensity of hunger and its satisfaction, and in the tension of a full bowel or bladder and the release of that tension in vacuation. The release can have a pleasure of its own, but, wherever an essential biological activity has been associated with prohibitions and restrictions, it becomes linked with ideas of guilt. Satisfactions are then incomplete. There are instances where satisfaction is so bound up with guilt that an individual may be unable to search for satisfaction except in circumstances which increase guilt.

A generation is growing up which is freer from guilt than previous ones, but, at the same time, boys and girls are exposed more and more to excitation of their developing sexuality. Many young boys and girls feel called upon to discuss and to experience some forms of sexual activity before they are emotionally prepared, and many seem just as vulnerable as their predecessors to the anxiety which is its accompaniment.

There is a good deal of inconsistency about parental and social attitudes to menstruation and seminal emissions. Some superstitions and irrational attitudes continue through the generations. There is folklore regarding menstruation which is associated with fears of contamination. In many cultures, women who are menstruating are compelled to keep themselves apart from the rest of the family, and are not allowed to touch any food that has been prepared for others. Many people in our own culture believe that it is dangerous for a menstruating woman to wash her hair or have a bath. Such prohibitions have no rational foundation, but are part of the embarrassment concerning the physical events which call attention to the sexual role.

Parents are equally embarrassed with regard to their sons if the bedclothes become contaminated with seminal emissions. Some boys and some parents regard emissions as something bad; they are unable to accept them as part of the normal process of growing up.

Physical Growth and Maturation

Generally, physical growth reaches its height in early adolescence, and the maximum seems to be reached at an earlier age than previously, perhaps because the better general standard of diet allows individuals to get their growing done earlier. Many young boys and girls approach their maximum height at the age of 14 or 15, but some do their growing at a later stage, up to 18 or 19 or even 20 years.

Much of the growing takes place in the long bones, particularly of the legs, and the growing process occurs in the cartilage which divides the shaft of the bone (diaphysis) from the two ends (epiphyses). Growth of these bones finally ceases when the last union of bone with bone takes place, replacing the cartilage; the vertebral column may continue to grow up to and sometimes after the age of 20 years by addition of bone to bone on the upper and lower surfaces of the vertebrae.

Nutrition and Health

Some illnesses have had a special association with adolescence. Tuberculosis, which formerly had a peak incidence in the late teens, is now rare, and is more responsive to treatment when it does occur. A severe form of anaemia used to be prevalent in young girls, perhaps because of the general standard of nutrition which was insufficient for the replacement of blood lost during menstruation. This kind of anaemia is uncommon now, but minor degrees of haemoglobin deficiency still occur. Where diet is inadequate, menstrual loss is still a significant factor in the general level of the blood count, and textbooks record a different "normal" blood count for women than for men. In many homes, a woman's diet was, traditionally, less substantial than that of the menfolk and, in addition, the loss of blood from the monthly flow and the extra demands on the body during pregnancies and lactation were not made up. At the present time, with increased care and higher living standards, men and women have similar "average" blood counts.

In some medical textbooks different norms for the two sexes are still specified. Similarly, physiology textbooks have described different types of respiration in men and women. Masculine respiration was described as "thoraco-abdominal", the muscles of the chest and abdomen moving with each breath. Feminine respiration was described as "thoracic", i.e. movements restricted to the muscles of the chest. It would appear that these physiologists had never seen a woman without her corsets!

Intellectual Maturation

The intellectual capacity of the individual is assumed to reach a maximum level during the period of adolescence for the purpose of calculation of many intelligence tests. Measurable growth of intelligence seems to cease in some individuals at an age between fourteen and sixteen years, but in some individuals measurable growth continues up to the age of eighteen or later. Perhaps there has been a false analogy of intelligence with height, and views about the cessation of intellectual growth at adolescence are not valid. It is recognized that some limitations which were formerly thought of as being an unalterable inherent quality are instead the product of the original potential together with the cultural experience. Growth is likely to finish early when there is cultural deprivation, and may be resumed if provision can be made of intellectual experiences that previously were missing. Thus it is possible to justify the continuation of education of young people at all levels of intelligence, but this would need the working out of educational principles which take into account the different needs and the different capacities of assimilation in different groups of young people. We must give a kind of education which is related to the personality of the individual and the mental framework which already exists. It is no use giving at any one time more than can be taken in at that time.

Here we can recall one of the propositions of Mayman, Schafer and Rapaport quoted in Chapter 14 which emphasizes that nothing can be absorbed unless it can be organized into a frame of reference which already exists, and that the assimilation of new experience occurs within the limits of emotional receptivity and endowment. Piaget makes the same point.

Leaving School

Separation of individuals into different groups has already occurred within the educational setting. Children are either in different kinds of secondary school or different types of class within the same school. A further separation occurs when some children leave school at the age of 16 years, and begin work, while others continue to attend school. Educational differences lead to social differences.

There is a difference between the kind of life of school leavers and of those who continue their education. Some young people find support for their educational life in the common purpose that exists in their own immediate neighbourhood, and are scarcely aware of the other world which has a different set of values. It is more difficult where there are neighbours or even other members of the same family who are enjoying a life which has more immediate satisfactions.

Leisure and Pleasure

The high earnings and leisure activities of the early school leaver may not be an undiluted satisfaction. The esteem that leaders of the community attach to intellectual ability and prolonged education, may give a feeling of unworthiness to those whose intellectual level makes them unsuitable for academic work. There is continued emphasis on educational opportunities, and there is an attempt to provide more efficient selection of a larger number of young people for higher education. Even although it is recognized that innate intelligence levels differ, there is an implication that those who are not selected have failed a test, and are somehow or other responsible for the failure. We must recognize that, even with an improvement in secondary-school education and with an increase in the number of places in tertiary education (Universities, Polytechnics and Colleges of Further Education), the majority of the population will not be able to be accepted for the highly valued experience of student life.

If this majority continues to be impressed with its inferiority, it cannot be surprising that the seeking of any pleasure that is available sometimes has an arrogant attitude. It is possible that one of the by-products of the particular emphasis on equality of opportunity in education is that there is a harmful effect when it is also implied that this equality of opportunity confirms the inferiority of those who are unable to benefit by it.

Further Education and Occupation

The recent cut-back in places for the education of teachers is symptomatic of a cut-back in expansion in higher education. For nearly a generation, education had taken place against a background of a continually expanding provision for tertiary education. This expansion has now come to an end (temporarily?).

The sharp distinction between academic and other forms of occupation has been blunted in the past by the voluntary "dropping-out" of young people with high educational qualifications, but who were able to return later, by choice, to the academic field. One could assume that the expansion of education (and thus of the academic professions) would make this possible. When expansion comes to an end, the "drop-outs", "push-outs", and those who do not find jobs, do not have a second chance.

Brief periods of so-called full employment should not divert attention from the perpetual problem of the jobless. There are young people whose fate it is to leave school without any reasonable prospect of a job. The accident of living in a particular town, or a particular region, or of being a member of a disadvantaged section of the community, may leave some young people with a well justified sense of unfairness, which will accompany them for the rest of their lives.

From the young persons' point of view, the way in which they are received into a job is very important. The change of status and of customs involved in passing from sheltered school-life to the more robust life of office or factory can be very disturbing for some. Many large firms arrange for a formal introduction of new employees, and for training schemes which make the role quite clear. In others, there are rivalries between old employees and a newcomer which are similar to those in a family when a new baby arrives. The old employees rag the newcomer, sometimes good-humouredly, and occasionally in a very cruel way. The newcomer who is able to "take" the ragging is readily accepted, but there are some who feel to be on the outside of the group, and who suffer very severe anxiety and distress.

Conflicts in the Home

Emotionally, adolescence is a disturbing stage. There are conflicts within the individual, and between the young person and the adult world. At one moment there is the wish to be independent, and to establish one's self as an adult, and, at another time, the wish to retain all the privileges of childhood. At some points of stress (and points of stress occur whenever there is a change of status), there is a need to go back, or regress, even further. At one moment behaviour is mature and responsible, and at another moment there can be tantrums resembling those of infancy.

There are similarly conflicting wishes within the parent, who may say to the child "Now you must take grown-up responsibility", and yet still wishes to guard against the danger that comes from bad companions, sexual activity and the choice of unsuitable jobs. The wish to see the child as a responsible separate individual is incompatible with the simultaneous wish to protect and to keep control.

Instability During Transition

Emotional instability in adolescence is partly due to the contradictory wishes of the individual. Many disturbances which, in an adult would be regarded as a symptom of mental illness, occur in the normal range of life of young people. At the same time, adolescents are vulnerable to criticism and sarcasm, and feel that even when being accepted, the acceptance is of no value because it is given on conditions. There is a special need during adolescence to be treated as potentially the equal of adults. There is the need for respect as individuals.

It is difficult to find the balance between providing guidelines on one hand and freedom on the other. One cannot treat the adolescent as an adult all the time. The feelings of the adult provide an even greater difficulty: few can retain within themselves the memory of the intensity and depth of turmoil in their own lives, and are inclined to measure present distress by the standard of a "mature" sense of proportion.

Responsibility is not something which can be forced on an individual. It is something that can be granted at the moment the child senses it and is ready for it. In some instances we find that when the adult is ready to grant it, it is already too late for the young person to receive it.

Notions of mature male and female roles are subject to change. An adult woman is no longer identified solely through her capacity to carry out the functions of a wife and mother. An adult man no longer has to derive his image more from his job than from his place in the home. Young people are therefore growing into roles which are being restructured. However, no matter what kind of part they will play as adults, they need freedom to rehearse one role after another, without at this stage committing themselves to any particular one.

Throughout adolescence, young people feel uncertain of themselves, and seek reassurance partly by entering into a conformity of standards with others of their age group. They need, in addition, the reassurance of those in authority and of the older ones of their own family that they are valued in the roles for which they are preparing.

Social Attitudes to the Adolescent

Some of the social problems of adolescence are similar to those that exist in any organization when a newcomer enters and seeks the privileges of the established members. Existing members are jealous of the traditions which they have helped to create, and feel that some of the privileges which have been earned over a long period are going to be demanded by the newcomer who has not, as yet, established a right. They also feel that the newcomer may want to alter or destroy that which had previously been created. Clubs protect themselves by selection of membership. A living culture cannot protect itself in this way. It is not possible to stop children from becoming adolescents, and adolescents from becoming adults. Antagonisms between the generations have some justification because, as a result of technical change and changes in education (for which the adult is most responsible), the young person has been brought up with a different set of values from those which the adult experienced.

Conflicts in the Community

The question of authority in the community and in the home over the young adolescent becomes a difficult one because the young person is now becoming equal in size and intelligence (but not in experience). Authority cannot now be enforced either by brute force or by illogical arguments. Authority at this stage is still necessary, but it has to be founded on previous good relationships, and reinforced where necessary by rational explanation. Rebelliousness is almost inevitable. The young people wish to test out the strength of the authority of parents and of the community, and sometimes they find weaknesses. They may also be reassured to find strength. They are attempting to assert their own individuality, and yet there can be uniformity within the adolescent age group, and the protests can fit in with, or be responsible for, particular fashions of the age. Young people may wear outlandish clothes—outlandish by adult standards, but conventional within their own group.

Those who wish to stand out from the crowd when diversity is the norm have to go to the limits of the bizarre: in variegated make-up, colouring, dress and hair styles, as exemplified at the time of writing, by "punk" culture.

Sometimes rebelliousness goes beyond that which can be contained within the ordinary standards of society, and many young people go through a phase of delinquency.

There appears to be a general impression that in this generation adolescence is a more turbulent phase than ever before. It would be more accurate to say that the stage of adolescence, which is the phase between the reaching of adult capacity and adult responsibility, has come to be looked upon as the entitlement of the population as a whole, instead of being restricted to that of the educated minority whose dependence and privilege is traditionally prolonged into adult life.

Jobless school leavers are contrasted with those in work. In large cities, black youth is contrasted with white. At the same time, some of the old divisions of male and female qualities are being upset. The notion that, when disturbed, girls are neurotic and boys are delinquent, no longer holds. Girls are claiming their share of violent behaviour, and neurosis can be recognized in boys. Sexuality has received its due recognition as a practice, not a fantasy; and the Gay Liberation movement challenges the idea that homosexuality is a disorder.

Some young people emphasize the quality of toughness in a stark simplicity of clothing—leather jackets and high boots which have a sexual significance. Others of both sexes wear make-up, their clothes are more fanciful, and the male clothing is feminized. Something that would be indicative of homosexuality in one individual is "fashion" when worn by thousands. The fashion reveals the *latent* homosexuality in the normal individual. In this present age, female fashions have included masculine items for a good many years. A girl may now wear clothes originally designed for the male, and, surprisingly, the result may be an enhancement of the feminity of her appearance. Fashions of long hair, and the use of cosmetics by males, may, in like manner, be not incompatible with masculinity. Unisex is not the absence of sex.

Preparation for Sexual Fulfilment

The young person's entry into adult sexual activity has its conflicts in youth and in the adult community. It is frequently stated that this is a permissive age and that youth receives encouragement for protest, for aggressiveness, and for the free enjoyment of sexuality. The word "permissive" may not always be appropriate because young people do not need to ask permission.

The contraceptive pill has separated the burden (and perhaps the satisfaction) of procreation from the pleasure of sexual union. Familiar addictive drugs, and some new ones, have become available to a population in which young people are prominent, and many adults are hesitant to condemn their use without indisputable proof that they produce irreversible harm. "Sex" and "drugs" are themes which stimulate social excitement and lead some of the adult world to take up an unduly repressive position, while others take up a position at the opposite extreme. Attitudes towards sexual activity and towards drug dependence are a good indicator of the position in which individuals stand in relation to ideas of authority and submission. Extreme permissiveness is the ultimate authoritarianism. It is as if one is saying, "I shall forbid you nothing; and then, whatever you do you will not have been allowed to do anything that I have forbidden".

Drugs, Delinquency and Social Excitement

No civilization has existed without the use of natural or manufactured products which are potentially addictive. Tea, coffee, alcohol and even cocoa provide a sensation of comfort, warmth and the relief of tension. It is something like the primal need of the infant to be fed and comforted, and is summarized in *My Fair Lady*:

> Lots of choc'late for me to eat,
> Lots of coal makin' lots of heat,
> Warm face, warm hands, warm feet,
> Oh, wouldn't it be luverly.[4]

The problem of drug addiction is confused by the attempts to define the behaviour in terms of mental or emotional illness. Delinquency provides another example of the use of a label, applied imprecisely to some kinds of behaviour, becoming regarded as the equivalent of a disease entity. Yet delinquency covers a wide variety

[4] Loewe F. and Lerner A. J., *My Fair Lady*, Chappell. © 1956.

of different acts in different circumstances, carried out by people of different family and personal background and with different kinds of motivation. There is the common characteristic that the law has been broken.

The behaviour of young people is often described in words that are intended to convey a precise meaning but which carry emotional overtones. Sometimes psychiatric and social services are called upon to deal with something that is described as a problem in young people, without having the authorization of a body of knowledge, of valid theories on which to base investigations, and practical methods of treatment. There are even more elusive problems of communication between professional disciplines and the mass media which have their own criteria in the selection of what is newsworthy. The mass media seem, at times, to be nearer to the problems of youth than professional people. These media are more sensitive to areas of excitement, to themes on the fringe of existing knowledge, and to the topics that arouse controversy.

Tolerance to Deviant Behaviour

It therefore follows that newspapers, popular journals, radio and television programmes, and the entertainment industry, find interesting material in the tentative explorations by young people of activities that had previously been forbidden. The use of this material by the "communicators" can serve many purposes. It provides a vicarious satisfaction for those who want to read, or look, but not take part. It may provide a further incentive for the breaking down of yet other taboos. It may *increase* the tolerance of the community to members whose behaviour is "deviant" when the deviancy is relative to cultural factors in the epoch in which people happen to live. It should not, however, be assumed that it is always progress for the community to become more tolerant to some particular aspect of behaviour or item of consumption. Whatever the ethical justification may be, there has always been a section of the community which has presumed to try to impose general limits on habits which they believed to be injurious to those who indulge in them. At the present moment, medical organizations are engaged in the exercise of attempting to *decrease* public tolerance to the practice of smoking tobacco in the form of cigarettes.

Public opinion is not uniform, consistent, or coherent. Some generalizations have wide acceptance, and value judgements are attached to the descriptive words; and categories of young people are created, each with its own image. A stereotype may become associated with a specific hairstyle or style of dress, and the stereotype is then made to represent rebellion, delinquency, promiscuity, and the abuse of drugs. At the other pole, there can be a reversal of values in which the established organization of society is considered to be invariably bad, and where there is a romanticization of rebellion against it.

Exploitation of the Young

These are areas in which youth can be exploited. There is financial exploitation (for example, in the use of drugs and pornography by criminal and by commercial interests). There is also emotional exploitation which can occur with the best of intentions on the part of worthy members of adult society. Many "pillars of the community" have secretly imagined that they alone in the adult world are completely in tune with the young. An inner core of a still living youthful enthusiasm and vitality tells them that the adolescent group is really the generation to which they personally have always belonged. None of us is unbiased, unemotional, or uninvolved in these themes.

Rebellion as an Exploration of Human Potential

Consolation can be found for those who are anxious about the experimentation of the young in the fact that a large majority of young people escape from these experiences unharmed. For some it is a creative exploration of human potentialities, and they are the means by which the standards of culture are altered. Others of these same people, however, become personal casualties.

With regard to sexual activity, there is justifiable protest against some of the repressive attitudes of a previous generation. New methods of contraception have allowed more freedom for the enjoyment of sexual intercourse outside the permanent relationships such as are envisaged in marriage. Many adolescents no longer need to defer the enjoyment of their sexual potential in the fairly long interval between puberty and marriage.

A large number of young people protest against society's rules and have no compunction in breaking the law, and may be instrumental in changing the law. Some pass through a delinquent period as a temporary phase before settling down into "respectable" adult life.

Some young people experiment with the use of drugs, simply because drugs are available and a sensual experience is available for the taking of it. Some of them feel that it heightens their sensitivity to external perceptions and inner fantasy life.

There are, however, young people who try out the experience of freely available sexual activity and, in spite of the availability of contraceptives, some have unwanted pregnancies, some get venereal disease, and some, who begin an association which is intended to be casual, find that one partner has become more involved than the other: contraception is not a protection against a broken heart.

Many young people try out the confrontations with the law, in company with their peers, and a proportion of them acquire criminal records that affect their future.

Amongst the number who experiment with drugs there are those who become hooked and who progress from the use of one drug to the use of others.

Rebellion Carrying Risks of Casualties

The young people of every generation have it in them to challenge the constraints which society (represented by their elders) imposes upon them. There is one thing that the adult world should not do and that is to compel the young to make the challenge for the vicarious satisfaction of those who have already passed through their own youth. After all, it is the young who carry the casualties.

It is one of the duties of the adult to show respect for the young, but it is also the duty of the adult to be adult, and to have adult ideas. The adult should be sensitive to the growth potential of the immature and, at the same time, be able to recognize the value in the immature. There is an immense contribution which the young can make while they are still young, and adolescence is long enough to be a period in its own right. H. W. Maier has called it "adolescenthood",[5] to match "childhood" and "adulthood".

Ego Ideal and Idealism

Adolescence has been described in the preceding section as a focus of conflict, but at the same time, during this period, young people are building into themselves an image of an ideal identity. The label "ego ideal" is applied to a process which is more deliberate and conscious than the infantile introjection of the irrational Superego. The ego ideal can be derived by the taking in of single qualities from a number of people, sometimes making a composite whole, and sometimes containing opposites. The ego ideal can be partly derived from literature or history, and its nature can also depend upon the trends of the moment.

It is a new feature in the life of young people that ideal representations are being found within their own age group. Teenage entertainment stars have an appeal for the teenage population, and, for that matter, an appeal for a wide section of the population of all ages. At least in the entertainment world, the teenage culture seems to be finding general acceptance.

In spite of the materialism and apparent cynicism in many young people, there is often an undercurrent of idealism, and many have much higher standards within themselves than they would be prepared to admit.

They feel underprivileged, and demand freedom and equality for themselves in comparison with adults. Sometimes they are able to direct this attitude into the seeking of freedom and justice for underprivileged members of the community in general. Many young people are willing to work for the right of people who are oppressed, and many have gone to far-off countries to fight for the rights of others. Some find an outlet in working for voluntary organizations which provide for the hungry in other lands. The same young people may occasionally seem selfish, and to view the world as if it were revolving round themselves, and yet often it is during adolescence that the outlook becomes broader, and, for the first time in an individual's life, the feelings of other people are taken into consideration.

Young people may begin to be interested in religion at this time. To some it merely means punishment for such sins as masturbation. Others become concerned with ideas of purpose in mankind and in the universe.

Cultural interests may take a new importance. Poetry, art and music—often of a bewilderingly modern type—maybe a kind of folk-art peculiar to a part of the young person's life. The tastes of young people may seem queer to older generations because each generation builds up its own culture. Unusual clothes and unusual art forms come together, and outlandish rhythms may be nothing more

[5] H. W. Maier, *Social Casework*, Jan., 1965.

than a confirmation to older people that younger ones are now a community in themselves.

Wider social contacts become possible in adolescence, and young people have the freedom to choose their experiences and their friends outside the family circle, and sometimes outside the circles of their own school or work. They may begin to lay the foundations of friendships with members of both sexes, and some of these remain friends for the rest of their lives.

Adolescence is still a period of development, and there are still developmental needs. There is the need for acceptance, there is the need for outlets of expression of the capacity or potential in physical, intellectual and emotional fields, and there is the need for standards with which to conform or against which to rebel.

Each generation of adolescents also provides a means of bringing out new qualities in those who represent the older generation. The young are their inheritors, supplanters, rivals and their future. They also represent, in some sense, the present. It was the older generation who created the jet and the electronic age, but the older generation has spent most of its time in the era before the existence of instruments which have transformed the nature of human activities and human perceptions. The young people have been born into this world, which is their birthright, and therefore it is the old who are the newcomers into it. Youth and age embody in their personalities something of one another, and each is constantly usurping the other's role.

17

Courtship and Marriage

DURING late adolescence and early adult life, new possibilities of interpersonal relationships are opened up. In childhood, the relationship of boy or girl with parents is at an unequal level. The essence of the oedipal situation is the inappropriateness of the assumed relationship between unequals. Both child and parent may attempt to distort the inequality by accepting a "pretend" relationship as if they actually were on the same level. The parent may inflate the child up to adult level, and the child may accept the obligations of this fantasy status. It often happens in such cases that the parent becomes alarmed by the power of the precocious adulthood in their children, and that the children feel overwhelmed by their inadequacy to meet the mature demands that they attempt to make upon their own selves.

During adolescence, when sexual excitement becomes possible with adult potentialities and consequences, young persons still may feel immature compared with the adults upon whom they are dependent. Many of the early feelings are reactivated either in relation to parents, or in relation to other adults who are objects of admiration and sources of identification or of rivalry.

Recapitulations of Early Stages

One can understand these phases of adolescence by comparing them with some of the earlier stages of development. It is almost as if, at each new phase, we have to recapitulate some of the previous stages. Adolescents, beginning to find sexual expression in a fuller way, repeat some of the situations of childhood which were described in terms of the oedipal situation. They re-experience some of the conflicting feelings which existed at the time between self and parents. Sometimes they act out the drama with other people instead of parents, idealizing some individuals, condemning others outright, as if unable to see individuals as complete persons with strength and weakness, goodness and badness. They have to abstract one particular quality from each, idealize it, and allow that one quality to represent a whole person. Most people pass through phases such as this, but some remain in this adolescent stage even after reaching adult life. All of us retain *something* of this stage, in our fantasies at least, and get enjoyment from the love stories which preserve the idea of the romantic love partner who can satisfy all our needs. The idea is that there is one particular individual in the universe who exists for each person. This individual is the "right" person, the right partner; and this partner must be met by some fortunate chance. If two people, who meet and marry, are the "right" people, then everything is all right. If, somehow or other, one meets the "wrong" person, then everything is doomed to failure. It is a simple life aim to seek the right person. It is a repetition of fantasy which we try to match in the personality of people who are important to us at all stages of our lives.

It was mentioned at an earlier stage that parents may behave in this way in their expectations of their children. Parents have in mind a perfect child, a fantasy child; and their own child can never come up to this fantasy. Children later learn that their parents are not perfect. They build up, in imagination, a picture of a perfect father and mother which their own parents can never be, although some parents are placed in a position of illusory perfection. Every individual is disappointed by reality and feels hurt. Parent, child, friend, courtship partner or marital partner—all fail to reach the standard of a mental representation. If the other person is expected to fit the role of the fantasy which has been treasured in imagination, then the real relationship is doomed to failure. Try as we will to deceive ourselves as to the perfection of those we love, human qualities break through and then we feel that someone has let us down.

In the relationship between therapist and patient during psychotherapy, the fantasy is called a "transference relationship" because in part it is brought ready-made to the situation. It is called a "positive" transference when the therapist is idealized, and a "negative" one when hostility is evident. Paradoxically we can regard a positive transference as being in some senses a negative one, because, when therapists are endowed by the patient with ideal qualities which they do not possess, the *real* personality is being rejected as insufficient. The idealization of one individual by another is no compliment. It is a demand that the therapist should be that perfect healer or answer for failure. It is equally important to remember that the therapist may demand perfection in the responses of the patient, and seek the satisfaction of patients who become cured.

There are other therapists who seek the satisfaction of a patient who remains uncured and therefore dependent, and this goes parallel with the relationship that some parents seek with a child who cannot be allowed to grow up.

If a parent idealizes a child, if the child idealizes a parent, if a husband idealizes a wife or vice versa, it is a demand that each should *remain* perfect. Therefore, it is a demand that none should ever be his or her own self. It is a rejection of the reality in favour of a fantasy.

Fantasy and Romantic Love

The ideal of romantic love is, nevertheless, encouraged when people derive their fantasy of the person they are going to marry from literature and not from their experience of living people. Young girls may picture their ideal man from adventure stories, such as those which form a continuing series where in each one the hero meets a girl in distress, saves her, but remains free for the next episode and to represent an ideal to all. To marry one would be to deny all others access to his perfection. The hero of the "Western" never actually stays with the girl whom he rescues from the bandits or Indians. He wins her heart, and then rides off alone into the sunset. These people never can really marry. They are unattainable and they have to remain the untested ideal—never tested by the reality of flesh and blood marriage.

Infatuation is the imposition of such a fantasy on somebody who would normally appear to be unsuitable. Infatuation has been defined ironically as an attachment to somebody one's mother doesn't approve of! This can be taken seriously because infatuation is an almost deliberate choice of someone not acceptable to the family of origin. As such, it is a turning to an individual, not because of any positive qualities within that person, but because of the qualities which are different from those approved by members of one's own family. There may be a difference of social class, of age, or religion, colour, race or cultural background, or even of the intellectual level. Marriage may be *sought* because of those differences.[1] It is not implied that marriage is necessarily unsuccessful between people with such differences. Many very sound marriages exist between people of very different kinds of background, but the chances are loaded against success if the differences are the *only* things that are sought; that is, if the marriage is sought for the differences themselves and not for positive qualities which could form a basis of an identity.

Mention must be made of arranged marriages. In the coherent cultures of immigrant groups, notably Asians, and, to a lesser extent, in Greek and Italian communities, the careful preservation of a girl's virginity is the prelude to an arranged marriage, and this implies careful chaperonage during adolescence. The freedom of school life in this country challenges the system. Girls may or may not actively rebel against these restrictions. The young males, however, while allowing freedom for themselves, often seek brides brought over for the purpose from the home country who are prepared to accept the traditional female role. There can be cases where the half-liberated girl, educated in this country, is left without an acceptable husband.

Choice of marital partner is influenced by many factors, conscious and unconscious, yet there is little need to examine the motives when individuals choose partners on the basis that two individuals, with something in common, are prepared to build up joint experiences. One could then think of marriage as the beginning of the relationship and not the final end; the beginning of a story where something new happens which could not have happened with either alone. The romantic ideal of perfect partners is, conversely, a static one of completely formed individuals. It is also an excuse for not doing anything personally about a marriage. One *has* found the right person, or *has not* found the right person; there is no need to do anything more oneself. The idea of two people building up something new together, in contrast to this, is an obligation which may be felt as a burden.

Conscious and Unconscious Factors in Choice of Partner

We have to allow not only for the deliberate and conscious choice (which must not be ignored), but also for the unconscious factors which depend upon the personal history of each partner. These owe a good deal to the personal experiences of

---

[1] See Chapter 9 (Rejection).

both individuals during adolescence, their friendships and their fortuitous opportunities, and they also owe a good deal to what has been absorbed about the marital roles from the parents in infancy. Children get their concept of male and female roles, the concept of their own role in marriage, and the concept of what would be the role of a marital partner, from the attitudes of parents. They get this not only from what parents say, but also from what they do, and how they behave towards each other.

There are satisfactory and unsatisfactory factors in every marriage and, sometimes, when these satisfactory and unsatisfactory factors are faced squarely, and not distorted or denied, children can just accept them as they grow up, and be content to repeat some of the satisfactory aspects of their parents' life together, or perhaps do a little better. There are some people who are able to derive their patterns quite satisfactorily in this way, and to link their lives with their own families with the satisfactory recollection of their own childhood in the family of origin. Sometimes there is the wish to reproduce the *perfection* of the parents' marriage, a perfection which was not a real one, and which depended upon denial or illusion. It can be very disturbing if the unsatisfactory features of the parents' marriage are still denied at the time when recognition of one's own unsatisfactory relationships begins to be realized. Feelings of failure arise when the *actual* marriage is compared with the *fantasy* of the perfect success of the parents' relationship.

Repetition of Pattern of Parents' Marriage

Sometimes, what is attempted to be reproduced is not the parents' relationship with each other, but the relationship of one parent with the child. Either partner may wish to reproduce the perfect relationship which is remembered as having been enjoyed in childhood with the mother or with the father. The man seeks another mother, or a woman seeks another father. Sometimes both want a relationship as with a parent rather than a relationship of marital partners, and neither can receive satisfaction. If an immature woman seeks a repetition of fathering from her husband, and manages to get it, the marriage may work satisfactorily at that level. It can also work when a man marries someone who is glad to be a mother rather than a wife. The choice, however, is not wholehearted and, sooner or later, one partner may protest against domination even though it was exactly that which had been sought. There is a resemblance at this stage to some of the features of adolescent rebellion. While seeking a mothering relationship, a young man can, at the same time, protest against it. He complains, as time goes on, of having a domineering wife, even if he had chosen her for this very quality and groomed her in the part in which he had cast her.

Sometimes in these marital dramas, the marriage has been undertaken in order to re-enact conflicts which have existed between the parents, almost as if it were to re-live the parents' life on their behalf and give *them* a second chance to do better by proxy. Sometimes, a child who has been aware of conflicts between father and mother will almost demand to repeat them in order to prove that he or she could have managed better. A girl who has been brought up in a family where a father and mother quarrel, and where father has seemed to be in the wrong, may have a feeling that if *she* had been mother the marriage would have been more satisfactory. She feels that although father behaved badly, this would not have occurred if he had received the level of love from mother that she herself would have been prepared to give him. She will repeat the situation through the choice of a man who is doomed to recapitulate the unsatisfactory behaviour of her father.

Sometimes, the attempt is to re-enact conflicts which have existed between the parents and child; not the perfection of the mother/child relationship but the imperfection of it. Not being able to relinquish the ancient struggle, a man with a nagging mother may marry a nagging wife, as if he could not be comfortable without the relationship.

Sometimes, there may be an attempt to alter the type of conflict, or to solve it, by choosing somebody opposite to the parent. A man who has been brought up in a very efficient, thrifty and austere home might seek a glamorous, provocative, vivacious wife and then, from the moment of marriage, try to convert her into a replica of his mother almost as if to prove that mother was right after all. Thus he marries somebody and then attempts to break the very qualities and spirit for which he had chosen her. The same thing can happen with a woman who has had a very worthy father, who seemed dull in his respectability. She may marry a reckless young man, and then regret the instability of the marriage and try to reform her irresponsible husband. Likewise, a girl whose father has been drunken and unreliable may marry a very steady young man and continue to regret the gay and frivolous life that she might have been able to lead with another individual.

Sometimes there is a tendency to solve the problem by alternating the person to whom the person is attached. This can occur before marriage or even after marriage. In some levels of society it is an accepted practice to have one type of person as a wife and another type as a mistress. Men may think of girls as being of two types; the good type such as one's sister or mother who would not have sexual intercourse, and bad ones who do. Some attempt to combine the two in some way. There are men who attempt to rescue a prostitute and make her into a *good* woman. First they have freedom to have sexual relationships because she is bad, and later have the moral satisfaction of trying to make her good. The attempt fails, as the recollection of previous promiscuity continues to haunt and torment the individual who feels that sexual relations are a contamination.

Sexual Problems in Marriage

Sexuality and marriage are not things apart but the activity of the whole personality. In marital problems, it is often some aspects of sexual relationship which is described as being the "cause" of the difficulties. In such cases, there is strong resistance to any request for description of life as a whole. There is resentment if questions are asked about life aims and past history. There is merely a search for a particular technique which will make everything all right. This is a way of denying the wholeness of marital life and of personal responsibility.

There are some overt sexual problems or patterns of behaviour which are sometimes presented as "the problem". A woman can be described as frigid, a man as impotent. There can be a preference for masturbation even within marriage. Some people can complain of, or be complained about, as being oversexed, or for lack of interest in sexual activity, and some for the practice of perversions.

Some of these will be discussed briefly.

There is *frigidity* which is an expression of inhibition of a complete sexual experience. Though the term is normally reserved for women, aspects of it can be seen also in male sexual behaviour. When women are allowed an active sexual role the distinction between frigidity and impotence (discussed below) can become blurred.

Frigidity may refer to failure to achieve full orgasm, even when the absence of orgasm is not complained of. It may happen that the act of intercourse becomes an enterprise, in which orgasm has to be imposed upon a somewhat reluctant partner. Some women can be aroused and never achieve climax, and others seem not to be able to be aroused at all. Those whose experience is that they do not "feel anything" may be expressing the idea they do not want to have anything to do with sexuality. It is the defence by which one estranges oneself from one's whole body. The extreme case is a complete refusal by a women of sexual intercourse; but it should not automatically be taken that this is caused by some sexual anomaly. It may occur when the would-be sexual partner has given ample justification for a hostile response.

One must however remember that many women happily give and receive sexual satisfaction, while seldom or never achieving orgasm. People look for "causes" of a refusal of acceptance of sexual activity, but it would be better to say that it is *associated with* patterns of behaviour, rather than say that it has a specific cause. It can occur in a woman who appears sexually attractive, and whose behaviour, is, in fact, provocative—a person who, almost deliberately, arouses sexual excitement and then refuses final satisfaction. As such, one can think of it as an aggressive reaction to the male. Although looking exceedingly feminine, she might resent and envy the role of the male as compared with that of the female. Such a woman may have latent homosexual tendencies. There is, however, in this field a continuum between what is abnormal and what is within normal limits. It is normal in our culture for a young girl, as she becomes aware of her feminity, to rehearse her sexual role and to see how attractive she can be without committing herself.

Sometimes, the explanation of refusal or of lack of satisfaction in intercourse is a clear, straightforward consequence of a breakdown of the marital relationship while the marriage still remains in existence. Where either partner has continually humiliated and destroyed the love of the other, it may not be the one who refuses sexual advances who needs psychiatric treatment, although sometimes the problem is presented as if all that was required was some treatment to make one partner respond to the sexual advances of the other.

There can be other aspects of sexual failure. There are those who fear losing control of themselves in sexual activity at the moment of the orgasm. This is the same kind of fear of losing control as that which finds expression as fear of death, or the fear of falling asleep, fear of insanity, fear of the violence within oneself. This fear of "letting go" is, in fact, not very different from the fear of letting go of the contents of the bowel and bladder. The fear of final "letting go" can inhibit sexual activity in either the male or female, and it can also inhibit any other form of expression of human activity.

Occasionally, repudiation of sexuality is complete. There is an exclusion of sexual expression that seems to be due to some aspect of personality structure, which can be perceived either as a deficiency or as the ultimate purity.

Impotence in the male is equally complex. A man might be impotent with one female and not another. A man may feel it is improper in every sense to have a sexual relationship with somebody whom he admires—with somebody who is "good". There are men who can be potent only with somebody whom they feel is already accustomed to sexual intercourse.

In some cases, a man may be impotent because of the fear of his own aggressiveness and the thought of his own violence in the act of penetration. He might look upon sexual activity as an attack. Early adolescent sexual fantasies frequently include some kind of violence as the essential part.

Impotence can also be due to the overvaluation of the sexual act as an index of a person's worth. This occurs when a man wishes to have sexual intercourse not for his own satisfactions, but because he wishes to prove that this is possible for him.

Sexual athleticism, which is the experience of some, the envy of many, and the conversation of even more, seems to be valued for its having occurred, rather than for the satisfaction of a need. Where it does occur in "mature" adults there seems to be little real satisfaction of sexual desire. More commonly, a man or woman not yet certain of adulthood, may seek sexual satisfaction not for itself, but for the reputation that it brings.

Sexual inadequacy can be associated with marital infidelity. There are persons who have homosexual qualities which are repressed and who do not seek sexual activities with others of the same sex. They seek heterosexual contact through a succession of partners without ever attaining full satisfaction. They may marry, become divorced, and remarry. Satisfaction still eludes such people because they are searching for something in someone else to make up for a feeling of deficiency in themselves. They may try to gain satisfaction by forcing satisfaction on to their partner. The partner's orgasm is their proof that satisfaction exists.

Another type of disturbance in marriage is where masturbation continues as the main satisfaction, sometimes accompanying actual sexual intercourse, sometimes as a substitute for it. Such an individual retains dependence upon fantasy and refuses complete involvement with another individual.

Reassurance about the normality of masturbation notwithstanding, anxieties remain in people of all ages about the continuation of the activity, and the accompanying fantasies, even when full sexual activity has been established. Sadistic and "perverse" fantasies remain even in those whose real life is sexually "normal". It seems necessary to give the added reassurance that such fantasies do not invalidate the normality, so long as the fantasies do not obsessively pervade everyday thinking, or emerge into some potentially disastrous actuality.

The Fact of Destructiveness

An added warning is that the universality of sadistic fantasy does not normalize the evils of torture and persecution. We cannot accept any statement that "we are all guilty"[2] (in our thoughts) because people generally do not translate such thoughts into action.

Sexual and behavioural abnormalities can sometimes be seen as immaturities. The "polymorphous perverse" phases of infancy would be psychosis if they passed unaltered into adult life. Each stage of development has its appropriate boundaries of normality and abnormality. At each stepping stone or crisis point there are some who try desperately to retain earlier childish or immature satisfactions. Others pass imperceptibly and happily into the next stage. The majority of people pass towards maturity with no more survival of the infantile patterns than a recollection which seems, by comparison, to enhance the enjoyment of the newer levels of experience.

Inconsistencies in Standards

"Wife swapping" is a phrase, at present in vogue, and which is used to describe a practice of changing partners in order to enhance sexual excitement. Equality of the sexes has not yet reached the point where it could be called husband swapping.

Sexual permissiveness, which is supposed to characterize contemporary culture, has still stopped short of regarding with equanimity the sexual activities in the physically handicapped and the elderly. Only recently have institutions for the handicapped permitted social and sexual contacts between the sexes, and even then there are instances where approval is dependent upon contraception or the sterilization of the female. Some questionable genetic hazards have been brought in to give a scientific authority to the moral and social problem of allowing parenthood to those who are seen to be imperfect. Sexuality in the aged has always been the subject of humour and there are traces of early oedipal fantasies, even in adults, with regard to their surviving parents.

---

[2] Erich Fromm, *The Anatomy of Human Destructiveness*, Jonathan Cape, 1974. Erich Fromm took up the theme of destructiveness in its application to the holocaust and to the idea that the actions of Hitler and tyrants can be explained in universal terms. He stated that when the word "aggression" is applied to destructive behaviour, it is often implied that the activity is normal because it is an innate quality, or beneficial because it utilizes forces that require to be released. Conversely, even when the word "aggression" is given an abnormal connotation, it may be linked with some pathological label and it becomes separated from the personality of the individual responsible for the behaviour. Thus, he showed, destructiveness is taken out of the moral sphere and becomes normalized, abnormalized or even trivialized.

18

Adult Life

HUMAN development has its analogies, and contrasts, with that of other living species. The early stages of the insect's life are a prelude to the *imago* which is the "perfect form". There is no climacteric and no senescence: perfection is followed only by death. Something of this is contained in ideas about human maturity. Adult life is the "perfection"; infancy, childhood and adolescence are the approaches to it; middle age and old age are a departure from it. On this basis, the stage of adult life is no fit subject in a book intended for workers in remedial and helping professions, unless there is some identifiable pathology. The assumption of an inherent normality (never mind perfection!) in adult life ignores the developmental aspect which is a continuing process in every stage.

For adulthood, as for childhood, alongside the concepts of normality and abnormality through which a diagnosis is made, we have to retain the idea of development continuing at different rates in different individuals, and leading to different levels of effectiveness in every aspect of personal and family life. For some purposes, we need to provide a chart of normality against which abnormalities can be identified, but we must remember that there are many anomalies of the developmental processes which can by no means be labelled diseases. There are, in fact, possible dissatisfactions in every aspect of living activity, and a host of professional workers may be called upon to deal with the marital, occupational, recreational, financial, sexual and behavioural details—normal and abnormal—in the lives of people who consult them.

Physical growth still takes place in the sense that the living cells die and have to be replaced. It is a salutary fact that, from early adult life onwards, the death rate of cells is somewhat higher than the growth rate. How fortunate it is that there is enough and to spare in our biological equipment!

Intellectually (notwithstanding the contention that mathematical geniuses have exhausted their potential by the age of 25), there are countless examples of original contributions and innovations by those who have changed the course of their professions in their middle age and later years. Modern technology makes the demand that workers adapt, and contribute to, knowledge and performances that did not exist in their early adult life. As with the physical qualities, an unused capacity exists (as well as possible erosions of earlier skills) and is the matrix for both development and change at all stages of life.

Emotionally too, development does not cease with the arrival of the capacity to have adult sexual relationships, nor with the ability to form a marital partnership, nor indeed with becoming a parent.

Maximum Responsibility

Adult life is the stage when individuals are expected to be able to take responsibility for their own care. During infancy and childhood, and, to a lesser extent, in adolescence, the individual is dependent upon others. In later life, external support may again be called for. In the adult stage of life, people are expected to take responsibility for their own selves, for their children, for their own old age which is yet to come, and perhaps for the care of older people who are part of their present family. This responsibility, and this care of others, may be accepted as an obligation which is purely personal, as an obligation within a larger family framework, or it may be delegated to the community in general through the contribution in taxation which the adult is called upon to make for the provision for social services organized by the state.

In addition to these responsibilities for the young and the old, there are also the burdens of those who are temporarily ill or injured, or for those who are permanently disabled, defective, or merely inadequate, who also receive care which can be a personal, family or a community service. There is a shifting balance of responsibility between the family and the "community", and it is on the adult members of the community that this responsibility rests.

Burdens can be privileges or even pleasures. Adults, in becoming responsible for their own life, may be able to direct it into paths which satisfy.

Sources of Satisfaction

The physical, intellectual and emotional aspects of personality all receive their fulfilment in the domestic, occupational and recreational life of the adult. Marital life, with the beginning of a new family, is the most important part of living for many people. Occupation is then looked upon as something to earn the means to maintain the home; and any recreational and social life is centered on the home. Others fulfil themselves in their job, and look upon the home merely as a place in which to recuperate for the next day's work. There are, again, others who seek a social life outside their jobs and their home, and who make that their most important goal.

Domestic life can be thought of in terms of the new family which is being created, and also it is necessary to take into account the links with the family of origin of each partner. A new family cycle is initiated, and the interrelationships and the emotional interchanges within the family depend upon the ideas that each married partner has of his or her role. The reader is referred to sociological and anthropological studies.[1]

---

[1] E. Bott, *Family and Social Network*, Tavistock Publications, 1957; Young and Wilmot, *Family and Kinship in East London*, Routledge and Kegan Paul, 1957.

A good deal of what is satisfactory is never studied, simply because there is no need to question it. Some facets of family life and participation are studied because we are aware of the changing nature of marital roles and of attitudes to different members of the immediate and wider family. There are changes in the attitudes to the wider network of grandparents, aunts and uncles when the move to other districts separates families, and there are additional changes where differing education and economic progress give young parents different cultural or material values from those of their own parents. Attitudes to children have changed in the last two generations along with the general diminution in family size. Children, being numerically fewer, become individually more important. Moreover, the smaller modern family is frequently the product of the first few years of married life, and child-bearing has become for many restricted to a period of five or six years in the early part of a young couple's married life. The children then grow up, together with their still youthful parents, in a family life in which no more planned children are born.

Patterns of living alter, and now with the reliability, as well as the availability, of contraception, some young couples choose to delay having a family for as much as perhaps five or ten years. Parenthood then becomes a very deliberate (and deliberated) step, and one which brings about a complete change in a settled life style. It is not necessary for us to say whether this is good or bad. It is sufficient to recall that conception can be largely controlled, and that sexual relationships can be enjoyed without reproduction. Wherever it becomes technically possible to control some biological function, people will use that possibility.

Similarly, feeding processes exist which allow the upbringing of infants without the necessity for breast feeding, and some proportion of mothers will feed their babies artificially whether they might have been able to feed them at the breast or not. Mothers, therefore, now have a freedom from some of the restrictions that used to be associated with the child-bearing function. A wife can be a mother for a limited period, and then still have an active social and recreational life that is (almost) as free as that of her husband. She may continue or resume her premarital occupational activities.

Sometimes the change of role of the woman brings about fresh problems. The wife and mother who goes out to work may still be expected to maintain the major responsibility for the running of the home. The fathering role has undergone some compensating alterations: the father's physical presence at the birth of the baby in hospital, which is a conscious acknowledgment of the need to repair some of the consequences of the separation of childbirth from family life in the home, can be a prelude to the father's participation in infant care.

The mother may still expect herself, and be expected, to take the main interest in the physical care and in the emotional ramifications of the lives of her growing children; and it is to her that all the family turn for nursing in times of illness. Sometimes it would seem that new-found freedom savours more of exploitation then emancipation.

The concept of any role of husband and wife, and the image of role that each has of the other, changes with each one's personal activities, and the pattern of family life must present a different picture to the children of each generation.

Occupational Fulfilment

The *occupation* of the male or female adult is something which can represent predominantly the physical, intellectual or the emotional aspect of life. *Physically*, the individual has reached the peak of height but not weight. Maximum strength is reached in the late teens or early twenties. The maximum can be maintained only for a short time. If an individual chooses physical activities as the ideal representation of personality, and is able to develop these gifts in an athletic occupation, then "prime of life" is going to be very limited. When a particular sport depends upon peak performance for a long period, athletes are "finished" at the age of 25; less strenuous activities may enable success and fame to be continued for much longer. As a leisure interest, appropriate physical activities can be a part of every stage of life.

There are some industries which demand extremely heavy work for high wages and where no provision is made for the period of life when that physical level of output can no longer be maintained. This leads to industrial casualties. There are other occupations which also still depend upon physical activity, but where an individual can maintain skill and usefulness for much longer periods so long as the rhythm of activity is maintained. Interruption caused by illness, accident or unemployment leads to loss of that rhythm, and it is sometimes impossible to return to that work.

In the days when full employment cannot be guaranteed, a thought must be given to the consequences of joblessness and of the problems of re-entering employment, or of finding new types of work. (What, for example, will happen to men working on the North Sea oil rigs when they are no longer capable of the necessary physical exertion?)

The idea of fixity of role, occupational or otherwise, in adult life is one that needs to be revised, and we ought to be able to think of development of personality as something which can continue in fresh ways even when some capacities have declined from peak levels.

Some individuals find occupations in which their *intellectual* attributes are their chief asset. Promotion tends to go with seniority and, therefore, it would seem that intellectual skills are expected to keep pace with increased demands. This fact of life stands out in contrast with notions derived from the results of some intelligence tests which reveal a falling off in the ability to give instant recall to data which remain available in a more unhurried exploration of the recesses of memory. In intellectual, as well as in physical activity, there is much work that can be originated or developed with the experience of maturity as well as with the freshness of unfettered youth. It has been suggested that the level of mental creativity is more likely to be maintained if there is a change of style of work, or change of direction of career, as there are limits to the possibilities of development in any one approach. Platt[2] quoted an idea that people should change their careers every twelve years in order to prevent the loss of originality which results from the diminishing returns when the same ideas or methods are followed for too long a period.

[2] R. Platt, Reflections on Ageing and Death, *Lancet*, 1–6 (1963).

The *emotional* aspects of personality can also be the material of the working life. Some occupations depend upon the professionalization of the use of relationships. The remedial professions have an origin in the desire to make provision for the care of people who are temporarily or permanently unable to make provision for themselves or to find help entirely within their own family.

The pattern of family life can be affected by what is put into occupational and leisure activities.

People who work in the "caring" professions, such as social work or medicine, utilize in their work the feelings that are ordinarily inherent in family life. A professional hazard is that such feelings receive their full satisfaction in working hours, leaving none to spare for home life. This is true to some extent in all work that involves human relationships, even if the relationship is incidental to another task, such as in salesmanship, law and accountancy.

Education is an example of where the importance of the relationship is stressed to different degrees according to the ages of the pupils, and the content of what is being taught. Here again, the teacher, as an individual, invests to an unknown degree a portion of his or her personal emotional life in the professional activity.

The successful teacher or social worker might deprive family members of very necessary understanding within the home. There are others who are better neighbours and friends than they are parents, and there are others yet again whose interest in the home leads them to give short measure in the job which provides the family income.

When the teacher, the therapist, the social worker act (sometimes unwittingly) in the role of parent, influence on the pupil, patient or client is incalculable. There is no denying the satisfaction that this gives to the professional worker who becomes aware of it. The choice of profession may sometimes be consciously determined by the opportunities that can be realized through a personal contact.

The period of full employment gave a choice in which some of the less esteemed jobs were left vacant, even though these included tasks which are necessary to keep a civilized community working. The salaries of firemen and policemen, for example, suffer in comparison with those of some professional and industrial occupations, but these jobs still have the attractions of prestige and security. Other forms of public service, such as transport, have drawn upon immigrant labour, but if these jobs are rejected by the indigenous population, they are unlikely to be attractive to the British-born children of immigrant parents.

An accelerating rate of inflation in all industrial countries imposes pressure on the wage structure. For a large proportion of the population, the wage scarcely keeps pace with the cost of what has become the minimum acceptable standard of living; but this has brought out a demand from those in jobs involving skills and training, to restore former differentials. Satisfaction appears to be relative. Also while choice of occupation may be partly voluntary, there are people whose particular occupation was imposed by economic processes and industrial developments over which they had no control.

There can also be a problem of simultaneous geographical and social mobility. Where there are frequent moves from one locality to another, either through promotion in an organization, or in the very nature of the job (such as in the Regular

Army), family and social life become subservient to occupational life. The children may suffer in their development, as a child will find it difficult to form emotional bonds with other children if these are likely to be destroyed by frequent moves to other areas. There is a tendency for any emotional relationships which are formed to become shallow.

Social mobility brings problems even when moves take place within the same locality. A husband and wife may have an unequal capacity for adaptation to the customs of different social classes, and in any case the transitional period is a difficult one. To remain in a former area with friends who may envy the social ascenders can be as difficult as moving to a new area where they may feel insecure. There are parallel difficulties with people who have declined socially or financially. If they remain in a district where they are unable to keep up their previous standards, the children are at a disadvantage as compared with the children of neighbouring households. If they move to another neighbourhood, they are told by their parents that they are superior to the children of the district, but find themselves treated as if they were inferior.

Limitations in Realization of Fantasies

We must return to a feature of all the problems which have been referred to—that of the image which we have of ourselves, and which we use as a standard with which to compare the reality as we perceive it. In the adult phase of life we have reached the point which has been looked upon as a fulfilment of all the previous preparation, and yet many people still preserve the image of themselves which they had during adolescence. This was the stage when our fantasy had no limits, and the realities of adult life may not compare favourably with adolescent dreams.

We preserve the idea of progress throughout adult life, and may go some little way towards realization of our fantasies, but there is an understandable tendency to preserve the ideal of the youthful stage when the future had no limits. The adult finds it hard to give up the personal picture of him or herself as a young man or a young woman. Some are able to accept their failures or the limitations of their success, and transfer the dreams and the problems to the lives of their children. Complete satisfaction eludes the majority of people who pursue it, and yet the belief in its existence seems to be one of the necessary illusions in our lives.

Paradoxically, the adult phase, which is notionally the stage of the burden of responsibility, is also the stage of comparative freedom from external restraint. No one can prevent the adult from remaining the perpetual adolescent, or the perpetual student who does not need to choose a final image nor is indeed compelled to secure employment.

It was stated at the outset that one of the reasons for the study of human development was the wish to make provision for human needs in sickness and in health. In adult life, use can be made of the qualities that have developed. Perhaps mental health is a balance of aspects of personality in the outlets that are available. Physical, intellectual and emotional qualities find fulfilment in the domestic, occupational and recreational life of each individual. The balance is not static in one individual, and in different individuals it can be attained in different proportions of involvement in each area of life.[3]

When dealing with provisions for the needs of children (Chapter 10) reference was made to the necessity for appropriate opportunities for expression of the child's potentialities and capacities. In adult life, we judge more by the performance than the potentiality, but even here there is the need for intake as well as output. The adult, like the child, needs love that is the acceptance of a separate individuality, and standards which, when their rules are observed, give recognition of an identification with a community. The triple needs, over and above material needs, are love, outlets and a framework within which one can be approved.

The Single, Widowed, Separated and Divorced

It is usually assumed that, for adults, the normal state is expressed in married life, which allows for the satisfaction of mature sexual needs and which provides a matrix for the upbringing of children. There are however, a significant proportion of people who do not marry, and, of those who marry, some are separated, some divorced and some suffer bereavement in the loss of a partner. In addition to those who marry and have no sexual fulfilment there are those who enjoy their sexual life and do not marry. There is marriage without children and there are children born outside marriage. Even if membership of a family is looked upon as being a criterion of statistical normality and a desirable state, the minority not in that state constitutes such a large number of individuals that we have no right to label them as abnormal. Most of them do not seek help and do not need help.

Of the single who never marry, in some cases it is by choice and in some cases there is a problem of availability of suitable partners at the time when a particular individual is mature enough for marriage. The different aspects of personality, referred to earlier as requiring outlets for fulfilment, grow at different rates; and the intellectual aspect may be finding rich fulfilment in occupational and social life, even to the exclusion of preoccupation with sexual activity. Some people, in times of social and occupational mobility, suffer the penalty of being in the van of progress. Rapid personal progress takes them away from the company of their former peers who could make close relationships with members of their family of origin. The need for close personal relationship of the kind found in marriage may make its appearance at a stage when it becomes a momentous individual decision, rather than one taken in the company of a group of young people developing together.

There is, however, a bisexuality in mankind which promotes some degree of satisfaction in sharing in imagination the experiences recorded in literature and available in various companionships.

The balance of satisfactions is never complete for anyone, and a large proportion of people build the structure of their personality as a whole out of the bricks that are available.

[3] A tantalizing observation on the comparative health of different sections of the population is that the most "healthy" category of all adults is that of unmarried women; and the next most "healthy" is that of married men.

There are similar problems for those whose marriages break down, and who suffer; yet here again the large number of open marital failures, in countries which permit easy divorce, makes one wonder whether the permanence of the marital state is something that can be regarded as the norm. There is even separation within marriage: separation of interests, e.g. the wife's life fixed on the children and the husband's on his work. There are men who work late, and even those who have two jobs. There are husbands who work in the daytime, and wives who work in the evenings. There are those who fall asleep in each other's company in the evenings, and there are families who silently watch television together, each member being more closely united with the scene on the screen than with one another.

Loss of the marital partner brings helplessness and social embarrassment to many males. Widowhood and divorce may make a woman sexually vulnerable. A large proportion of men and women who lose their partners are, however, able to re-marry or form a new stable relationship. A large number of adults married or single, find a measure of fulfilment in the sharing of adult interests with working colleagues; and, with the lengthening of life beyond the reproductive stage, this capacity for corporate adult enjoyment becomes increasingly important.

19

Middle Age

MIDDLE age has biological and cultural boundaries. At one time, each period of life was marked out by special clothing, and stages were distinct. The middle-aged man and woman each wore an altered style of dress in accordance with the dignity of the new status of middle age. The period of middle age probably extended from the middle forties to the age of 60, when old age began. The change of status and change of clothing corresponded with alteration in physical capacity. It was assumed that peak performance was over, and yet the individual who accepted the status of middle age could feel entitled to respect that did not depend upon physical competition with the young adult.

The intellectual and emotional aspects of personality undergo changes which are not necessarily at the same rate, or in the same direction. The sequential changes which have relevance in early stages of development no longer seem to be inevitable in the cultural divisions of adult life. The personal image in the forties and fifties may savour more of a maturing than of a decline, and even in the later years of life there are many who preserve an inner care of youth. The qualities at one time attributed to middle age are being transferred to the "elderly", and even that is a category from which many old people would exclude themselves.

Notwithstanding the actual structural changes which affect physical, intellectual and emotional life, the relevant image at any one time carries a relationship to the part of the life span still to come. With a greater expectation of life for the middle aged, there is much more in life which is still in store.

With regard to changes in reproductive capacities, there are important biological differences between the sexes. It has already been mentioned that girls reach puberty earlier than boys. An even more significant sex difference is that the number of ova is finite and countable, and that a woman reaches a stage when she is no longer fertile simply because no fertilizable ova remain. The effect of the "pill" on the duration of fertility is as yet unknown.

The menopause is a biological stage in a woman's life. It is identifiable, and is indeed an aspect of feminine identity.

The existence of a female menopause has had its impact on notions of male sexuality, but there is no comparable physical change in the middle life of men. The single release of an ovum at fairly regular intervals in the reproductive life of a woman is contrasted with a profuse and variable number of potential seminal emissions each with millions of spermatozoa.

These sex differences are part of the process by which the genetic inheritance retains its chance character. It is also an inescapable difference that the period of male reproductive capacity continues into old age.

Imbalance in the time span of fertility has contributed to ideas about "creativity" in general. At one time, "creativity" in a woman was restricted to the notion of child-bearing and child-rearing, whereas men then seemed to have arrogated to themselves the monopoly of artistic creation, and scientific invention. Ideas are said to be "seminal" not "ovular", but the balance is restored when one speaks of the "gestation" of an idea.

Physical Wear and Tear

As regards the physical attributes, tissues begin *noticeably* to show signs of degeneration. Body tissues wear out unevenly. There is some "wear and tear" at every stage of life. Tissues degenerate and become damaged, and, although some become repaired by natural processes, there is always a certain amount of permanent effect of the wearing out process which accompanies even the early stages of growth.

People who work in heavy industry or who do heavy manual work may wear out selectively, begin to show signs of degeneration in the cardiovascular system, and become unable to continue in their occupation.

In some instances this problem is circumvented by promotion to supervisory posts where appointments are made by seniority. Although this practice may often have successful results, there are many individuals who are unable to teach or to control those who have been previously their equals. Some workers may, in any case, have to continue in a heavy job with diminishing physical capacities, and increasing anxieties. The result may be a loss of confidence and self-esteem even if employment is maintained. This applies particularly to people who continually work close to the limits of capabilities and resources. As a rule, any individual can increase output to a surprising degree for a limited time if there is sufficient motivation for it, but that is because there usually is something in reserve. Those who work nearer to the limits of their capacity find themselves living on their reserves in order to maintain the balance of energy exchange in daily life. When there is a reduction in their total capacity, the reserves become exhausted and there is nothing left but to break down.

Alteration in Image of Self

As the reserves in an individual's physical capacity become reduced, there should be a corresponding alteration in the image of the self, which would allow a reduction in expectations of performance. Perhaps for that reason the custom of changing the fashion of clothing for different periods of life was a good thing.

As the years advance, some adults deliberately attempt to preserve the "differentials" in performance as against a younger generation, continuing to outmatch the efforts of new recruits in occupational activities, or even in their recreation. Sometimes individuals return to some sport or to some working activity which they had previously relinquished to the newcomers. They may attempt a physical movement based on the recollection of the kind of movement that they would have made a number of years before. There can be minor or major consequences of inappropriate overexertion, ranging from the rupture of a tendon, to cardiac "strain". Many adults are saved from having to compete in this way by the good fortune of "a bad back".

There are illnesses which are associated with selective degeneration of tissues, such as cerebral or cardiovascular disease, and, there are illnesses such as cancer which seem more prevalent now because with a longer span of life, people are living long enough to suffer from them. This applies in general to illness where the incidence is greater in later years of life.

Intelligence is said to suffer decline, but there are compensations in the contribution that experience can make to the use to which intellectual capacity is put. The young person may grasp problems much more quickly, but the middle-aged person, especially if originally of high intelligence, can bring recollections of previous experience, which might help to reach a more balanced judgement than was possible in earlier years.

In many professions, middle age is the time when a few rise to administrative posts because of having entered the profession at a time when it was expanding. Some such, often exceptional in personality, may not have had the training which is provided as a matter of course for the new recruits who become their subordinates. They may credit the newly trained workers with a knowledge that nobody really could have, and expect the training to provide a skill which exists only in people's imagination. This is a process with which we are familiar in the relationship between clients and the professional worker. The clients attribute to the professional worker powers which they feel *ought* to exist but which they cannot quite believe in. They wish the worker to have that power but at the same time try to prove that it does not exist. The same processes also occur in the relationships between parent and child, child and parent. The parent has an image of the perfect child; the child attributes perfection to the parent; both are disappointed at the failures. There are the same reciprocal processes between colleagues of different ages, and this may become expressed in arguments about the value, or otherwise, of new concepts of professional work. The young new recruits, with the latest training, may feel at first that they are being held back by old-fashioned traditions, but, at the same time, they might have a hidden and perhaps exaggerated veneration for the wisdom of the older person in charge. These processes are referred to in the concept of the transference and counter-transference relationship.

The emotional life of the individual is bound up with the physical and intellectual qualities, as the image that is entertained of the personality as a whole depends upon every aspect of personality. The children may now be grown up, and a new kind of relationship has to be established between husband and wife.

Fertility and Sexuality

There is the question of the importance of sexual activity at this stage. Fertility usually ceases in the late forties or early fifties, in a woman, but at the time of the menopause, irregular bleeding, which may have a physiological or even a pathological basis, may still be associated with ideas of the possibility of pregnancy. The danger here is that pathological bleeding may be treasured as evidence of fertility and, therefore, youth.

Some women feel that it is inappropriate or even wrong to continue with sexual activity after the menopause. Others are released from inhibitions and find new sexual freedom in the removal of any fear of pregnancy.

Although there is no male physical equivalent of the female climacteric there may be anomalies in sexual interests and activities. Reduction in potency, or heightened interest in sexuality are usually a psychological phenomenon. There are some cases where there is a physical stimulus to sexuality associated with an enlarged prostate.

Some men and some women make what seem to be irresponsible attempts to get the satisfaction which had so far eluded them in the past, in what they feel to be the little time left to them, or to try to store up experiences to last them for the barren years ahead.

Women may feel a sense of relief that one episode of life is over and that new status and new potentials are opening out. The children of the family now no longer need close support. The constant responsibility for the family has gone, although some may try to maintain the dependence of the children, cherishing the burden long after it is appropriate. In some cases the menopause is treated as being the end of a sexual life which had never really been fully realized.

For many, a new phase of life begins in relation to the children—sometimes at this stage the children have married and have left home. If there are grandchildren, a new level of relationship emerges which is different from that between children and their parents. The grandchildren can receive from the grandparents that part of parenting which is accepting and free, without the part of parenting which is restricting.

In the interwar years a cultural gap developed between the generation of parents and grandparents focusing on restrictive as against permissive patterns of child rearing. Parents would often resent the attempts of grandparents to "interfere" with their authority.

For the moment, there appears to be more tolerance for different contributions; many grandparents seem to be able to accept contemporary patterns of upbringing; while many parents positively value the extra dimension of family life which grandparents can give, and they are rewarded by the availability of benevolent baby sitters!

There remains however a diversity in patterns of child-rearing with regard to regional differences, brought into notice by social mobility in the indigenous population. Immigrant cultures may also stand out sharply in contrast with generally accepted standards, particularly in matters of punishment, and attitudes towards authority. The differences, however, often seem no more than the continuance of a pattern that was generally accepted in this country only two generations ago.

Conflicts, Anxieties and New Levels of Fulfilment

Many people are able to renew themselves with a change in direction of occupation which is undertaken voluntarily in middle life. A married woman may return to a previous occupation after a child-rearing period, and many have never left this work completely, although it was subsidiary to family cares. Middle life provides a renewal of full engagement with some of the excitements and rewards of a life outside the home.

In many cases women who have been tied to a home may seek a more drastic change, taking up academic or other kinds of training for professional work. With men, the tendency for change of occupation may not be so obvious, but there are many who seem to have extracted all the fulfilment that is available in their first career, and seek a second one. In many other cases, the move is made for them by the technical changes in industry and by the administrative reorganizations which alter the character of their work to the extent that an original training is no longer relevant to the current activities. Unemployment, redundancies, and take-overs, of large firms, force a change of occupation onto a growing proportion of the adult population at all ages.

To a certain extent, these changes can be welcomed even when compulsory. Middle age, then, can be a second adolescence in which change is an introduction to new opportunities, and to fulfilments which were missed on the first time round.

As with the first adolescence, there is a good chance that the fulfilment of fantasies will remain as elusive as ever. The emotional turmoil of this period is manifested in an increase in the number of divorces and remarriages.

It is possible that in a previous generation a large number of successful people did not live long enough to savour the experience of emptiness which disturbs many successful people of today. The Jungian School of dynamic psychology offers a great deal to the understanding and treatment of these dissatisfactions in this period of life.[1]

The emotional aspects of middle life are, therefore, complex, and should not be considered from the point of view of any one individual but as an interaction between members of a family which may extend to three or four generations.

Sometimes emphasis is placed on those aspects of middle age which are seen as sources of disturbance and anxiety. It is just as frequent, however, to see changes which become the basis of new levels of satisfaction and of fulfilment. At the point of change there may be anxiety. Anxiety could be felt in relation to loss of previous status and also in relation to the imagined happenings which face an individual in the next stage of life. There are values that can be found in each new status and these values come from the acceptance of the differing quality of an individual's capacity at each phase of life. Each new status can be experienced as a personal discovery which adds to the contentment of life. It becomes a new level of maturity.

Some of the emotional changes in middle age are linked with the reality of death. There is a gradually increasing mortality rate as people get older and, therefore, those who survive become more aware of the loss through death of others closely connected with them. It is a time when the middle-aged person becomes likely to suffer from the loss of parents, or other elderly associates, and the loss of colleagues who succumb to one or other of the disturbances and diseases which can come in

[1] C. G. Jung, *Collected Works*, 2nd ed., 12 vols., Routledge and Kegan Paul, 1966.

middle life. The mortality of middle age has to be considered then, not only for itself, but also for the effect on others.

The death of parents in particular can be a shattering experience at any age, and yet it is inextricably a part of human experience. There is a sense in which this experience confirms a degree of independence in the individual. Identity, however, is rooted in the past, and looks out towards the future; and there is an even greater tragedy in the loss of a place in the continuing stream of life in the case of parents who survive their children.

Depression in Middle Age

The characteristic mental or emotional disturbance in middle age and later middle age is depression; and depression is described as occurring in two categories. There is the *endogenous* type of depression which is associated with changes which occur within the body, i.e. metabolic changes or chemical changes of various kinds, and there is the *exogenous* or *reactive* depression which is associated with external events. It is possible to link these two kinds of change with each other and consider all depression, in some way at least, as being associated with loss. There is the loss of closely related individuals through death, loss of possessions and, sometimes, loss of one's own esteem, which can be associated with a good many conditions, including the fear of loss of potency. If we think of depression as being associated with loss, we can bring together *endogenous* depression, where there is internal loss in the form of loss of the image of the body as a vigorous and sexually fertile individual, and *reactive* depression where the losses are external.

The Need to Mourn

Depression was associated by Freud with mourning. He compared depression, which is pathological, with grief, which is normal; and the difference is one of degree. With the death of a member of the family or a close associate, the loss means losing some part of one's own self. People need a period of mourning to accommodate that loss. People need a period of mourning in order to redistribute their own feelings within themselves. In fact, mourning is a healing process; it is a necessary process in which people adjust to their feelings about the situation.

Mourning begins to take place early in life. There is a link between the mourning which takes place with regard to the death of people who are close to us and the losses which occur in the changes from one status to another in childhood and onwards. A child who is weaned loses the close association with the nipple and has to accommodate to a new type of feeding experience. Here, as mentioned before, there are some advantages in the new status. All loss is a stage towards personal independence, and even our mourning can be a process which helps us, not only to accommodate the loss, but also to re-establish, within our personality, a representation of the person to whom we have been closely attached.

Individuals are sometimes robbed of their mourning processes by being "jollied" out of their grief, and by being prematurely consoled. There is a saying in the Talmud: "Do not console the mourner in the presence of his dead". It is just as inappropriate to attempt to hurry along people's developmental stages at a rate faster than they can accommodate.

Regression at Points of Change

When people appear to pass from one stage of development to the next too quickly, they sometimes have to go back again to stages that seem more infantile than the one from which they had just passed. We call this "regression".

Developmental stages all take time. It takes time to recover from the severance of ties to people and places when we move house. Even journeys should take time. People who travel by air take some time after they arrive before they "catch up with themselves". It is almost as if they have left themselves behind, and they have to wait at their destination until they arrive!

The attitude to illness, to operations, to childbirth, has become more and more mechanistic. It is for very good reasons that people are discharged from hospitals two or three days after an operation or after a confinement, and for very good reasons that they are got up out of bed at early stages after operations. There is a tendency for clotting to take place in deep veins when a patient is kept too rigidly at rest. Early movement helps the circulatory system. But, because of this new trend towards early activity, people generally tend to make too little of their illnesses and their operations, and women of their confinements. They no longer allow for the time which is necessary to accommodate themselves to the changes involved, or, in the case of operations, for the insult to the body. They do not allow themselves the time to make adjustments to the alteration necessary in the body image. People are cheated out of some necessary regression, and of the comfort of being nursed back to levels of adult responsibility, if they are expected to take their illnesses in their stride.

Deferring Satisfactions

Financial affairs can be a factor in the emotional aspects of middle age. Some people at the beginning of adult life incur obligations which help them to live at a particular rate. They buy houses with mortgages which permit the cost to be paid off over a period of (say) twenty years, and in the course of paying off these mortgages they have accumulated a certain amount of capital. They may also make arrangements to save money at the same time, by taking out insurance policies, and they may be able, in addition, to add to their household possessions. Some people try to save money for unexpected expenses. This habit of putting something aside for the future becomes a habit of deferring enjoyment and deferring satisfactions. It contrasts with hire purchase, which is a way of getting immediate enjoyment in the present at the cost of the future. Saving becomes a way of *not* having something in the present for the sake of what is *going to be had* in the future[2] and this, to some extent, can be an inevitable process in the arrangement of the lives of many people in the middle classes.

[2] As a result of the unprecedented rates of inflation in recent years, the prudence of saving as against borrowing has been questioned.

Some people accept the need to save for the future, and then begin to find satisfaction in the process of saving and planning for the future, and not in the enjoyment of the present. A time comes when some of the aims have been realized; the mortgage has been paid off, an insurance has matured, or a particular post has been reached, and yet in the end there seems to be no satisfaction in it. All the satisfactions have been channelled into the process of preparation, and none for the arrival of the actual benefits. Sometimes, then, the cause of depression is not a loss, but a gain. It may be that it is not what people *do not get* but something that they *get* which seems to initiate a period of depression. People can become depressed at attaining a very long-deferred ambition or aim because they have pictured the happiness that awaited them when financial security had been reached; and yet when the material success is attained, happiness seems to be no nearer.

Depression and Attainment of Aims

Life is unsatisfactory for everybody to some extent. There is always a feeling that it is going to be satisfactory at a particular stage in the future. If that stage arrives, and the individual still finds that life is more or less the same, it is devastating. If the aim still remains some distance ahead, there can still be the feeling that perfect happiness, to which we feel that we are entitled, is there, if only we could reach it. Thus there is depression which follows the *attainment* of a particular kind of ambition.

Depression and Losses

But there are actual losses: financial losses and failures in one's occupation or ambition. Some people not only save, but speculate. Some gain and some lose. If people gain, they may feel that they have some kind of special worth which has entitled them to that gain. If they lose, they may become angry—with the universe, with other people, and sometimes with themselves. They feel that they have lost a sense of worth within their own selves. Sometimes a financial loss sets up a train of events which leads to depression. People may worry unduly about a particular small financial transaction or an unfortunate purchase—a purchase which promised to be a bargain but wasn't. Often it is a purchase where the article itself carries some value to the individual. Many people link their status with external objects such as motor-cars. Many a person has become much more concerned and depressed over an unfortunate transaction concerning the exchange of a motor-car than might have been expected from the dimensions of the transaction itself. The conclusion is that the loss which causes depression (as against transitory regret) is *the loss that we cannot afford*. The loss that we cannot afford is the loss which makes a difference to our estimate of ourselves.

Thus the concept of loss comes into the picture of depression in every aspect discussed so far.

Depression and Physical Factors

Pollitt divides depressive illnesses into two main groups, psychological or physiological.[3] He calls the former type "J" (justified) and the latter type "S" (somatic). The emphasis in the type "S" is on symptoms and signs of characteristic bodily changes dependent on persisting altered function in the central nervous system. These changes have been referred to by Pollitt as "the depressive functional shift". This refers to symptoms such as early morning waking, loss of appetite, loss of weight and loss of sexual desire—irrespective of the severity of the depressive mood accompanying the changing functions. Attempts have been made to find characteristic metabolic features, such as alterations in the rate of water excretion, the carbohydrate metabolism, or disturbances in the balance of sodium potassium or cholesterol levels. It is suggested that a coordinating role for all these different physiological functions is to be found within the hypothalamus, which is one of the vital centres situated deep in the brain. These observations at a physical level are the justification for the search for forms of physical and chemical intervention in the treatment of depression and these efforts have been eminently successful, within a narrow clinical field. The process is still empirical as the action of the drugs is not closely related to discoverable relevant alterations in body processes. Moreover, the use of these drugs should not divert attention from the search for disturbances of intrapersonal and interpersonal conflicts.

There is no justification whatever for giving these drugs in a routine way for the frustrations, discomforts, and conflicts that come within the broad range of ordinary satisfactory and unsatisfactory human experiences. Neither is the use of drugs a justifiable alternative to the attempt to explore the possibility of gaining access to better material resources or to the better use of the personal internal resources.

Drug firms advertise their products in the medical press giving examples of an overburdened mother in a high-rise flat, or a man just made redundant from his employment. It is implied that these people are suffering from an illness which can be diagnosed as depression, and that the remedy is a particular drug. What is bad about this is the further implication that people are not entitled to feel badly when bad things happen to them, unless the feelings can be attributed to illness.

Physical treatments are dependent upon producing profound changes in the central nervous system. One example is treatment by artificially induced convulsions. In the first form of this kind of treatment, convulsions were produced by the intravenous administration of powerful drugs in small doses. Later, convulsions have been produced by electrical methods. An electrode is placed over each side of the area of the skull corresponding with the frontal lobes of the brain, and an electric current is passed. This is known as ECT (electroconvulsive therapy) or electroplexy, and, in this treatment, a convulsion is followed by a brief loss of consciousness.

The convulsions involve contractions of the muscles of various parts of the body which could be so powerful as occasionally to cause fracture of the bones. The modern modified treatment is given under a general anaesthetic. A drug which

---

[3] J. Pollitt, *Depression and its Treatment*, Heinemann, 1965.

temporarily paralyses the muscles is also used, and this prevents the contractions, but the neurological equivalent of the convulsion remains.

The physical treatment methods are remarkably successful in shortening the course of severe depression and may avert the danger of suicide.

Physical methods of treatment are empirical, i.e. there is no clear explanation of the way in which the successful results are obtained. One suggestion with regard to ECT is that there is a temporary blocking of the pathways between the forepart of the brain (which carries the higher mental processes, including sensitivity to anxiety) and the centres in the deeper parts of the brain, or basal ganglia (which are the areas of the brain linked with primitive drives and emotions). The temporary blockage of pathways during ECT has been compared with the permanent and deliberate cutting of nervous pathways in the operation known as prefrontal leucotomy.

Another type of explanation of the benefits of ECT on dynamic lines is that the treatment is a symbolic death, which is what a depressed person is looking for. It is noteworthy that, where an individual has made a determined attempt at suicide and is rescued by medical or other treatment, the depression often seems to clear up along with the recovery from whatever injury has been inflicted.

An alternative to the use of ECT which has now been largely superseded, is provided by drugs such as the Imipramine Group (e.g. Tofranil) or Monoamine Oxidase Inhibitors (MAOI). These drugs act in a powerful way and need to be given under close psychiatric supervision. They cut short some of the severest depressive illnesses, which previously carried high risk of suicide. Even in cases where the depression can be related to psychological causes, it may be necessary to administer suitable drugs before the patient can become an active participator in a psychotherapeutic process.

One further point is that the danger of suicide is sometimes greatest at the stage when a patient is beginning to recover from the deepest phases of depression, where there had been such a degree of apathy as to make it impossible to carry out any effective purpose. With treatment, a patient may improve just enough to be able to put self-destructive drives into action.

Taking Charge of the Patient

The problem of treatment is that there are instances of depression where we should leave people alone and there are other instances where it is necessary to take charge of the patient.

There is an ethical issue in the assumption that the professional worker has the right to, and the responsibility for, preventing someone from committing suicide. The justification is that some people who make determined attempts, and fail, or who are rescued, live to enjoy the new life which has been granted to them (or imposed upon them). There are, however, others who continue to make suicidal attempts, until finally, they succeed. It also needs to be noted that there are many instances where conscious and deliberate choice of suicide seems to be the only practicable course in some unusual circumstances of an individual's life.

New Levels of Development

Apart from its theological message, the Bible story of Job can be interpreted as the experience of a man who lost possessions, family and physical health, and who eventually survived the grief to find a new life, with a new level of maturity. We can use this theme to point out that depressive illnesses have a positive function in adapting individuals to a new status in life.

Jung[4] has dealt extensively with the symbolism of burial and rebirth. It is a frequent experience for people to find a fulfilment in work and in personal relationships which had not seemed possible before some change in the pattern of life has occurred.

An individual may have a particular aim in life and an appropriate image of himself or herself for every stage. In our culture, there has been an exaltation of youth or of early adult life as the part of life which matters. Other stages of life have been thought of as being either the stage of "becoming" or the stage of "having been". We should, instead, look for the new levels of maturity which are achieved for the first time in later life.

At a *physical* level, we have been accustomed to thinking that all growing stops at the end of adolescence. It is true that height cannot increase once the bony structure is complete. Perhaps it was on the analogy of this that it was thought that intelligence reached its maximum before the beginning of adult life. Psychologists now are prepared to think of further stages of intellectual development, and there is no structural limitation for this such as there is for physical growth. Ideas about *emotional* growth have never been able to be expressed in precise language, but it seems credible that every relationship with another individual can add something to one's personality. This is part of the process of growing-up which can continue even into the stage of life when we must admit to growing old.

Value in Each Stage of Life

Each stage of life has its separate importance. Childhood has an identity of its own and it is not the stage of being an immature adult; adolescence has been prolonged to the extent of being more than an in-between stage; and adult life has received an extension into and beyond an active middle age. Therefore, there could be new subdivisions of the adult phase according to functional capacity, self-image, and cultural expectations. Each change of function can have some element of growth, but this growth should not conceal the reality of degeneration of some of the tissues, with consequent diminution in some kinds of performance. Growth can still take place within the hitherto unused potentialities of physical, intellectual and emotional performance.

Some people preserve the image of youth too long, as when men and women well past middle age refer to themselves as "girls" and "boys".

Growth takes place through parenthood, grandparenthood, and in more indirect contacts with younger colleagues at work.

[4] C. G. Jung, *Symbols of Transformation*, The Collected Works, Vol. 5, Routledge and Kegan Paul, 1966.

Melanie Klein describes how the personality characteristics laid down in infancy can still influence the adult interactions at every age; she deals with the origin of envy and greed in the infant. Greed makes demands which exceed anything which can be received, but envy is worse because the coveted object has to be spoiled to prevent any other person's enjoyment of it. When, however, good experiences predominate over the bad, it becomes possible to work through primitive anxieties; and the processes of reparation and of gratitude come into operation. "If gratitude for past satisfactions has not vanished, old people can enjoy whatever is still within their reach. Furthermore, with such an attitude, which gives rise to serenity, they can identify themselves with young people."[5]

[5] M. Klein, *Our Adult World, and other Essays*, Heinemann, 1963.

20

Retirement, Old Age and Death

FROM the practical viewpoint of medical and social services, old age presents the problem of a large and increasing population in need. Patients over the age of 65 take up 48% of psychiatric hospital places (we have chosen the word "places" rather than the conventional term "beds" which implies inactivity), over 50% of all general hospital "beds", and an entire specialist geriatric service.[1] Social Service Departments face a demand for residential places in homes, and hostels, and an apparently limitless obligation to provide counselling, meals, assisted holidays, and other forms of support for old people living in their own homes. Chiropodists and physiotherapists give their specialist skills, and health visitors and home nurses provide domiciliary social and nursing care.

Added to these are the special housing provisions in council-owned property: housing that is purpose-built, or adapted for the convenient living of older people in the same way as is authorized for the disabled, through cooperation between Social Service and Housing Departments.

Financial provision, apart from retirement or other pensions given as of right, can be made through Social Security Departments.

The entitlement to general medical care through the general practitioner is retained, along with the growing tendency to look for specialist geriatric medical attention.

With all this provision, sometimes an actual reality, but only too often an empty promise of services in the process of preparation, it may seem surprising that the vast majority of old people live in their homes, or in the homes of daughters, sons, or other close relatives, without seeking, and apparently without requiring, any special help beyond that which is applicable to the population at large.

The ever-present burden on public services of large numbers of old people, diverts attention from the much larger population of old people who remain invisible among the rest of the community. The unnoticed large section of old people, however, may include many who are living in financial privation, deplorable residential accommodation, and, sometimes in conflict with members of family or close neighbours.

---

[1] In 1975, of the 87,000 resident patients in psychiatric hospitals, 48% were over the age of 65 (and 25% over the age of 75 years). In general hospitals, the patients over the age of 65 years occupy approximately half the beds, but form only $2\frac{1}{2}\%$ of the population of people over that age. (Figures given in detail in *A Happier Old Age*, a DHSS Discussion Document on Elderly People in our Society).

Great as the *ascertained* needs might be, the *potential* use of clearly designated entitlements to benefits would, if realized, be far beyond the capacity of available staffing and material resources. If all who are entitled to claim the Supplementary Benefits of National Insurance, or even the holiday grants offered by some Local Authorities, took up the advertised offers, the yearly budget allocated for the purpose, would be exhausted within the first few weeks.

At the time of writing, Area Health Authorities and Local Government Departments are being asked to make cuts in their budgets, thus further depleting already scarce resources.

All these themes need to be explored from a number of viewpoints: the capacities of old people (physical, intellectual and emotional); the interactions in families; the social problems and their attempted solutions; and the changing cultural backgrounds in which old people have developed and with which they continue to interact in new ways.

Population Trends

At the beginning of this century, only one in twenty-one of the population was over the age of 65. In 1963, the proportion was one in eleven, and in the late 1970s it was approximately one in seven. Projections of the proportion of old people in the community of the future have been calculated, for the old, the older, and the very old. For example, in 1979, there were 9,636,000 people over the age of 60, i.e. 17% of the 54 million population of the U.K. The calculated increase in this group for the year 2000 is $3\frac{1}{2}\%$.

In the same year there were 2,978,000 over the age of 75, and the calculated increase for the year 2000 is 21%.

For those over 85 years, the 1979 figure was 535,000, but the tendency to longer life is so great that the projected increase over the same period for this group reaches the figure of 40%.[2]

The increase in longevity of the population is due to the fact that more people attain the possible span of life than previously, and it is not an increase in the total span of life available.[3]

There are limits to the duration of life which are genetically determined and linked with sex chromosomes. On average, women live longer than men. A social consequence is that in sponsored outings, holidays, and old people's clubs, women overwhelmingly outnumber the men. The greater preponderance of widows over widowers, is due, however, only partly to the genetic factor in the longer life of females. Other factors are, first the tendency for the male to be the older of a marital pair, and secondly, the greater occurrence of occupationally-related deaths in mid-adult life among men.

---

[2] Figures supplied by Age Concern in 1979.
[3] F. J. Kallmann, "Genetic Factors in Ageing", in *Psychopathology of Ageing*, by P. H. Hoch and J. Zubin, Grune and Stratton, New York, 1961.

Retirement as Normal Expectation

Retirement as a general experience is a comparatively new feature of our society. Previously, it was taken for granted that people lived on what they earned, or what they had saved, or what was provided for them by members of their family, or, if all these failed, by residential or other provision under the humiliating conditions of the old poor law. The word "retirement" was reserved for the gentleman of means who had voluntarily relinquished his post or his own business.

The "Welfare State" is an aspect of an industrial society in which the "right to work" is at times an obligation and, at other times, a privilege for those who fit comfortably into the political and economic structure. Those who do not work receive support according to statutory regulations; retirement is compulsory for the majority of workers in industry and the passage from work to retirement is usually the entitlement to a pension which is gradually enclosing a contributory element, with payments related to former earnings. Payments coming directly from state funds may supplement work-related pensions, or they may be the only means of support for those outside the occupational field. In one sense, the pensions are an indication of the wealth of the society which provides them; in another sense, the pensions are the reparation for the compulsory exclusion from former occupation.

In times of industrial depression, scarce jobs have to be reserved for younger people who may be heads of families.

A more general feature is the recognition that failing physical and mental capacity may make an employee no longer suitable for the post that he or she had been occupying.

To many people, retirement is the arrival at freedom from the burden of unsatisfactory conditions of work, or the opportunity to carry out activities for which the working life gave no time. There still remains a large number of people who are able to arrange a continuation of some kind of paid work with scarcely a pause between.

The balance of life at all stages is a continuation of physical, intellectual and emotional expression. If occupational life seems to predominate at some stages, it is still necessary to explore the way that satisfactions are achieved or are lacking. Those whose life seems to have no component other than work, derive their self-image from that work and have nothing left to enjoy when work ceases. To these, compulsory retirement is a reluctant departure, sometimes with a ritual disrobing on the last day at the work.

In no case however should work occupy one's whole existence. Women more than men are able to derive some image of themselves from their activities in the home, but the sharp dichotomy of women in the home, and men in jobs, no longer holds (if it ever did).

What some men and women feel at retirement resembles the experiences in women at the natural menopause or the artificial one of hysterectomy. A capacity which is linked with the self-image is lost, and, unless there is enough left to be enjoyed and developed, the loss is one which leads to depression.

There is a falsity in the deliberate substitution of activities which would not have been valued by the individual if the opportunity had been there while he or she was still working. Work should always have been balanced by play, relationships with others balanced by individual fulfilment, and activities which have an end product should be balanced by the freedom to enter into thoughts and feelings which may have unanticipated consequences.

At all ages of life, there is room for creativity which is associated with the undirected and the ambiguous. In childhood, play is recognized as having a value that goes beyond learning specified tasks. The amount of play exceeds the amount of work. During the later years of education, the balance alters, sometimes to the extent of stifling imagination. This continues for many in working life. Retirement comes best to those who could always keep a part of their time uncommitted to specifically planned activities.

The use of time provides an illustration of contrasting attitudes. Some of our time is contracted to other people for specific purposes, and some of it is unbound. Yet many people find ways of committing their unbound time to purposes that are deliberately invented so that no time should be seen to be wasted. Every uncommitted moment has to be given a use, and every wandering thought has to be transformed into a rational principle.

It may not be easy to keep a balance between free and disciplined activity, to find comfort in uncertainty as well as certainty, or to keep some time in hand that is not committed to a definite task. Some people take on an extreme as an enduring standard by which to live their lives. Reward will come, in Kipling's words,

> "If you can fill the unforgiving minute
> With sixty seconds' worth of distance run".

Others would commiserate even with the success of the principle, and ask with W. H. Davies,

> "What is this life if, full of care,
> We have no time to stand and stare?"

Preparing for Retirement

The theme of retirement is now the subject of many studies made under the aegis of government departments, voluntary bodies such as Age Concern, and educational institutions. Professional organizations and industrial concerns run classes dealing with preparation for retirement.

Much of this literature includes sound practical advice about availability of concessions and supportive services, the use of free time, and the development of new interests. Some give recipes for living in "cook book" style.

Others enter another dimension by calling attention to the diversity of needs and personality among the retired and the elderly. For example, Sidney Jones[4] discusses the variety of possible perceptions of older people and the dangers of assuming that they must inevitably degenerate physically. For most people, however old or inca-

---

[4] S. Jones, *Learning and Personality in Later Life*, A Report of a seminar arranged by the Department of Adult Education, University of Keele, the Beth Johnson Foundation, and the Pre-Retirement Association of Keele, September 1976.

pacitated, there are areas of knowledge and experiences which can still be opened up. Learning in retirement is more than a time user: it is a fulfilment.

Categorization as "old" has to be seen as a recognition of biological facts which might or might not entail special needs. Categorization is necessary for some administrative purposes, but it should not deny the general quality of continuity of life, nor the individual aspects of any one person. Any problem of the old ought to be treated as a problem in its own right. It is only a matter of convenience to make generalizations on the characteristics of old people and it is done in order to legitimize the allocation of resources.

The majority of old people can live their lives without the need for any personally directed help. Pensions, concessionary fares on public transport, and price reductions are welcomed even by those not in dire need. The categorization is, indeed, readily accepted when it brings a tangible benefit.

Social Problems of Dependence

There are, however, numbers of old people who have survived their apparent economic usefulness, and who urgently need assistance in order to maintain normal standards of living. It is a sad fact that even with this assistance, the circumstances of a large number of old people fall far below national standards.

The existence of a large number of underprovided individuals lies heavily on the conscience of the community, because these were the previous working generation and are the parents of the present one. Not all of them are dependent now, but those who are, may be seen as a burden and obligation on public funds, or as a personal responsibility of their own families. The present working generation has learned to accept increased obligations for those who are dependent at both ends of life. Childhood and adolescence have been prolonged, and so has old age.

Perhaps members of the working adult population have come to regard themselves as representing the whole of the community and all the others as a race apart. Individual adults at times feel and act as if they personally had never had a childish dependent state, and as if they have no intention of becoming dependent in their old age. Thus, at times, it seems that there are distinctive races of man—children, adults and old people—rather than a people in which each individual has a series of different stages of the same life and personality.

In less cynical moments, one might comment on the extent to which the community is in fact prepared to provide for those who are no longer capable of looking after themselves. There is a good deal of feeling of compassion and concern for those who are dependent, but we must be aware at the same time that there are two aspects of feeling about carrying the burdens of others. Resentment and hostility is the other aspect of the ambivalent picture. Occasionally people can conceal their ambivalence by being able to express their wish for provision to be made for old and other dependent people, but make it clear that this care should be carried out by "The Government". Their concern and hostility can both be expressed in criticism of existing provision.

Sometimes we hear people speaking resentfully or in a hostile way of some burden that they are carrying, and in this case the hidden part of feeling is the tenderness which makes them able to do it at all. Others conceal the hostility under elaborate care which over-protects their dependent relatives and which restricts their freedom of action. Beyond ambivalence lies undiluted hostility.

Some of the problems with regard to old people are related to the conflict between the generations. It is implied that problems at the present time are greater than formerly, yet there always has been some distinction between the elderly and the young adults. In some cultures, old people have been venerated to an extraordinary extent as the carriers of wisdom, and treated with almost religious adoration.[5] Perhaps it was their scarcity value, in cultures where most people died young, that allowed this special treatment. Those who survived must indeed have had some special qualities!

Carrying the Culture

Some old people in our culture are able to express themselves well, and are carriers of the culture of their youth and may have added some appreciation of contemporary culture to their personal experience of previous generations. Some old people convey to their intimate family this feeling of being somehow special. An eighteenth-century writer said, "Old age is such a charming condition. What a pity it lasts such a short time"—and perhaps there was something personal in the feeling. One remembers that George Bernard Shaw, on reaching his ninetieth birthday, was very concerned at the idea of mortality, and felt that at least for a few selected people there should be some lengthening of the ordinary span of life.

Many people are reluctant to let go of life itself, and some are unwilling to let go of a particular position which they have held in life. This may be the position of power or authority in a family, where a woman is reluctant to let go the burdens of housekeeping, or a man to let go the responsibility for making the important decisions which affect the lives of other members.

Problems arise on an economic level when people are able to maintain their positions and block the promotion of younger people. Such individuals, if in a managerial or ownership position, may hold on to power and financial responsibility, and not only impede other people's advancement, but also hamper the progress of the concerns which they are directing. This may happen also in voluntary organizations where a chairman holds on to the position for a period long past full usefulness to the committee.

Reluctant Abdication

It may happen that an individual gives up wealth or position yet still wants to keep the disposal of it. We may think of this as a modern practice which has grown up to save the payment of inheritance taxes, but a similar story occurs in Shakespeare's *King Lear*. In this play a whole range of human conflicts is depicted

---

[5] Felix Post points out (1965) that man stands out in the animal kingdom by reason of his capacity to store and elaborate life experiences mentally, and to transfer them by speech to other members of his species. In a wider sense than the merely biological one, he remains useful to his race after his reproductive role is over. (*The Clinical Psychiatry of Late Life*, Pergamon Press, 1965.)

with a depth of understanding which goes far beyond that which modern psychiatric writers are capable of revealing.

One facet of the story concerns Lear's decision to divide his kingdom between his three daughters. Regan and Goneril express their love for him in acceptable words at his request, and are correspondingly rewarded. But Cordelia, the youngest daughter is unable to deny the complexity of her intense feelings—her share is therefore refused her and divided between the other two. When ex-king Lear arranges to stay, in turn, with the two daughters who are his inheritors within his lifetime (much as an elderly father of today may stay with his married children in turn), the daughters begin to feel that he is still competing with them for the authority that he gave away. His very vigour disturbs them. His daughters plead with him to accept the consequences of his new status and obey the orders of those who know better than he does what is good for him (or them).

> O Sir, you are old;
> Nature in you stands on the very verge
> Of her confine: you should be Rul'd and led
> By some discretion, that discerns your state
> Better than you yourself,

says Regan. Later she commands "Being weak, seem so"! He is made to carry the consequences of the illusory strength of his rebellion. His family cast him out into the storm, which he defies, and he fights impotently against the elements. It is a matter of our choice whether we think of his madness as coming from the degenerative process of old age in which his behaviour becomes troublesome, or whether we think of him as justly rebelling against, and being driven mad by, the ingratitude of his daughters.

As in Greek Tragedy, death for Lear is the inevitable outcome of his character and actions. At the moment of death, he is joined by Cordelia in the dying, and in the discovery of their concealed love for each other.

None of the problems of old age—personal, family or communal—are new. What is new is the fact that more people live to a greater age, and therefore any problems which exist are multiplied. The economic aspects have to be faced, and it may become more important that ever to find value in the capacity and competence that old people still have in family, social and occupational life.

Changing Functions

It is still appropriate to deal with the life of old people in the different aspects—physical, intellectual, emotional and social. The physical changes include the continuation of degenerative processes, or wear and tear of various tissues. There are changes which are to be expected and which we call normal. The rate of metabolism is reduced, i.e. the tissues work at a lower rate and chemical interchanges go on more slowly. Some tissues may shrink, and many old people find it convenient to eat less and become thinner. This may happen imperceptibly as, when the output of energy becomes less, the food intake may be reduced, and appetite, which is partly a matter of habit becomes less. Many people accommodate themselves very well to the metabolic change by slowing down many of their activities, and yet finding themselves able to preserve some interest in restricted fields. There may be a change in the rate of working and even a change in the rate of thinking about one's work.

There are some characteristic patterns of mental life in old age. Memory for recent events may be lost while the recollection of events long passed may still be preserved.

Changes take place in the central nervous system, particularly in relation to the cells in the brain tissue, and the total amount of mental activity is reduced. Thus, amongst the normal changes, there is some deterioration in intellectual capacity. The deterioration seems less marked in those of high intelligence, and it is one of the unfair aspects of nature that those who have more, have it longer.

Mental Disturbances: Functional and Organic

Old people sometimes become separated from members of their family on account of their lack of capacity to enter into the day-to-day life of the home. Sometimes this lack of capacity is increased by the reluctance of other members of the family to share the knowledge of day-to-day events with old people, perhaps because they are slow to grasp them. There may be a tendency to exclude the elderly from family councils, to make decisions without any consultation, and, sometimes, without conveying the decision. Important events occur in a household, and the old person has no foreknowledge of them. This can lead to a feeling of confusion, of uncertainty, and to the expression of a belief of being no longer valued in the household. And next comes the feeling of being disregarded, and being talked about behind one's back. The actual reality resembles the delusional feelings which are characteristic of paranoia, and there is a danger that a clinical diagnosis of paranoia might be made in cases where an individual is actually suffering from the reality of being excluded. Nevertheless, paranoid states of varying degrees of severity do, in fact, occur frequently in old people.

Depressive illnesses can occur from endogenous or from exogenous causes in the same way as in middle age. These can be variations of mood or exaggerations of ordinary feelings that people of all ages can have from time to time. Sometimes there is an exaggeration of personal characteristics which had been present previously in a milder form. It is no longer easy to conceal various personality traits, which differ from individual to individual, when the older person is no longer in complete control of all the faculties. Meannesses, hatred, maliciousness, and a variety of minor or major antisocial tendencies become revealed. An older person may sometimes become a caricature of the former self once the lifting of controls and inhibitions reveals qualities which had previously existed but which had been kept within what appeared to be the normal range.

Physical, intellectual and emotional characteristics thus become linked with one another in the changing nature of behaviour which results from the degenerative processes. There are the social implications, too, with regard to the various aspects of care and treatment. Some of the mental changes might be thought of as due to organic or structural changes, and many of the mental illnesses are ascribed to senile degeneration and are labelled "Senile Psychosis".

Many of the changes, however, seem to be "functional" rather than structural, and they are not necessarily permanent mental disorders. This is important and there is a tendency to look upon the mental changes in old people as irreversible, and therefore to seek permanent residential placement for those who become mentally ill. Some patients improve rapidly when transferred to hospital. There may be a degree of benefit from the very fact that in a psychiatric hospital individuals have *permission to be abnormal*. They are allowed to be themselves. They can be legitimately confused and are not forced to fit into the pattern of an effective younger self that can no longer be sustained. They become able to make a new adaptation at a level which actually is within their capacity.

Some of the implications of the label "senility" will be discussed later.

Problems of Residential Accommodation

There is a serious clinical as well as social problem with regard to the fact that residential accommodation is sought for the elderly person with mental symptoms. Provision is made under a variety of medical and social services. A patient suffering from some limitation of function as a result of mental or physical illness may need long-term treatment. Some patients are there for the purpose of receiving active medical and nursing treatment, and some are there because there is nowhere else for them to be.

It was one of the purposes of the 1959 Mental Health Act to place responsibility for social, rather than medical, care on to local authorities instead of the hospital boards, and it was expected that some people who have had a long stay in hospital should be returned to the community. It was, however, impracticable to discharge people from a hospital which was their only home, and the one which they had known for many years. Perhaps the most that we can do is to see that this type of hospital population is not added to, and we can consider alternative types of residential accommodation to prevent new admissions of this type to hospitals.

Varieties of Hospital, Hostel and Housing Provision

Apart from psychiatric and general hospitals there are some hospitals which specialize in the treatment of chronic and disabling illnesses, and there are geriatric wards especially for old people. Outside the hospital system, the Social Service Departments of the local authorities have the responsibility of providing homes for old people who are unable to provide homes for themselves and who have no relatives who find it possible to provide a home for them. In addition, Housing Departments make special housing provision where old people can live independent lives with the minimum of supervision. Finally, one of the duties of the Social Service Departments of local authorities is to provide hostels for elderly people who have mild mental illness which may not call for, or be amenable to, hospital treatment.

There is an increasing demand for all these different kinds of accommodation, and it is a frequent topic of social workers that families of old people are no longer willing to take responsibility for them. Nevertheless, by far the largest proportion of old people live in their own homes with their families, and often quite happily and on good terms. Difficulties can occur, and some of these are due to the changing patterns of living and technical "progress". The very nature of progress in housing can present a difficulty. Slum clearance and the rebuilding of houses in new suburbs is often carried out in a manner that fits the nuclear family consisting of a father and mother with two or three children. The two- or three-bedroomed house or flat becomes the most frequent unit. Spare bedrooms are less frequent, and the demands for higher standards of accommodation and hygiene make is more difficult to fit in an old person as an extra resident within the family. Even where there is a spare bedroom it may be of a kind which is lower in status, size and amenities than the principal bedrooms.

The fittings of a modern house, with its streamlining and electrification of cooking and working equipment, form a different setting from the homes in which many of the old generation were brought up. It is difficult for an old person to find a place where he is comfortable and does not damage valuable furnishings. Kitchens have become workshops and not living rooms, and, where furniture is precious and easily damaged, the old person is less acceptable in the home. In some cases, as a result of rehousing, the bathroom becomes a sign of the new status and of the improved standards of living. A chamber pot is looked upon as something archaic and if, as a result of the difficulty of finding the way to the bathroom at night, accidents happen, the old person feels ashamed and may be subjected to criticism or abuse. Incontinence may be a social rather than a physical phenomenon.

In the smaller family, the physical burden of looking after an old person who becomes feeble is greater than in the large family where the duties are shared. If husband and wife go out to work there may be no one at all to take the responsibility for an aged parent or relative. There are, therefore, a good many reasons why there seems to be pressure to get special places for old people, and yet in many families all that is asked for is some help in order to maintain and keep the old people within the family circle.

When help is given at an early stage, before distress and conflict have reached a high level of intensity, the integrity of the family can be maintained. In some cases a short stay in hospital gives relief to all concerned. Sometimes an old person is admitted for the weekend to give the family a rest; in other cases, during the week, when the family are out at work. Ideally there should be day hospitals where patients can find occupation, as well as treatment, and return home to sleep, and night hospitals where people can sleep and go out to work in the day-time if still able to do so.

The structure, architecture and siting of the various types of residential accommodation is a matter of controversy. There are mansions in the country where provision is made for old people on a grand scale but in complete isolation from their families or from the community in general. There are small blocks of houses on the fringe of housing estates, or special types of accommodation scattered amongst ordinary housing. There are old people's homes in which there are resident wardens and provision for some medical supervision; and it has been said that the ideal site for an old people's home would be one with a public house at one corner, a Woolworth's store at another, and a fish and chip shop at a third corner!

Amongst the considerations for siting of such hormones are the arguments as to whether old people should intermingle with younger ones or not; whether they would lose patience and be disturbed by the noise of young children, or whether they would wish to see them running about. The relationship is often mutually supportive, but in some cases there is conflict arising from the intolerance of the old or the young.

Dependence and Independence within the Family and Community

When all these considerations have been discussed are we not taking responsibility, even with the best intentions, for the way that old people *ought* to feel, without giving them an opportunity to work out what they *actually do* feel? We arrive at the best decision that we can, and expect the old people to be grateful. "Being *old*, seem so!" we say. The question arises as to whether it might not be possible for old people to have a more independent life of their own, productive, and with emotional satisfactions appropriate to their needs and capacity.

In many homes, the grandparents still serve as a stabilizing influence, receiving, and therefore justifying, respect, and building up a special kind of relationship with grandchildren or great-grandchildren.

It is the suddenness of change of function which leads to loss of status and loss of self-respect within the personality of the old person before other people begin to share in this process of devaluation. The industrial pattern may need to change in order to use the productivity of old people, if self-respect is to be preserved. At this stage of life, mental disturbance is more noticeable in the male than in the female in relation to the clearly marked and sudden change of status on the day that retirement takes place. Nevertheless, there are many women in these days who carry the impact of retirement from valued employment for which the substitution of housework is no compensation. Conversely, there are many men who gain a new self-valuation, status and satisfaction from tending the garden and improving the home. Together some retired couples find a new harmony, and this stands out in sharp contrast with the cases where a wife resents the presence of a husband in her own domain and in the time she has allocated to her own tasks. It is a modern cynicism: "I married him for better or for worse, but not for lunch."

Senility

Senility, which comes to some people, implies a life that has survived the capacity for action and thought; even feelings may be no longer credited to those who are labelled senile. There is a physical basis to senility, but perhaps some of the features are the mental acceptance of a status which is imposed on some old people who have lost the power to determine the events and circumstances of their lives. This loss of status is what many people fear even more than dying in pain. Relatives are

disturbed by the enfeeblement of the old who go on living, when what is left seems
to be a caricature of the former self, with some of the old faults highly exaggerated.
Death, in some cases, comes as a relief to the living.

Survival from illnesses, even in old age, can be perceived as a rebirth, and give a
reassurance of a goodness such as people may emerge with from a depression.

> All these things God may do to a man,
> again and yet again,
> bringing him back from the pit
> to enjoy the full light of life.[6]

Facts of Death

Children ask about the facts of death as urgently as they ask about the facts of
life, and the answers to the questions on death are often more incomplete than the
information that is given about sexuality and birth. There is a reluctance in those
who are in early adult life to contemplate their own death or the death of young
children, but these deaths occur. It seems difficult to come to terms with a universe
in which death can come through the chance of injury or disease, and not through
the inevitability of reaching the limit of life. Doctors and social workers are hesitant
in discussing the topic of death even with those suffering from incurable illness at
the terminal stages, yet the dying need professional care and the involvement of
their families; and the relatives of those who die, whether suddenly or after long
illness, need some preparation and consolation.

Death itself is something which is feared at many stages of life. At some stages
the fear can be denied, but there are times when this fear takes a greater intensity,
and people become concerned about leaving some effect or trace of themselves as a
living immortality. They seek to influence their children during their lifetime, or
afterwards, by instructions and conditions which they can lay down. Sometimes this
wish becomes frantic when the capacity for present-day activity and influence seems
to be becoming reduced. Many people, however, achieve a serenity during old age
and feel they can afford to let go of life and be content with what they have given
and received.

The inevitability of death is contrasted with "the declared aim of the remedial
services, which human beings have created ... to cure or prevent diseases and, it is
implied, to prevent death".[7] But there are illnesses which are incurable, and death
does not always await old age. There are untimely deaths which leave survivors
unprepared except for the comfort that the deceased did not suffer long. Families
may be left bereaved of members who would otherwise have long remained an
essential element. The contrast is between inevitability and hazard.

Although we know why some diseases and misfortunes occur, and why in the
civilized world that we live, we face hazards of accident, as well as of ill fortune, we
do not know which particular person will suffer a calamity in which there is a
statistically precise, predictable incidence.

[6] Job 33: 29-30. NEB (2nd ed), Oxford and Cambridge, 1970
[7] J. H. Kahn, *Job's Illness: Loss, Grief and Integration*, p. 158, Pergamon Press, 1975.

Old age and death form an inherent quality of life, even when a person may steadfastly deny that it would actually happen to him or her. In his protest against his suffering Job says: "I thought I would die with my powers unimpaired."[8] Some people do die in possession of all their faculties and in the middle of some task.

While life continues, an old person needs to be able to look forward to some change and development in what is yet to come, but there is also a need for permission to look backwards on past satisfactions and dissatisfactions. The permission is needed to be able to talk about these things, and therefore it is part of the relationship with younger people.

Fear of Death

In 1967, Hinton[9] pointed out that the main argument for euthanasia was the lack of provision for the total care of the dying. There is also the tacit assumption that dying is painful, as indeed it often is. Cicely Saunders[10], who has written of her experience in St Christopher's Hospice, refers to the control of pain by medication, but more importantly, she writes about those who have an instinctive belief in survival. They are able to communicate their fear to someone who still respects their independence. She states that she does not believe that we should step in to cut short the mental suffering that we hate to see, and thus deprive a dying man of the accompanying reconciliation and peace, in which the helper should have a share.

Communications with the Dying

McIntosh has studied the communications between medical and nursing staff and patients in a cancer ward. He describes some of the evasions, but comments on the difference between patients who ask explicit questions, who want to know, and those who ask indirectly, and would rather welcome the faint hopes that go with uncertainty. He submits that it is as unwarranted to tell a patient who might not want to know as it is not to tell a patient who does.[11]

The policy of not telling even when the cancer is curable perpetuates the lay belief that it is a dread and uncurable disease. When a patient dies, the diagnosis is no longer secret, but those who are cured may not be known about.

Those responsible for the care of the dying patient should sit down with the patient and take seriously any minor or incidental discomforts or disturbances such as digestive disorders, and treat them as if the patient had a life time still ahead. It would be so easy to dismiss them as if they were of little account in comparison with the seriousness of the major pathology.

---

[8] Job 29: 18, NEB.
[9] J. Hinton, *Dying*, Penguin, 1967.
[10] C. Saunders, The treatment of intractable pain in terminal cancer', *Proceedings of the Royal Society of Medicine*, **56**, 1963.
[11] J. McIntosh, *Communication and Awareness in a Cancer Ward*, N. Watson, New York, 1977.

Counselling and Anticipatory Mourning

Frankness is not a virtue in itself, but it has been presented in opposition to the superstitious belief present, even in the sophisticated, that the word has the power to create the fact. If you tell a person that he or she is dying, (or even mention the possibility), that in itself can make it come true. But, just as reassurance can be for the benefit of the helper, who cannot bear the hopelessness of an approaching death, so can frankness be part of the "virtue" of the helper who has scorned to be associated with hypocrisy. It takes discretion and skill, as well as courage, to employ frankness for the benefit of the dying. Some people wish, and need, to know that they are dying, in order to be able to put their material and spiritual affairs in order. Others like to employ a conventional concealment that does not deceive anyone, but which keeps alive a spark of hope and makes it possible to look forward to the next day of the life that remains (and who knows how many more days?).

The frankness of communication includes a process of anticipatory mourning. Sometimes this anticipatory mourning precedes an unexpected recovery, and in such circumstances the recovery does not receive an unmixed welcome. Relatives may say sympathetically, "But won't he have to go through all this again?"

In an illness with a long delayed fatal outcome, even in a child, emotions may be exhausted well before the end. It can be said, as of King Lear:

> He is gone indeed
> The wonder is he hath endured so long:
> He but usurp'd his life.

Death as a Fulfilment

The experience of grief, however, can enrich the lives of families. It is always to poets that we must turn to find language adequate for these feelings. Tennyson, in "In Memoriam" speaks of birth as well as of death; and Milton, of untimely death says:

> For Lycidas is dead, dead ere his prime . . .
> . . . .
> He must not float upon his watery bier
> Unwept, and welter to the parching wind
> Without the meed of some melodious tear.

Yet death may come as a fulfilment as in the Job story:

> So Job died, being old, and full of days.

Afterword

A STUDY of human development is usually carried out by tracing the progress of an individual through the various stages of maturation and growth. There is an assumption that this takes place against a fixed background of "the culture"—unless it is "the culture" that is being studied. We have found it difficult to turn from "the individual" to "the culture", and vice versa; but we considered the effort had to be made.

We have introduced the theme of ethnic differences in our population, wherever we have thought it appropriate to do so.

The ethnic distribution of our child population is now a major issue in any planning for general welfare provision. In our view, it is unsatisfactory to concentrate only on the literature that is specifically designed to call attention to the disadvantaged status of some groups. We need also to be able to listen to the voices of those in each community who are trying to express their aspirations, their identity, and the changes in their identity.

There was a "pre-run", at the beginning of the twentieth century, in the experiences of a Jewish immigrant community, of some of the features of the present day settling-in of new arrivals from the West Indies, Africa, the Indian subcontinent and the Far East.

The Jewish experiences were given recognition by Anglo-Jewish writers, notably by Israel Zangwill, who dealt with Jewish immigrant life in London, and who was also recognized by the wider host-community as a significant writer of his generation.

Each community needs a literature which explores the richness of its own culture; and this literature should be accessible, and of interest, to the population at large. At least some of it should become part of "English Literature".

V. S. Naipaul has written about the culture and experiences of Indian communities in India, in African States and in this country. One of his titles, *In a Free State*, points to the special problem of adaptation to a new culture, when the original culture has also been, for some time, in a state of transition.

The West Indian Community in this country is, in its turn, producing a rich literature of its own; but, for the most part, unknown to the population at large. This is in contrast to their conspicuousness in the avant-garde in entertainment, which perhaps contributes a disproportionate amount to their public image.

Ethnic minorities, for all their distinctive characteristics, merge in diverse ways with the general community. Some of their members enter the mainstream of the

211

culture through entry into established occupations and professions, some by inter-marriage, and some by public activities. There is still, however, a tendency, in many organizations and institutions, for the "token black" to be given an exaggerated importance.

Current history may be repeating, in a different way, the experiences of the children of early Jewish immigrants who enthusiastically entered a culture which was partly closed to their parents. Sometimes, this took the form of complete assimilation into the host culture. However, some individuals managed to retain an identity within their parent culture, and yet find a place and a significant change of personal identity in the new culture. This was often achieved by entering pro-fessions and industries which were themselves undergoing rapid technological change, and were, therefore, attractive to those who could contribute to and, some-times, anticipate trends.

The experience of adaptation, or of failure to adapt, of the children of ethnic-minority parents could be used as a paradigm of the general experience of the emergence of all adolescents into the adult community. Within the last few decades, a whole generation of schoolchildren has received an education which has been extended from a school-leaving age of thirteen, to fourteen, to fifteen, and, now, to sixteen years. Whereas a sizeable proportion of schoolchildren are, by now, "second generation" secondary-school pupils, a much smaller proportion are "second generation" university students.

The widening of education has been accompanied by technical change which has taken young people into realms that their parents have never known; even though it was the parents' generation that laid the foundation for the new knowledge and the new techniques.

Some of the disadvantages suffered by immigrant communities could be used to call attention to the problems of young people in heavily populated urban areas—which seem to escape notice, because they are in the indigenous population. Rates of delinquency show a differential distribution in relation to schools, quite as much as to family and to other environmental factors, and this has been well annotated by Power, and, more recently, by Rutter.[1] We wish, however, to refer to the study by Downes,[2] who puts forward the thesis that young people attempt to surmount dispiriting features of their surroundings. Some use the school positively, and escape through educational success; others may be unable to do this, either because of lack of the necessary ability, or because of the unattractive way in which edu-cation is so often presented. These latter may choose what Downes calls "the delin-quent solution", in which a delinquent reputation is deliberately built up into the image of identity. In this connection, we could spare a thought for those who achieve neither educational success, nor delinquency, and who remain dispirited.

Communities change, and adapt; and it is misleading, if we think of change as invariably being desirable progress. A new culture, whether it be from the varying degrees of adaptation of minority groups or from the innovations of contemporary

[1] M. J. Power, R. T. Benn, and J. N. Morris, Neighbourhood, school, and juveniles before courts, *British Journal of Criminology* (1972) 12, 111–32; and Rutter *et al.*, *Fifteen Thousand Hours: Secondary Schools and their Effect on Children*. Open Books, 1979.

[2] D. M. Downes, *The Delinquent Solution*, Routledge and Kegan Paul, 1966.

culture as a whole, may have no consistent pattern which could represent an entire population.

Innovation has values which are in competition with the continuing traditions that have survived from previous centuries. Some sections of the population make it their task to preserve these. Those who hold up their hands in horror at the sexual freedom or revolutionary political activities of a new generation are the counterpart of those who reject everything which pre-existed their current preoccupations.

What is called the generation gap closely resembles the gap between minority groups and the rest of the population. It is impossible to escape from the attribution of values to cultural trends. Innovation does not lead instantly to identified consistent characteristics which can claim approval. The problem of those who deviate from their parent culture is that attempts at creativity may appear as confusion, even to themselves.

Some people have sought to recognize any departure from established custom (even insanity) as a desirable liberation from the repressions of society; but undirected thoughts and activities are not all of equal merit. The small number of writers and artists who shatter traditional boundaries do so because they have something new to say which cannot be said within existing conventions; and they are originators who, in turn, become the subject of challenge. On a larger scale, dissatisfaction with the existing framework may lead to nothing more than cults which give a transitory group cohesion in which the message is protest against something, rather than the arrival at a satisfying substitute. What we wish to avoid is on the one hand approving all innovation, or, on the other hand, labelling it as pathology.

We must recognize that the task of anyone in an existing institutionalized profession is to be able to extend its boundaries and to be able to contemplate entirely unanticipated thoughts and behaviour; to be prepared to find positive values in it; and also to be able to recognize the distress of those who are making efforts in vain to find an identity which so far has no pre-existing model with which it can be compared.

In contemplation of what we have written elsewhere in the book, the major theme we wish to convey is that of continued development, and the avoidance of any impression of finality in the recording of studies of any aspect of development.

Moreover, although our studies are intended to help professional workers to provide themselves with a perspective of development against which to view the task that they undertake, we have to recognize the unpredictability of social trends in a community which is carrying considerable tensions, as well as potentialities for economic and cultural growth.

Our final word is that this plea for toleration of what is unanticipated is accompanied by recognition of the need for a framework within which to make our observations and carry out our work, and within which the value judgements of goodness or badness can, however tentatively, be attributed to the results.

Bibliography

Ainsworth, M. D., *The Effects of Maternal Deprivation.* Public Health Papers No. 14. W.H.O., Geneva, 1962.

Allport, G. W., *Personality—a Psychological Interpretation.* Henry Holt, New York, 1937. Revised 1963.

Barbour, R. F. *et al.,* Eneuresis as a Disorder of Development. *Brit. Med. J.,* 5360 (1963).

Bernstein, B., Aspects of Language and Learning in the Genesis of the Social Process. *J. of Child Psychol. and Psychiat.* (1961).

Bernstein, B., Social Structure, Language and Learning. *Educational Res.,* **3**, 173–6 (1961).

Birch, H. G. *et al., Mental Subnormality in the Community.* Williams & Williams, Baltimore, U.S.A., 1970.

Bott, E., *Family and Social Network.* Tavistock Publications, 1957.

Bowlby, J., *Attachment and Loss (Vol. 1: Attachment).* The Hogarth Press, 1969.

Bowlby, J., *Maternal Care and Mental Health.* W.H.O., 1958.

Bowlby, J., The Nature of the Child's Tie to his Mother. *Int. J. Psychoanal.,* **39**, 1958.

Bruner, J. S., *Towards a Theory of Instruction.* Norton, New York, 1966.

Burton, L., *Care of the Child Facing Death.* Routledge & Kegan Paul, 1974.

Caplan, G., *An Approach to Community Mental Health.* Tavistock Publications, 1961.

Caplan, G. (ed.), *Prevention of Mental Disorders in Children.* Tavistock Publications, 1961.

Clarke, A. M. and Clarke, A. D. B., *Early Experience: Myth and Evidence.* Open Books, 1976.

Clegg, A. and Megson, B., *Children in Distress.* Penguin, 1968.

Court, J., The Mother Who Injures Her Child. *Social Work Service,* December 1973.

Davis, Hunter, *The Creighton Report.* Hamish Hamilton, 1976.

D.E.S., *The Continuing Needs of Immigrants.* Education Survey No. 14. H.M.S.O., 1972.

D.E.S. *Special Educational Needs:* The Report of the Committee of Enquiry into the Education of Handicapped Children and Young People (Chairman Mrs. H. M. Warnock). H.M.S.O., 1978.

D.H.S.S. *Fit for the Future.* The Report of the Committee on Child Health Services (Chairman Professor S. D. M. Court). H.M.S.O., Cmnd 6684, 1976.

Donaldson, M., *Children's Minds.* Fontana, 1978.

Downes, D. M., *The Delinquent Solution.* Routledge & Kegan Paul, 1966.

Duche, D. J., Schonfeld, W. A. and Tomkiewicz, S., Physical Aspects of Adolescence Development, in Caplan, G. and Lebovici, S. (eds.), *Psychiatric Approaches to Adolescence.* International Congress Series 108, 1966.

Ellenberger, H. F., *The Discovery of the Unconscious: The History and Evolution of Dynamic Psychiatry.* Allen Lane, 1970.

Erikson, E. H., Identity and the Life Cycle: Selected Papers. *Psychological Issues* (Monograph), I:1, International Universities Press, N.Y., 1959.

Escalona, S. K., *The Roots of Individuality.* Tavistock Publications, 1968.

Fairbairn, W. R. D., *Psychoanalytical Studies of Personality.* Tavistock Publications. 1952.

Feldman, L., *Care Proceedings.* Oyez, 1978.

Flower, F. D., *Language and Education.* Longmans, 1966.

Frank, L. K., Therapeutic Play Techniques. *Amer. J. Orthopsychiat.* (1945).

Freeman, J., *Gifted Children: Their Identification and Development in a Social Context.* MTP Press, 1979.

Freud, A., *Normality and Pathology.* Hogarth Press, 1966.

Freud, S., *The Origins of Psycho-Analysis: Letters to Willhelm Fliess,* Drafts and Notes: 1887–1902. Imago Press, 1954.

Fromm, E., *The Anatomy of Human Destructiveness.* Jonathan Cape, 1974.

Gesell, A. and Amatruda, C., *Developmental Diagnosis.* Paul B. Hoeber Inc., 1960.

Gillman, B. (ed.), *Reconstructing Educational Psychology.* Croom Helm, 1978.

215

Glover, E., *Psychoanalysis*. Staples Press, 1939.

Greenson, R. R., *The Technique and Practice of Psychoanalysis*. The Hogarth Press, 1967.

Gunter, M., Instinct and the Nursing Couple. *Lancet* **1**, 575 (1955).

Halsey, A. H., Genetics, Social Structure and Intelligence. *Brit. J. Sociol.* **9**, 15–20 (1958).

Harrison, G. A. *et al.*, *Human Biology*. Oxford University Press, 1964.

Hawthorn, P. J., *Nurse, I Want My Mummy*. Royal College of Nursing, 1974.

Henry, J., *Pathways to Madness*. Jonathan Cape, 1972.

Hill, D., On the Contribution of Psychoanalysis to Psychiatry: mechanism and meaning. *Brit. J. Psych.* (1970).

Hinde, R. A., The Nature of Imprinting, in Foss, B. M. (ed.), *Determinants of Infant Behaviour*, Vol. 2. Methuen, 1963.

Hinton, J., *Dying*. Penguin, 1967.

Hoffmeyer, H., *The Feminine Role and Motherhood*. W.H.O. Seminar, Athens, Working Paper EURO. 206 2/WP6, 1962.

Hourd, M. L., *Coming into Their Own*. Heinemann, 1959.

Hudson, Liam, *Contrary Imaginations*. Penguin, 1967.

Hull, C. L., *A Behaviour System*. Yale University Press, 1952.

Illingworth, R. S., *The Development of the Infant and Young Child, Normal and Abnormal*. 6th Ed. E. S. Livingstone, 1975.

Jackson, B. and Marsden, D., *Education and the Working Class*. Penguin, 1966.

James, W., *Pragmatism: A New Name for Some Old Ways of Thinking*. Longman, Green & Co., 1907.

Jelliffe, D. B. and Jelliffe, E. F., *Human Milk in the Modern World*. Oxford University Press, 1978.

Jones, S., *Learning and Personality in Later Life*. A report of Seminar arranged by the Department of Adult Education, University of Keele, the Beth Johnson Foundation, and the Pre-Retirement Association of Keele. September 1976.

Jung, C. G., *Collected Works*. 2nd Ed. Routledge & Kegan Paul, 1966.

Jung, C. G., *Symbols of Transformation. The Collected Works*, Vol. 5. 2nd Ed. Routledge & Kegan Paul, 1966.

Kahn, J. H., *Job's Illness: Loss, Grief and Integration*. Pergamon Press, 1975.

Kahn, J. H., The Newham Community Mental Health Services, in Freeman, H. and Farndale, J. (eds.), *New Aspects of the Mental Health Services*. Pergamon Press, 1967.

Kahn, J. H. and Nursten, J. P., *Unwillingly to School*. Pergamon Press, 1964. 3rd Ed. 1980.

Kahn, J. H. and Nursten, J. P., School Refusal: a Comprehensive View of School Phobia and Other Failures of School Attendance. *Am. J. Orthopsychiatry*, **32**, 708 (1962).

Kahn, J. H. and Redman, J., Personality Development in the Mentally Subnormal. *Social Work*, Jan. 1969.

Kallmann, F. J., Genetic Factors in Ageing, in Hoch, P. H. and Zubin, J. (eds.), *Psychopathology of Ageing*. Grune & Stratton, New York, 1961.

Kelly, G., *The Psychology of Personal Constructs*. Norton, N.Y., 1955.

Kempe C. H. *et al.*, The Battered Child Syndrome. *Journal of the American Medical Association*, No. 1, 1963.

Kempe, C. H., Franklin, A. W. and Cooper, C. (Eds.) *The Abused Child in the Family and in the Community*. Selected papers from the 2nd International Congress on Child Abuse and Neglect. Pergamon Press, 1980.

Klein, M. and Riviere, J., *Love, Hate and Reparation*. The Hogarth Press and the Institute of Psychoanalysis, 1937.

Kovel, J., *A Complete Guide to Therapy*. Penguin, 1978.

Lambert, W. E., A Social Psychology of Bilingualism. *Journal of Social Issues*, No. 23, 1967.

Lerner, A. J. and Loewe, F., *My Fair Lady*. Chappell, © 1956.

Lindemann, E., Recent Trends in Preventive Child Psychiatry, in Caplan, G. (ed.), *Emotional Problems of Early Childhood*. Basic Books, New York, 1955.

Loewenfeld, M., *Play in Childhood*. Gollancz, 1935. Reprinted 1965.

Lorenz, K., *King Solomon's Ring*. Methuen, 1952.

Loring, J. and Holland, M., *The Prevention of Cerebral Palsy: The Basic Facts*. The Spastics Society, 1978.

Luria, A. H., *The Mentally Retarded Child*. Pergamon Press, 1963.

McIntosh, J., *Communication and Awareness in a Cancer Ward*. N. Watson, New York, 1977.

Maddox, B., *Half-Parent: Living with Other People's Children*. Deutsch, 1975.

Maier, H. W., *Three Theories of Child Development*. Harper & Row, 1965.

Mayman, H., Schafer, R. and Rapaport, D., Interpretation of the Wechsler-Bellevue Intelligence Scale, in Anderson, H. and G. (eds.), *An Introduction to Projective Techniques*. Prentice-Hall, New York, 1951.

Mead, M., *A Cultural Anthropologist's Approach to Maternal Deprivation—Deprivation of Maternal Care.* W.H.O., Public Health Papers 14, 1962.
Medawar, P. B., *The Art of the Soluble.* Methuen, 1967.
Midwinter, E., *Education and the Community.* Allen & Unwin, 1975.
Miles, M., The School Psychological Service: A Headmistress's View. *Bulletin of the British Psychological Society,* July 1963.
Morrice, J. K. W., *Crises Intervention: Studies in Community Care.* Pergamon Press, 1976.
Newson, J. and Newson, E., Breast Feeding in Decline. *Brit. Med. J.* 5321 (1962).
Newson, J. and E., *Infant Care in an Urban Community.* Allen & Unwin 1963. (Patterns of Infant Care, Penguin, 1965.)
Opie, I. O. and P. O., *Lore and Language of School Children.* Clarendon Press, 1959.
Peters, R. S. (ed.), *John Dewey Reconsidered.* Routledge & Kegan Paul, 1977.
Piaget, J., *The Child's Conception of Number.* Routledge & Kegan Paul, 1952.
Piaget, J., *The Child's Construction of Reality.* Routledge & Kegan Paul, 1955.
Piaget, J., *Play, Dreams and Imitations of Childhood.* Heinemann, 1951.
Piaget, J., and Inhelder, B., *The Psychology of the Child.* Routledge & Kegan Paul, 1969.
Platt, R., Reflections on Ageing and Death. *Lancet* 1–6 (1963).
Pollitt, J., *Depression and its Treatment.* Heinemann, 1965.
Post, F., *The Clinical Psychiatry of Later Life.* Pergamon Press, 1965.
Power, M. J., Benn, R. T. and Morris, J. N., Neighbourhood, School, and Juveniles before Courts. *British Journal of Criminology,* 12 (1972).
Ravenette, A. T., *Dimensions of Reading Difficulties.* Pergamon Press, 1968.
Read, H., *Education through Art.* Faber & Faber, 1943.
Richman, N., Depression in Mothers of Pre-school Children. *J. Child Psychol. and Psychiat.* **17,** 1976.
Robertson, J., *A Two Year Old Goes to Hospital.* (Film) Tavistock Child Development Research Unit, London, 1952.
Rose, J. A., The Prevention of Mothering Breakdown associated with Physical Abnormalities of the Infant, in Caplan, G. (ed.), *Prevention of Mental Disorders in Children.* Tavistock Publications, 1961.
Rutter, M., *Maternal Deprivation Reassessed.* Penguin, 1976.
Rutter, M. *et al., Fifteen Thousand Hours: Secondary Schools and their Effect of Children.* Open Books, 1979.
Saunders, C., The Treatment of Incurable Pain in Terminal Cancer. *Proceedings of the Royal Society of Medicine,* **56,** 1963.
Schaffer, H. R., *The Growth of Sociability.* Penguin, 1971.
Schaffer, H. R. and Emerson, P. E., *The Development of Social Attachments in Infancy.* Child Development Publications, Indiana, 1964.
Sheldon, W., *The Varieties of Temperament.* Harper, New York, 1942.
Sheridan, M., The Developmental Progress of Infants and Young Children. *Reports on Public Health and Medical Subjects,* No. 102. H.M.S.O., 1960.
Shuttle, P. and Redgrave, P., *The Wise Wound: Menstruation and Every Woman.* Gollancz, 1978.
Skinner, B. F., *The Behaviour of Organisms.* Appleton—Century—Crofts, 1938.
Skinner, B. F., *Science and Human Behaviour.* MacMillan Co., 1953.
Smail, D. J., *Psychoanalysis: A Personal Approach.* J. M. Dent, 1978.
Soffietti, J. P., Bilingualism and Biculturalism. *Journal of Educational Psychology,* No. 46, 1955.
Tanner, J. M., *Foetus into Man.* Open Books, 1978.
Tanner, J. M., *Growth at Adolescence.* Blackwell Scientific Publications, 1962.
Tizard, B., *Adoption: A Second Chance.* Open Books, 1977.
Tizard, B., Play, the Child's Way of Learning, in Tizard, B. and Harvey, P. (eds.), *Biology of Play.* Heinemann, 1977.
Watson, J. B. and Rayner, R., Conditioned Emotional Reactions. *J. Exp. Psychol.* **3,** 1920.
Watson, J. *The Juvenile Court.* Shaw & Sons, 1970.
Williams, C. D., Maternal and Child Health Services in Developing Countries. *Lancet* **1,** 345 (1964).
Winnicott, D. W., The Depressive Position in Normal Emotional Development, in *Through Paediatrics to Psycho-Analysis.* The Hogarth Press, 1975.
Young, M. and Wilmot, P., *Family and Kinship in East London.* Routledge & Kegan Paul, 1957.
Yudkin, S. and Holme, A., *Working Mothers and their Children.* Michael Joseph, 1963.

Further Reading

(additional to works cited in the text)

Bell, N. W. and Vogel, E. F., *A Modern Introduction to the Family*. Collier MacMillan, 1969.
Benedict, R., *Patterns of Culture*. Routledge & Kegan Paul, 1935.
Blackburn, J., *The Framework of Human Behaviour*. Routledge & Kegan Paul, 1947.
Blackburn, J., *Psychology and the Social Pattern*. Routledge & Kegan Paul, 1945.
Bowlby, J., *Child Care and the Growth of Love*. Penguin 1953. 2nd Ed. 1965.
Bowlby, J., *The Making and Breaking of Affectional Bonds*. Tavistock Publications, 1979.
Bruner, J. S., *Relevance of Education*. Allen & Unwin, 1972. Penguin, 1974.
Burlingham, D. and Freud, A., *Infants without Families*. Allen & Unwin, 1944.
Caplan, G., *Theory and Concepts of Mental Health and Consultation*. Tavistock Publications, 1971.
Carstairs, G. M., *This Island Now*. Hogarth Press, 1963.
Daws, D. and Boston, M. (eds.), *The Child Psycho-Therapist*. Wildwood House, 1977.
D.E.S. *Children and their Primary Schools*. A Report of the Central Advisory Council for Education (England) (Chairman: Lady Plowden). H.M.S.O., 1967.
D.E.S. *Half Our Future*. A report of the Central Advisory Council for Education (England) (Chairman: J. Newsom). H.M.S.O., 1963.
English, O. S. and Pearson, G. H. J., *Emotional Problems of Living*. Allen & Unwin, 3rd Ed. 1965.
Erikson, E. H., *Childhood and Society*, Norton, N.Y., 2nd Ed. 1963.
Ferard, N. L. and Hunnybun, N., *The Caseworker's Use of Relationships*. Tavistock Publications, 1962.
Flugel, J. C., *Psychoanalytic Study of the Family*. The Hogarth Press, 1921.
Fraiberg, S. H., *The Magic Years*. Methuen, 1968.
Fransella, F., *Personal Change and Reconstruction*. Academic Press, 1972.
Freud, A., *Introduction to Psychoanalysis for Teachers*. Allen & Unwin, 1931.
Freud, S., *An Outline of Psychoanalysis*. Hogarth Press, 1969.
Freud, S., *The Psychopathology of Everyday Life*. Benn, 1948.
Illingworth, R. S., *The Normal School Child*. Heinemann, 1964.
Illingworth, R. S. and Illingworth, C., *Babies and Young Children*. 6th Ed. Churchill & Livingstone, 1977.
Isaacs, S., *The Nursery Years*. Routledge & Kegan Paul, 1932.
Jolly, H., *The Book of Child Care*. Allen & Unwin, 1975.
Jolly, H., *Diseases of Children*. Blackwell Scientific, 1976.
Lello, J., *The Official View on Education*. Pergamon Press, 1964.
Lenneberg, E. H. and E. (eds.), *Foundations of Language Development*. Academic Press, New York, 1975.
Levy, D. M., *Maternal Overprotection*. Columbia University Press, 1943.
Linton, R., *The Cultural Background of Personality*. Routledge & Kegan Paul, 1947.
Luria, A. R. and Yudovich, F. I., *Speech and the Development of Mental Processes in the Child*. Penguin, 1971.
Medawar, P. B. and J. S., *The Life Sciences*. Wildwood House, 1977.
Mead, M., *Coming of Age in Samoa*. Penguin, 1943.
Miller, E., *The Generations*. Faber & Faber, 1938.
Milner, Marian, *A Life of One's Own*. Penguin, 1952.
Newson, J. and E., *Seven Years in the Home Environment*. Allen & Unwin, 1976.
Newson, J., Newson, E. and Barnes, S. P., *Perspectives on School at Seven Years Old*. Allen & Unwin, 1977.
Pearson, G. H. J., *Emotional Disorders of Children*. Allen & Unwin, 1951.
Piaget, J., *The Moral Judgement of the Child*. Routledge & Kegan Paul, 1932. Penguin, 1977.
Pincus, L., and Dare, C., *Secrets in the Family*. Faber & Faber, 1978.
Pringle, M. K., *A Fairer Future for Children*. MacMillan, 1980.

218

Pringle, M. K. *The Needs of Children*. Hutchinson & Co. Ltd., 1974.
Pritchard, D. G., *Education and the Handicapped 1760–1960*. Routledge & Kegan Paul, 1963.
Reisman *et al.*, *The Lonely Crowd*. Yale University Press, 1950.
Rutter, M., *Helping Troubled Children*. Penguin, 1975.
Segal, H., *Introduction to the Work of Melanie Klein*. Heinemann, 1973.
Sheehy, G., *Passages: Predictable Crises of Adult Life*. E. P. Dutton, 1976. Bantam Books, 1977.
Skynner, A. C. R., *One Flesh: Separate Persons*. Constable and Co. Ltd., 1976.
Storr, A., *The Integrity of Personality*. Heinemann, 1960. Penguin, 1963.
Tinbergen, N., *Social Behaviour in Animals*, 2nd Ed. Methuen, 1965.
Thompson, S. and Kahn, J. H., *The Group Process as a Helping Technique*. Pergamon Press, 1970.
Winnicott, D., *The Child, the Family and the Outside World*. Penguin, 1964. Wolheim, R., *Freud*. Fontana Modern Masters, 1974.

GENERAL READING

The Bible: Book of Job

Albee, E., *Who's Afraid of Virginia Woolf?* Jonathan Cape, 1962. Penguin, 1970.
Bellow, S., *Herzog*. Weidenfeld & Nicolson, 1965. Penguin, 1969.
Barstow, S., *A Kind of Loving*. Michael Joseph, 1960. Penguin, 1962.
Eliot, George, *The Mill on the Floss*.
French, M., *The Women's Room*. A. Deutsch, 1978.
Fromm, E., *To Have and to Be*. Jonathan Cape, 1978.
Hoban, R., *Kleinzeit*. Jonathan Cape, 1974. Picador, 1976.
Ibsen, H., *The Wild Duck*. Heinemann Educational, 1958. Methuen, 1968.
Jong, E., *Fear of Flying*. Secker, 1974.
Millet, K., *Sexual Politics*. Rupert Hart-Davis Ltd., 1971.
Naipaul, V. S., *In a Free State*. A. Deutsch, 1971.
Osborne, J., *Look Back in Anger*. Evans Brothers, 1957.
Pirsig, R., *Zen and the Art of Motorcycle Maintenance*. Bodley Head, 1974. Corgi, 1976.
Pinter, H., *The Caretaker*. Eyre Methuen, 1967.
Scott, P., *Staying On*. Heinemann, 1977.
Shakespeare, W., *King Lear*.
Stoppard, T., *Rosencrantz and Guildenstern are Dead*. Faber & Faber, 1967.
Zangwill, I., *Children of the Ghetto*. Heinemann, 1899. Leicester University Press Facsimile Ed. 1977.

Index

221